English Gardens in the Twentieth Century

English Gardens in the Twentieth Century

FROM THE ARCHIVES OF COUNTRY LIFE

TIM RICHARDSON

AURUM PRESS

For Katherine, Rebecca, Emily and Sofia

First published in Great Britain 2005 by
Aurum Press Limited
25 Bedford Avenue, London WC1B 3AT

Text copyright © 2005 by Tim Richardson
Photographs © *Country Life* Picture Library

All rights reserved. No part of this book may be reproduced or utilised in any form or by any means, electronic or mechanical, including photocopying, recording or by any information storage and retrieval system, without permission in writing from Aurum Press Limited.

A catalogue record for this book is available from the British Library.

ISBN 1 84513 071 5

10 9 8 7 6 5 4 3 2 1
2009 2008 2007 2006 2005

Design by James Campus
Originated by Colorlito-CST Srl, Milan
Printed and bound in Singapore by CS Graphics

Frontispiece: *Felley Priory, Nottinghamshire.*
Front endpaper: *Branklyn, Tayside.*
Rear endpaper: *Little Sparta, South Lanarkshire.*

THE COUNTRY LIFE PICTURE LIBRARY

The *Country Life* Picture Library holds a complete set of prints made from its negatives, and a card index to the subjects, usually recording the name of the photographer and the date of the photographs catalogued, together with a separate index of photographers. It also holds a complete set of *Country Life* and various forms of published indices to the magazine. The Library may be visited by appointment, and prints of any negatives it holds can be supplied by post.

For further information, please contact the Librarian, Camilla Costello, at *Country Life*, King's Reach Tower, Stamford Street, London SE1 9LS (*Tel:* 020 7261 6337).

ACKNOWLEDGEMENTS

I would like to thank Michael Hall for asking me to write the book, Clare Howell for editing it with such skill and patience, James Campus for his care in designing it, and Kathryn Bradley-Hole for her useful comments on the text. At the *Country Life* Picture Library, Camilla Costello and her colleagues Paula Fahey and Lara Platman have been unfailingly helpful and good-humoured even as the archive was filleted and then put back together again. I would also like to thank the staff at the Lindley Library of the Royal Horticultural Society, as well as the staff in the Rare Books reading room of the British Library. Finally, I would like to thank the owners of all the gardens featured in this book, and all the gardeners who have maintained those gardens – this book is really a testament to their skills and dedication.

Page 183: From *Derek Jarman's Garden*, Derek Jarman. Text © 1995 Estate of Derek Jarman. Reprinted by kind permission of Thames & Hudson Ltd., London.

LIST OF ARTICLES

The following is a list of *Country Life* articles for which the photographs reproduced in this book were taken. The photographer's name is given in brackets, where known.

Alderley Grange, Gloucestershire: 9 October 1969 (Alex Starkey).
Ammerdown, Somerset: 2 March 1929 (A. E. Henson).
Antony House, Cornwall: 3 May 2001 (Jerry Harpur).
Arley Hall, Cheshire: 24 December 1904 (Charles Latham).
Ashford Chace, Hampshire: 18 December 1920.
Athelhampton Hall, Dorset: 2 September 1899 (Charles Latham); 2 and 23 June 1906 (Charles Latham).
Barnsley House, Gloucestershire: 26 September 1974 (Alex Starkey).
Barrow Court, Somerset: 18 January 1902 (Charles Latham).
Beacon Hill, Essex: 2 May 1925 (Arthur Gill).
Belvoir Castle, Leicestershire: 27 August 1898 (Charles Latham).
Bentley Wood, Sussex: 26 October and 2 November 1940 (Thompson).
Beth Chatto Garden, Essex: 27 May 1993 (Marianne Majerus).
Blagdon, Northumberland: 8 August 1952 (F. W. Westley).
Bodnant, Denbighshire: 17 July 1920; 26 September 1931 (Arthur Gill).
Bradfield, Devon: 2 January 1904.
Branklyn, Tayside: 2 June 1966 (P. Ayres and Jonathan Gibson).
Brickwall, Sussex: 29 September 1900.
Bridge House, Surrey: 1 April 1916.
Britwell Salome, Oxfordshire: 5 October 1972 (Alex Starkey).
Brockenhurst Park, Hampshire: 23 and 30 November 1901.
Bulbridge House, Wiltshire: 8 July 1965 (Alex Starkey).
Burford House, Shropshire: 6 September 1973 (Alex Starkey).
Buscot Park, Oxfordshire: 21 October 1916.
Buttersteep House, Berkshire: 2 January 1942 (A. E.Henson).
Cambo Hall, Fife: 8 January 2004 (Val Corbett).
Campsea Ashe, Suffolk: 15 July 1905.
Charters, Berkshire: 24 November, 1 and 8 December 1944 (F. W. Westley).
Chiswick House, London: (Charles Latham).
Clifton Hall, Nottinghamshire: 12 May 1900.
Compton End, Hampshire: 23 April 1919.
Coleton Fishacre, Devon: 31 May 1930 (A. E. Henson).
Cornwell Manor, Oxfordshire: 24 May 1941 (A. E. Henson).
Cothay Manor, Somerset: 22 October 1927 (Arthur Gill and A. E. Henson).
Cottesbrooke Hall, Northamptonshire: 17 March 1955.
Cranborne Manor, Dorset: 7 December 1901.
Crathes Castle, Kincardineshire: 25 September 1937 (A. E. Henson).
Cray Clearing, Oxfordshire: 6 April 1967 (Alex Starkey).
Crowhurst Place, Surrey: 5 and 19 July 1919.
Ditchley Park, Oxfordshire: 9 and 16 June 1934 (A. E. Henson).
Dowles Manor, Worcestershire: 16 March 1945 (A. E. Henson).
Easton Lodge, Essex: 23 November 1907.
Eaton Hall, Cheshire: 20 April 1901.
Eltham Palace, London: 4 September 2003 (Jerry Harpur).
Eric Geddes' Penthouse: 19 October 1935.
Eridge Park, Sussex: 30 September 1965 (Jonathan Gibson).
Essex House, Badminton, Gloucestershire: 1980, unpublished (Alex Starkey).
Faringdon House, Oxfordshire: 19 May 1994 (Clive Boursnell).
Felley Priory, Nottinghamshire: 20 June 1996.
Fiddler's Copse, Sussex: 10 December 1964 (P. Ayres, Jonathan Gibson).
Folly Farm, Berkshire: 28 January and 4 February 1922.
Fulbrook House, Surrey: 31 January 1903.
Garrowby Hall, Yorkshire: 5 August 1949 (A. E. Henson).
Gledstone Hall, Yorkshire: 20 April 1935 (A. E. Henson).
Glyndebourne, Sussex: 27 May 1939 (Thompson).
Goddards, Surrey: 30 January 1904; 1981, unpublished (Jonathan Gibson).
Goodnestone Park, Kent: 16 May 1985 (Alex Starkey).
Gravetye Manor, Sussex: 3 April 1997 (Clive Boursnell).
Great Chalfield Manor, Wiltshire: 18 June 1998 (Clive Boursnell).
Great Tangley Manor, Surrey: 30 July and 6 August 1898; 21 January 1905 and 22 September 1906.
Gribloch, Stirlingshire: 12 and 19 January 1951 (F. W. Westley).
Haddon Hall, Derbyshire: 1 June 1901.
Hamblyn's Coombe, Devon: 9 August 2001 (Laurel Guilfoyle).
Hardwick Hall, Derbyshire: 13 October 1900 (Charles Latham).
Harewood House, Yorkshire: 3 August 1995 (Anne Hyde).
Harleyford Manor, Buckinghamshire: 4 June 1910.
Hartham Park, Wiltshire: 7 August 1909.
Hascombe Court, Surrey: 26 September 1936 (A. E. Henson).
Heathbrow, London: 9 May 1963 (Alex Starkey).
Heronden, Kent: 11 and 18 August 1960.
Herstmonceux Castle, Sussex: 9 March 1918 (A. E. Henson and Frederick Evans).
Hestercombe, Somerset: 10 and 17 October 1908; 23 September 1976 (Alex Starkey).
Hidcote Manor, Gloucestershire: 22 February and 23 August 1930 (A. E. Henson).
High and Over, Buckinghamshire: 19 September 1931 (Newbery).
High Glanau, Monmouthshire: 23 February, 8 and 15 June 1929 (Ward, Arthur Gill and F. W. Westley).
High Sunderland, Selkirk: 15 September 1960 (Alex Starkey).
Hilles, Gloucestershire: 7 and 14 September 1940 (A. E. Henson).
Howick Hall, Northumberland: 27 February 1997 (Clive Boursnell).
Huntercombe Manor, Buckinghamshire: 6 May 1899.
Iford Manor, Wiltshire: 28 September 1907.
Jenkyn Place, Hampshire: 3 June 1965 (P. Ayres, Jonathan Gibson).
Jestico House, London 1999 (*New Eden*).
Joldwynds, Surrey: 15 September 1934.
Julians, Hertfordshire: 4 July 1947 (A. E. Henson).
Kelmscott Manor, Oxfordshire: 20 August 1921 (A. E. Henson).
Kingston Bagpuize House, Oxfordshire: 24 June 1999 (Clive Boursnell).
Lasswade (16 Kevock Road), Midlothian: 11 February 1960 (Alex Starkey).
Lees Court, Kent: 12 August 1922 (F. Sleigh).
Leith Hall, Aberdeenshire: 12 March 1938 (A. E. Henson).
Little Boarhunt, Hampshire: *Gardens for Small Country Houses*, L. Weaver and G. Jekyll, *Country Life* 1912.
Little Paddocks, Berkshire: 12 May 1934 (A. E. Henson and Arthur Gill).
Little Sparta, South Lanarkshire: 18 July 1996 (Clive Boursnell).
Little Thakeham, Sussex: 28 August 1909.
Littlecote Manor, Wiltshire: 5 November 1927 (Arthur Gill).
Lyme Hall, Cheshire: 17 December 1904 (Charles Latham).
Marsh Court, Hampshire: 19 April 1913.
Master's Garden, Lord Leycester Hospital, Warwick: 10 April 2003 (Chris Linnett).
Mathern Place, Monmouthshire: 19 November 1910.
Moor Close, Berkshire: 31 May 1924 (F. Sleigh).
Mountains, Essex: 14 March 1925.
Mounton House, Monmouthshire: 13 February 1915.
Munstead Wood, Surrey: 8 December 1900.
Nether Lypiatt Manor, Gloucestershire: 19 May 1934 (A. E. Henson).
New England, Surrey: 16 March 1961 (Alex Starkey).
Newby Hall, North Yorkshire: 6 September 1984 (Alex Starkey); 24 September 1998 (Anne Hyde).
No 41, Trafalgar Square, London: 16 February 1935.
North Luffenham Hall, Rutland: 12 April 1919 (Guy Fenwick).
Nymans, Sussex: 17 and 24 September 1932 (A. E. Henson).
Odiham, Hampshire: (Alex Starkey).
Olantigh, Kent: 24 and 31 July 1969 (Jonathan Gibson).
Old Sleningford, North Yorkshire: 22 March 2001 (Steven Wooster).
Old Vicarage, Firle, Sussex: 25 September 1975 (Alex Starkey).
Orchardleigh Park, Somerset: 21 December 1901 (Charles Latham).
Orchards, Surrey: 31 August 1901.
Overbecks, Devon: 4 August 1994.
Packwood House, Warwickshire: 4 January 1902 (A. E. Henson).
Penshurst Place, Kent: 18 March 1899 (Charles Latham).
Port Lympne, Kent: 19 and 26 May 1923; 4 February 1933 (A. E. Henson; Arthur Gill).
Private Garden, Knightsbridge: 15 November 1979 (Alex Starkey).
Prospect Cottage, Kent: 3 June 1993 (Alex Ramsay).
Red House, Bexleyheath, Kent: 10 July 2003 (Martyn Goddard).
Rodmarton Manor, Gloucestershire: 4 April 1931 (F. W. Westley).
Roughfield, Sussex: 25 September 1950.
Saighton Grange, Cheshire: 23 May 1908.
School House, Langford, Oxfordshire: 24 September 1981 (Alex Starkey).
Serenity, Surrey: 14 September 1958 (Charles Latham).
Shore Hall, Essex: 10 June 1999 (Clive Boursnell).
Shoreditch Electricity Showroom, London: 2000 (*New Eden*).
Sissinghurst Castle, Kent: 11 September 1942 (A. E. Henson).
Sleightholmdale, North Yorkshire: 18 May 1995 (Clive Boursnell).
Snowshill Manor, Gloucestershire: 1 October 1927 (F. Sleigh).
St Catherine's Court, Somerset: 24 November and 1 December 1906 (Charles Latham).
St Nicholas, Yorkshire: 12 December 1936 (Arthur Gill).
St Paul's Walden Bury, Hertfordshire: 22 March 1956 (Alex Starkey).
Stanwick Park, Yorkshire: 17 February 1900.
Stoke Park, Buckinghamshire: 1 August 1903.
Stone Cottage, Leicestershire: 22 September 1977 (Jonathan Gibson).
Strawberry House, London: 14 November 1985.
Sudeley Castle, Gloucestershire: 3 April 1909.
Sutton Place, Surrey: 21 March and 13 June 1996 (Clive Boursnell).
The Coach House, Dorset: 13 June 2002 (Melanie Eclare).
The Cottage, Badminton, Gloucestershire: 20 May 1976 (Alex Starkey).
The Deanery, Berkshire: 9 May 1903 (Charles Latham).
The Garden House, Buckland Monachorum, Devon: 9 August 2001 (Clive Boursnell).
The Garden of Cosmic Speculation, Scottish Borders: 23 October 1997 (Clive Boursnell).
The Hill, London: 23 February 1918.
The Homewood, Surrey: 22 July 1993 (Mark Fiennes).
The Laskett, Herefordshire: 16 January 1997 (Clive Boursnell).
The Manor House, Bledlow, Buckinghamshire: 6 June 1996 (Tim Imrie-Tait).
The Manor House, Sutton Courtenay, Berkshire: 16 and 23 May 1931 (A. E. Henson).
The Menagerie, Northamptonshire: 12 October 1995 (Simon Upton).
The Old Rectory, Burghfield, Berkshire: 16 March 1978 (Alex Starkey).
The Old Vicarage, Rickling, Essex: 12 June 2003 (Clive Boursnell).
The Priory, Kemerton, Worcestershire: 4 September 1986 (Alex Starkey).
The Salutation, Kent: 13 September 1962 (Alex Starkey).
Tigbourne Court, Surrey: 23 September 1905.
Tintinhull, Somerset: 12 and 19 April 1956 (Alex Starkey).
Trent Park, Hertfordshire: 20 July 1929 (Arthur Gill).
Tyringham Hall, Buckinghamshire: 25 May and 1 June 1929 (Arthur Gill).
Upper Wolves Copse, Sussex: 4 December 1958 (Alex Starkey).
Valewood Farm, Surrey: 13 October 1928 and 21 September 1935 (A. E. Henson and Mason).
Waddesdon Manor, Buckinghamshire: 4 September 1997 (Anne Hyde).
Wardes, Kent: 30 August 1919 (A. E. Henson).
Waterston Manor, Dorset: 12 February 1916.
West Bitchfield, Northumberland: 28 September 1940 (A. E. Henson).
Westonbirt Festival of Gardens, Gloucestershire: 8 August 2002 (Clive Boursnell).
Wightwick Manor, Staffordshire: 18 April and 15 August 1996 (Anne Hyde).
Wilton House, Wiltshire: 28 May 1904.
Windle Hall, Lancashire: 28 July 1983 (Alex Starkey).
Yorkshire Sculpture Park, near Wakefield, West Yorkshire: 14 January 1999 (Clive Boursnell).

CONTENTS

Introduction

6

Old England's Dreaming: 1900–1914

8

'A Little Peace and Some Surprises' – Gertrude Jekyll

28

Arts and Crafts Ascendant: 1900–1939

50

Border Cultists: 1900–1939

72

Monumentality: 1900–1939

92

Hidcote and Sissinghurst

110

The Modernist Garden: 1920–1999

120

Romance and Restraint: 1940–1969

142

From Smart to Art: 1970–1989

164

Making it Over: 1990–1999

184

Bibliography

204

Index

206

The twentieth century was an exceptionally rich period in English garden history, marking as it did the appropriation of ornamental gardening as a pastime by a much wider section of society than ever before. From the high watermark of Arts and Crafts and the gardens of Gertrude Jekyll and Edwin Lutyens in particular, the connoisseurial plantsmanship of mid-century and its exciting experiments in Modernism and monumental Italianate gardens, to the artistic innovations and new planting ideas of the 1980s and 1990s, English gardens in the twentieth century have proved remarkably diverse. As the photographs in this book bear witness, the English lavished extravagant amounts of care and attention on their gardens through the decades.

This is a book about gardens, not horticulture. Gardens are to the English what cuisine is to the French and the aim here is to provide an overview of a century's development of the garden as England's vernacular art form. It is in many ways a success story, since the twentieth century established England's reputation as the pre-eminent gardening nation, with the international status of gardens such as Sissinghurst and Hidcote a reflection of the symbolic power of the English cottage garden.

Post-war English gardens have not been the subject of much critical analysis as there has been a tendency to view them chiefly in terms of the two principal movements in design – Arts and Crafts and Modernism. But distinctions in styles are extremely blurred in gardening (it is, after all, a notoriously imprecise and ephemeral art form) and there have been many recurring strands in garden fashion through the decades – not least the English obsession with plantsmanship. Perhaps this stylistic complexity, which often verges on the idiosyncratic, derives in part from the amateur status of so much of garden design, dependent as it has been on the make-up of specific social circles and patronage.

It is not just the interweaving of styles that has made much of the history of twentieth-century gardens elusive, it is also because the type of gardening popular for much of the twentieth century was predominantly horticultural – focused on the herbaceous border and the growing of perennial plants in particular. The gardens of the 1940s, 1950s, 1960s and even the 1970s are cases in point, because so many of them were based on plants and were therefore constantly remade in new forms. Gardens do not survive, unless they are tended, and even if they are, they inevitably change when their ownership changes – it is virtually impossible for a successor to garden in quite the same way. However, every garden retains traces of its previous incarnations which can be discerned, or uncovered 'on the ground', and contemporaneous photographs are an invaluable tool for the garden historian in this respect.

Country Life's photographic archive is an exceptionally valuable resource because it contains over 100,000 images of gardens, taken since its inception in 1897, which capture gardens at a particular moment. Its photographs record not only celebrated gardens, but also gardens which have been lost to posterity. They reveal that broad stylistic movements in planting and garden design can be detected from decade to decade. These trends move slowly, and there are some multiple overlaps, but they give lie to the claim, sometimes heard in gardening circles, that this is a subject somehow immune to the whim of fashion.

The images in this archive are remarkably wide ranging. *Country Life*'s sympathies have moved, in tune with the tastes of successive gardening editors, from the Arts and Crafts heyday of the Edwardian era to pioneering Modernism in the 1930s, from rhododendron obsessions in the 1970s to herbaceous exuberance and individualistic artistry in the 1990s. The selection of photographs made for this book necessarily reflects the magazine's predilections: certain designers, such as M. H. Baillie Scott, or genres such as the suburban garden, may have figured only occasionally in its articles, while others, such as Edwin Lutyens, were very much part of the family, but they are all discussed in the book. Included, too, in this survey, as representatives of unusual and individual creations, are seminal gardens in Scotland, such as those of Ian Hamilton Finlay and Charles Jencks, and several in Wales, including Lord Aberconway's horticultural extravaganza at Bodnant.

Capitalising on the richness of the archive, the book is structured chronologically, using only photographs contemporaneous with the period under discussion to represent the garden as it appeared at that moment. The publication date (where known) of the photographs used in this book is given in brackets as part of the caption.

Finally, it has been a great pleasure to realise that the history of the English garden in the twentieth century ended at a high point, a period of rich diversity and experimentation on par with the heyday of the Arts and Crafts movement in the 1910s and the 1920s. Everyone likes a happy ending. But, of course, things have already moved on.

Tim Richardson

◂ *Lyme Hall, Cheshire (1904).*

1 · Old England's Dreaming 1900–1914

At the turn of the century, England's gardens remained largely in thrall to the horticultural obsessions and decorative predilections of the late nineteenth century: there was no seamless transition from Victoriana to Edwardiana. In fact, if one looks at the garden scene as a whole rather than at singularly dramatic examples, the much-vaunted Edwardian revolution in taste – represented primarily by the architects of the Arts and Crafts movement and the plantswoman Gertrude Jekyll – arrived only stealthily and haltingly. In most places, in the first years of the new century, the principal change was in the tone and atmosphere of the garden, in part due to changes in planting style rather than in an overhaul of the general layout and architectural design. Outwardly, 'Victorian' gardens continued to be the norm at England's grander houses, even while their atmosphere was subtly but significantly changing.

The Victorian garden – and particularly the practice of carpet bedding, still seen today in many municipal parks – came to be widely derided and caricatured during the twentieth century. But late-nineteenth-century gardens at their best can be glamorous, impressive and uplifting, and it is easy to see why owners (and, just as importantly, head gardeners) were reluctant to change them. At one extreme, there are the exuberant abundance and horticultural profligacy of a Stanwick Park, Yorkshire; at the other, there sare the restrained, perfectly scaled parterres of an Eaton Hall, Cheshire.

The High Victorian garden was packed with decorative incident and horticultural variety: magnificent parterres or flowerbeds cut into the grass contained hundreds or thousands of annual flowers laid out in embroidery patterns in geometric beds; decoratively planted tubs and urns were arranged on terraces or on gate piers; formal rose gardens became engorged with colour and scent for the summer months alone; fountains, pools, statues and clipped hedges helped enliven and direct the scene; and carefully arranged long borders of flowers were immaculately tended.

Balustraded Italianate terraces, dotted with comfortable chairs, afforded long views over wide lawns fringed by thick shrubberies, where old yews and cedars cast long shadows as evening drew on. Broad gravel walks, edged by rhythmically planted, height-ordered flowerbeds (the tallest plants at the back) and overlooked by long lines of small trees, standard roses or planted urns, led to fully stocked walled gardens with serried ranks of vegetables and fruit trees trained on the walls. Visitors might discover dramatic rockeries, gardens devoted solely to the rose, iris, lily or

lupin, and perhaps a rhododendron dell or a garden in any one of a number of national or historical styles, from Moorish to Japanese (Victorian gardens were stylistically as well as botanically acquisitive). Hothouses nurtured orchids, botanical curiosities or exotic fruits for the all-important dessert course, and ferneries, conservatories and indoor winter gardens provided a paradise of cool green filigree where tea might be taken in comfort.

These Victorian extravaganzas were rich and eclectic places designed to be lived in and enjoyed – and also to be marvelled at. Pleasure gardens such as those of the Rothschilds at Gunnersbury, Ascott, Tring Park and Waddesdon, balanced decorum with luxuriance. While the decorative taste of the late nineteenth century is often derided for its uncontrolled eclecticism, at many an old hall or great house the opposite approach was adopted: the garden was left relatively unadorned – seemingly blank, even – as if it was somehow uncouth to ornament the surroundings of an ancient building (as at Longford Hall). And in many instances (Wilton, Knebworth and Panshanger Hall, for example) the parterre arrangements below the terrace or fronting the orangery, inspired by

French, Italian or Dutch precedent, harmonised success-fully with the architecture of the building – both in spatial terms, and as a complementary decorative scheme on a horizontal plane.

So Victorian gardens were not the disaster area described by so many writers in the early twentieth century. Yet the Victorian look, and particularly the choice of flowers and their 'unnatural' arrangement in the borders and beds, enraged certain commentators and was the catalyst that eventually led to a new movement of planting and design that is labelled 'Arts and Crafts'.

William Robinson led the attack. This irascible and ener-getic Irishman started life as a professional gardener and went on to become a prolific journalist and publisher of magazines, including the long-lived *The Garden* (a prede-cessor of the Royal Horticultural Society's journal, which later took over the name). In his books, *The Wild Garden* (1870) and *The English Flower Garden* (1883) and their many revisions, Robinson's main target was carpet bedding, which was then at the height of its popularity. He encouraged gardeners instead to plant in what he saw as a more naturalistic way – specifically to develop the

ABOVE:

● *Stoke Park, Buckinghamshire (1903). The wide, empty, immaculate south terrace, with potted plants from the conservatory laid out for summer. There was a restrained glamour and taste for exoticism in the High and late-Victorian garden – a tone that was to be challenged in the Edwardian era.*

RIGHT:

● *Orchardleigh Park, Somerset (1901). The view from the wisteria-clad terrace of this 'Elizabethan' style mansion built in the late 1850s. The juxtaposition of the perforated balustrade and the decorative urns illustrates the synthesis of 'Old English' and Italian Renaissance of the period, while the wistful photo-graph attempts to appropriate the place for Arts and Crafts.*

woodland garden and its fringes, to experiment with hardy perennials, to melt shrubs into the scene, and to arrange species (even the imported exotics) so that it appeared they were growing in place quite naturally.

Robinson did not originate all of these ideas – they had been brewing in some form for several decades before 1870, most notably in the guise of the cottage-garden cult and through the work of other original-minded gardeners – but he was responsible for refining and popularising them. He also became famous because he pulled no punches. Reading *The English Flower Garden*, it seems at times as if Robinson is incapable of going for more than a few sentences without insulting or traducing someone, explicitly or implicitly.

Robinson's focus in *The Wild Garden* is almost entirely on the planting of the garden rather than its structure, but else-

where he is as much concerned with art as with nature. Take for example his observation in *The English Flower Garden*: 'Nature is a good colourist, and if we trust to her guidance we never find wrong colour in wood, meadow, or on mountain.' This might sound like a plea for a *laissez-faire* attitude to horticulture of the type preached in some quarters today, but such an interpretation was anathema to Robinson, who saw no contradiction between formality in design and his own 'natural' style of gardening (a fact borne out by the substantial formal areas in his designs for North Mymms and in his own garden at Gravetye). To Robinson, the new horticulture amounted to artistry: he saw no paradox, for example, in the way he used newly introduced exotic plants from China and North America in his 'natural' planting schemes, just as long as the gardener arrayed them artistically.

◄ *Wilton House, Wiltshire (1904).*
A Victorian parterre could be quite magnificent when scaled correctly and paired with fine stonework and statuary.

● *Eaton Hall, Cheshire (1901).*
At the start of his career, in 1897,
Edwin Lutyens designed this perfectly
weighted 'Italian' parterre garden in
High Victorian spirit for the first Duke
of Westminster. It is easy to
understand why so many garden
owners found it difficult to give up
such formal features well into the
twentieth century.

As time went on, Robinson formulated more precise prescriptions for flower gardening in the modern style, as this passage from *The English Flower Garden* shows: 'Plant in naturally disposed groups, never repeating the same plant along the border at intervals, as is so often done with favourites. Do not graduate the plants in height from the front to the back, as is generally done, but sometimes let a bold plant come to the edge; and, on the other hand, let a little carpet of dwarf plants pass in here and there to the back, so as to give a varied instead of a monotonous surface. Have no patience with bare ground, and cover the border with dwarf plants; do not put them along the front of the border only.' This tells us as much about typical Victorian planting style as it does about Robinson's own ideas. He goes on to suggest that the gardener should allow smaller cottage plants to mingle and intertwine freely with others – a typically Jekyllian technique. The John the Baptist of herbaceous planting, as he has been nicknamed, then widened his attack to cover everything he considered to be the formal mode in gardening – which included the majority of gardens that could be described as Victorian. Despite seeming dated, *The English Flower Garden* proved so

powerful and persuasive to gardeners that it remained relevant, influential and in print until the mid-twentieth century.

It is true that Victorian gardens could go disastrously wrong. At its worst, the Victorian period represents the nadir of British gardening. The source that helps confirm this attitude is the *Country Life* archive and the number of photographs therein that depict gardens which appear paltry, denuded and prissy, characterised as they are by large expanses of stately emptiness punctuated by bursts of frenetic activity that unbalance the composition (Enville, Powis Castle and Adcote are good examples). In such images, many major Victorian gardens appear remarkably untended and unadorned compared with what was to come, despite the reputation of late-nineteenth-century gardens for horticultural quality and detail. Undignified, out-of-scale flowerbeds of globular or triangular shape interrupt the lawns or cower beneath yew hedges and brick walls, while lines of standard roses stretch away like street lamps, punctuated by the traffic-light effect of canna lilies, roundabouts of circular flowerbeds and fountain pools, and traffic-jam rows of diminutive identical trees or shrubs.

Tightly organised, compartmentalised Victorian planting schemes can look as absurd to modern eyes as they did to William Robinson's, since we have been conditioned throughout the twentieth century to idealise the Arts and Crafts mixed border above all. Victorian flowerbeds are sometimes profuse but always strictly height-graded, with lines of low annuals at the foot of the border (like the 'skirts' supposedly placed round Victorian table legs), with small, single-species clumps, rather than long drifts, and little intermixing. A predictable, orderly repetition of plant combinations is apparent as one looks along the bed, giving rise to a palpable sense that all the plants have been deliberately placed, rather than arisen as a result of a free hand or (heaven forbid!) self-seeding.

Robinson's radical horticultural ideas were important, but the atmosphere of turn-of-the-century gardens was influenced at least as much by two other factors: a fervour among gardeners, architects and writers for the rediscovery of the atmosphere of old English country houses, and the middle-class craze for cottages and cottage gardens.

The ideal of the country cottage became a key aspect of English rural nostalgia back in the eighteenth century, but it reached fever pitch in the last quarter of the nineteenth century, when squads of watercolourists blessed with varying degrees of talent would decamp from the capital to the Home Counties in search of 'picture-perfect' cottages to paint and sell on to an eager market. One of the foremost,

Myles Birket Foster, used to perform a kind of reverse commute, from London into the Surrey countryside, although several artists, including Helen Allingham, bought country cottages themselves.

The work of these watercolourists – among the best are Allingham, Arthur Claude Strachan, Lilian Stannard, Beatrice Parsons and Ernest Rowe – is best placed in the context of growing industrialisation and the concomitant middle-class yearning for lost rural ways. The dream had started to become a reality by about 1900, when rural Surrey in particular became popular as an alternative to London living, mainly for an artistic or monied set who did not need to travel up to town every day. The garden element of these cottage scenes is in fact generally given more attention than the house and often forms the backdrop to some gentle narrative of country life – a decorous peasant chore, or children playing by a path. However, in the work of Allingham especially, a garden is sometimes depicted as being of interest in its own right. The cottage gardens in these pictures seem to overflow with simple 'old-fashioned' flowers – sometimes termed 'Shakespearean' in the literature, but by no means necessarily native to Britain or always in pastel shades – such as phlox, lupins, foxgloves, dog roses, zinnias, marigolds and campanulas, all ostensibly arranged in an artless fashion by the humble but happy cottager.

There was considerable crossover between these feudalistic, pre-urban fantasy images and horticultural and children's literature; indeed, many cottage-scene artists made their names by providing illustrations for books, and the first of several exhibitions devoted to new cottage art was held in 1886. Some cottage-garden books had a practical flavour, such as E. Hobday's *Cottage Gardening* (1901), which is aimed in part at the monied cottager: its first chapter is devoted to flowers rather than vegetables, when everyone knows that 'flowers do not make the pot boil', as one old rural saying has it. But most were romantic in tone. One highly popular children's serialisation was *Mary's Meadow* (1883–84) by Juliana Horatia Ewing, in which the eponymous heroine makes a flower garden inspired by John Parkinson's famous compendium of plants, *Paradisi in sole, Paradisi terrestris* (1640). Taking her cue from Robinson and other writers, Ewing declares that the humble cottage garden has been the sole repository and saviour of the old-fashioned flowers of England, a bogus idea that is continually repeated by cottage cultists.

It is not that the cottage paintings were fakes – there were hundreds of suitable cottage gardens for the artists to seek out and paint – but they represented a highly selective vision. In the late nineteenth century, rural England was dogged by bad harvests, agricultural depression and the exodus of youth to the towns. The vast majority of villagers were living in or close to poverty in dilapidated, cold, unsanitary buildings; there was usually neither the time nor the space to make a garden for food, let alone for flowers. In many places, the only space available for cultivation was a narrow strip of earth against the front of the dwelling, or else a utilitarian allotment at some distance from the house.

In contrast to the ideas of middle-class sentimentalists, gaudy florists' flowers and even carpet-bedding schemes on a small scale were much loved by these cottage gardeners, who were supposedly ignorant of fashion, and rows of pink chrysanthemums or dahlias would probably have been as commonplace as old-fashioned flowers. Jekyll, at least,

appreciated this tendency, as her apparently eccentric endorsement of common scarlet pot geraniums indicated.

The cottage cult was a romanticised, popular, unintellectual aspect of cutting-edge gardening fashion at the turn of the century, whereas the architectural approach to gardens was scholastic, antiquarian and professional in flavour – although in its own way just as romantic. This period saw a steady output of journalistic articles and impressive illustrated books about the history of English gardens and garden architecture. Notable examples include: *Garden Craft Old and New* (1891) by John Dando Sedding; *The Formal Garden in England* (1892) by Reginald Blomfield; *A History of Gardening in England* by Alicia Amherst (1895); *English Pleasure Gardens* by Rose Standish Nichols (1902); and *Formal Gardens in England and Scotland*

◆ *Clifton Hall, Nottinghamshire (1900). The immaculate Italianate stonework of the Victorian era, if allowed to become slightly over-grown, could also create the mood of romance and antiquarianism which was suddenly so fashionable in the early 1900s. The* Country Life *article on this garden in 1900 dwelt at length on the qualities of the stone-work and particularly the steps.*

(1902) and *Garden Craft in Europe* (1913), both written by H. Inigo Triggs.

Revivalism of historical styles had been a key component of Victorian garden design (the concept of the 'old-fashioned' garden had been current since at least the 1870s), but these new authors seemed to be seeking a deeper vein of inspiration – something which tapped into the very essence of English history and culture, something more than an opportunistic raid on the history of the decorative arts. The unifying theme of these new 'histories' was a veneration of 'Old English' formal gardens of the seventeenth century, such as Montacute and Hardwick Hall, as well as earlier models: Medieval, Tudor, Elizabethan and Jacobean. Their literary heroes were Francis Bacon and John Evelyn, as well as the herbalists. These authors broke new ground in that they reprinted illustrations from original manuscript sources and also included line drawings of features such as garden terraces and enclosed courts, small pavilions and sundials, all lovingly treated (in Triggs's books especially). These elements were to become part of the design vocabulary of later Arts and Crafts designers.

The distinction between Old English and Old Italian was consistently blurred at this time – both on the page and on the ground – and in many cases the two styles amounted to the same thing in terms of overall atmospheric effect. A book such as *Italian Gardens* (1907) by the painter George

Samuel Elgood fits easily into the genre of English gardening history, as the terraces and enclosed courts of Italian Renaissance gardens had provided inspiration for their equivalents in England. Add to this Elgood's portrayal of exuberant flowerbeds in the English tradition, and for the Edwardian reader the main discrepancy between English and Italian gardens seems to be climatic rather than stylistic.

The rather overlooked commentary to Elgood's *Some English Gardens* (1904) was written by none other than Gertrude Jekyll, who describes the metamorphosis of English-Italian gardens from the sixteenth century onwards: 'So grew into life and shape some of the great gardens that still remain; in the best of them, the old Italian traditions modified by gradual and insensible evolution into what has become an English style.' This apparent stylistic synthesis did not in practice relax the inherent tension between the humble simplicity and Englishness of the cottage garden on the one hand, and the luxuriance, decadence and 'foreignness' of the Italian garden on the other. In the ensuing decades, Arts and Crafts gardens would frequently display elements of both idealised traditions. Such tensions are often the wellspring of original artistic endeavour, and these contradictions would become one of the underlying strengths of gardens of this period – culminating in the triumph of Old English/Old Italian that

is Hidcote (see Chapter 6). It should be emphasised that the turn-of-the-century idea of Italian gardens was quite different in spirit to the High Victorian version of Italianate style exemplified by Sir Charles Barry. His parterres and terraces at Trentham Hall and Shrublands, for example, were viewed as modern and ornamental rather than antique and 'authentic'.

J. D. Sedding's discursive and digressive *Garden Craft Old and New*, published posthumously in 1891, could not be more different in tone to his architectural colleague Reginald Blomfield's treatise. Sedding, one of the founders of the Artworkers' Guild and therefore a pioneer Arts and Crafts designer, gave voice to the growing aesthetic conviction that Old English country houses and their gardens 'embody ideas of ancient worth ... they render into tangible shapes old moods of mind that English landscape has inspired'. These somewhat nebulous, even mystical ideas were appealing to the developing Arts and Crafts sensibility, and Sedding's concentration on the tone and atmosphere of Old English gardens was to prove more attractive to the next generation of garden designers than Blomfield's more practical enjoinments.

Oldness in itself was considered a virtue for a garden at this time, and it was a quality not easily replicated. Crucially for young designers, however, Sedding also insisted upon the freshness and immediacy of the new old-fashioned gardens: 'True that there is about the Jacobean garden an air of scholarliness and courtliness; a flavour of dreamland, Arcadia, and Italy – a touch of the archaic and classical – yet the thing is saved from utter affectation by our English outdoor life which has bred in us an innate love of the unconstrained, a sympathy that keeps its hold on reality, and these give an undefinable quality of freshness to the composition as a whole.' Two of the three designers who came to represent the heart of the later Arts and Crafts movement, Ernest Gimson and Ernest Barnsley (the third was Edward Barnsley), trained under Sedding, and something of this admixture of the freshness of new design and the antiquity of the vernacular can be appreciated in their work at Rodmarton and elsewhere.

This same synthesis can be detected in some of the new garden histories of the time. Rose Standish Nichols' *English Pleasure Gardens* (1902) is all couched in the past tense but clearly written with contemporary gardens in mind.

ABOVE:
▲ *Bradfield, Devon (1904). The cones of yew and box in this garden are typical of the old topiary found in many late-Victorian gardens. Such topiary could easily be assimilated into the new Arts and Crafts look in the first decades of the century.*

RIGHT:
▲ *Brickwall, Sussex (1900). Oldness was considered a virtue for a garden at the beginning of the century. This garden, with its massive yew topiaries planted in the late-seventeenth century, found favour as an apparently surviving vestige of medievalism. The architect George Devey had worked hard at accentuating these qualities in the mid-nineteenth century.*

Nichols' examples include Penshurst Place, Haddon Hall, Hatfield House, Longleat, St Catherine's Court, Packwood, Hampton Court and Levens Hall – all of which contain the high hedges, topiary shapes and sequestered spaces that help create the desired tone of Old England. Several of her exemplars were not authentic examples of old-fashioned gardens in that they had been remodelled to appear more 'old-fashioned' – most notably Penshurst Place, which George Devey had reorganised in this spirit as early as the 1850s. Indeed, there had been an abiding interest in old-fashioned gardens throughout the late nineteenth century, encouraged by the poetry of Tennyson and by Pre-Raphaelite painting. There were several isolated instances of gardeners remoulding their gardens in this light: Lady Louisa Egerton's garden at Hardwick Hall is a prime example, and Rossetti's appreciation of the broken-down garden at Brickwall was also influential.

Nichols' own drawn plans of these gardens – intended in part as a sourcebook for designers – emphasise the essentially practical rather than historical tone of her treatment: these were gardens to be copied more widely. Her description of the Elizabethan flower garden is of more relevance to the gardening aspirations of 1902 than the realities of 1602: 'Pleasure gardens were always connected as closely as possible with the house, to form a prolongation of the living rooms. If practicable, the drawing room opened onto a parterre of flowers; if not a terrace formed the means of intercommunication.' Historical accuracy has here been superseded by the contemporary aspiration for old-fashioned gardens: whether or not Elizabethan houses had 'drawing rooms' is a moot point.

A necessary partner for Old English and Old Italian architectural detail was clipped topiary in yew and box. There had been a craze for such decoration since the 1870s – with topiary chessmen and apostles as its most extreme incarnation – but now old hedges began to be perceived in the light of the new ideas about Old English gardens. At Athelhampton, Dorset, in the 1890s, F. Inigo Thomas new-planted conical yews and hedges for his antiquarian-minded client, in imitation of Old English precedent. The Elizabethan garden at nearby Montacute became, perhaps, the epitome of the Old English garden to Edwardian eyes, and it was reprised at Athelhampton in the tall obelisks and graceful curves of a stone enclosure called the Corona. Old hedges and topiaries could be incomparably powerful creators of atmosphere in any 'old-fashioned' garden. It is this kind of transformation that is at the heart of the prototype Arts and Crafts gardens – above all a transformation of tone and atmosphere.

▲ St Catherine's Court, Somerset (1906). The view down the grass stairway. Gertrude Jekyll described the garden in Country Life in 1906; 'Here ... we have a purely English garden with, what to many would appear to be, Italian features. But it remains a purely English garden, because there is no striving after Italian mannerism.'

BELOW:
◀ Brockenhurst Park, Hampshire (1901). Italianate statuary meets 'Old English' topiary. For Gertrude Jekyll, writing in 1904, Brockenhurst typified 'the old Italian traditions modified by gradual and insensible evolution into what has become an English style'.

Our best guide to the burgeoning gardening spirit of the age is Eleanor Vere Boyle of Huntercombe Manor, Buckinghamshire, who as 'EVB' produced evocative, poetic pæans to old-fashioned gardens, chiefly her own, across three decades from the early 1880s. Given the fertile crossover between gardening books and children's literature, it comes as no surprise that Boyle made her name as an author and illustrator of fairy tales. She came to garden writing relatively late, in her fifties, after the death of her curate husband, a younger son of the Earl of Cork.

Boyle's early writing was ostensibly horticultural, concerning the remaking of her own garden from the evening in 1875 when she decided to plant yew hedges at Huntercombe in order to make it look more 'old-fashioned'. Some of Boyle's ideas anticipate Jekyll's, while in certain respects she seems to go even farther in her prescriptions, particularly in terms of freedom in gardening. 'Colour effects, wherever they appear, are seldom planned in our garden,' Boyle writes in the early 1880s. 'But it is quite an exquisite delight to find the most beautiful accidents of colour in unexpected places all about the garden. Then these chances may give hints, which we may take or not … Under the trees, one meets a pallid columbine looking like a ghost, and just by chance in the lilac iris bed, occurs one rich carmine rose.' This is modern gardening, in which happenstance and serendipity play their part,

Haddon Hall, Cheshire (1901). Steps and balustrades were repeatedly illustrated by Country Life *in the first years of the century: a flight of steps disappearing into the undergrowth was one of the best ways of creating a sense of romantic mystery.*

informed as much by considerations of atmosphere as by horticulture.

Where Jekyll was to emphasise artistic control, colour theory, technical expertise, and picture-making in her gardening, Boyle highlights the emotional, romantic appeal of this type of garden with comparable skill and exactitude. Perhaps Jekyll was essentially a visual artist, whereas Boyle was at heart a poet? If so, we should take with a pinch of salt Boyle's claim, of the main border at Huntercombe, that 'We give it neither care nor culture, and it gives back to us, for nothing, the treasure of its sweetness'; this notion of the ungardened garden is a poetic conceit, although the liking for more unruly flowers such as foxgloves, rambling roses and clouds of gypsophila in garden borders gave them a certain savour of anarchic weediness. A looser maintenance regime went hand in hand with a desire to create an atmosphere of languor.

Boyle was not alone in her predilection for old-fashioned gardens – most descriptive garden books of the time eulogise the romantic, timeless qualities of gardens. Her finest work is probably *A Garden of Pleasure* (1895), one of the most sensual evocations of gardens in the language, in which the author displays an ecstatic, hedonistic delight in the close observation of nature, like John Ruskin drunk on fruit liqueurs. Of an old wall in her garden, she writes: 'Ancient rugged pear trees grow up against it, and their outstretched knotted old limbs are set now with knots of flowers, and young, tender leaves, and the half-transparent shadow of every flower and leaf lies still, or trembles on the wall.' The poetic, minutely recorded appreciation of nature was more important to Boyle than considerations of colour: her own borders at Huntercombe were divided into squares devoted to favourite plants, in pairs or alone – ranunculus, lilies, pinks and native anchusa. The planting was uncomplicated and (supposedly) often left to chance.

Which is where *Country Life* comes in. In 1897, Edward Hudson, the monied but barely educated scion of a family of businessmen, took over a failing horse-racing paper called *Racing Illustrated*, renamed it *Country Life Illustrated* on a hunch, and gradually introduced more and more material designed to appeal to a new constituency interested in rural living. Then as now, property advertising provided more than enough financial support for the magazine's occasionally esoteric interests, and it has appeared every week for over a hundred years.

Country Life's chief contribution to English garden history, aside from its role as a journal of record, is that it became in effect a manifesto of the new taste and atmosphere of gardens until the First World War, reflecting in its

◣ *Chiswick House, London.*
The eighteenth-century English landscape garden had fallen from favour in the Victorian period, and was still considered old-fashioned by early-twentieth-century designers. But in an overgrown state, even a garden such as Chiswick could be considered sympathetically by Country Life.

generously illustrated country-house and garden articles (the series 'Country Homes and Gardens Old and New' started to appear in 1898) the fashion for a romantic, slightly dilapidated garden atmosphere. The covert design mission of the country-house articles was later elucidated by H. Avray Tipping, one of the magazine's most distinguished writers, in an article for the one thousandth number of the magazine in 1916: 'Each one has been so treated as to show some merit, teach some lesson, and exercise some influence on the taste of today.'

This was a very English kind of art manifesto, however. *Country Life* was first of all a commercial operation. Its *raison d'être* was not the artistic edification of mankind but the sale of units and of advertising space, and to achieve those ends the magazine had to stimulate its own market by giving its readers new ideas as well as reflecting existing ones. So the types of gardens illustrated in the magazine's glossy, highly produced pages ranged from the ultra-romantic 'new old-fashioned' gardens which appeared to have been left almost to rack and ruin but nevertheless looked effortlessly charming, to typical High Victorian extravaganzas where neither a pansy petal nor a tiny nugget of coloured gravel was out of place.

In the choice of photographs and the style of photography, as much as in the actual appearance of the gardens, *Country Life*'s turn-of-the-century garden articles evoke powerful images of civilised Edwardian country life. In this sense, the magazine's early photographs are more akin to sophisticated late-twentieth-century advertising images than historical documents: they are not fakes, but they are not quite authentic, either. They tell a story. They are distinctive and individual. They inspire a sense of community or clubbability among readers. They create an agreeable world in which one can become completely immersed for a few pages and minutes. They represent something to which readers might aspire. The celebrated woodcut by John Byam Shaw which framed the titles of the country-house articles, depicting quintessential themes such as topiary and peacocks, was in a sense the trademark of the *Country Life* approach.

In its photographs *Country Life* can be seen to have encapsulated most of the ideas about gardens which had been

● *Cranborne Manor, Dorset (1901). The* Country Life *photographs of this Tudor manor are the most stage-managed of all. Redolent of Pre-Raphaelite painting and the early photographs of Julia Margaret Cameron, they are also strongly contemporary – the heavy oak furniture and aesthetic planters are Arts and Crafts statements.*

● *Campsea Ashe, Suffolk (1903). Old topiarised hedges became something of a cult in the Edwardian period. 'These fantastic forms are indeed made of such stuff as dreams', wrote Rose Standish Nichols in 1902. 'In the sunshine their shapes are vaguely outlined behind the gayly hued flowers; but as the light grows dim, shadows lengthen, and colours become indistinguishable, the quaint images of men and beasts, moving darkly forward from the background, have a mysterious fascination and transform the garden into a new and strange wonderland.'*

brewing for the previous two decades, while at the same time moving taste forward. First, there is the 'old-fashioned' tone, which can be expressed as simple Picturesque dilapidation (as at Derwent Hall and Clifton Hall); as misty Romanticism or heavy mystery (Sedgwick Park, Campsea Ashe or Etwall); as a vision of ancient simplicity and decorum (Sudeley Castle); or even as a self-conscious version of Pre-Raphaelitism (the remarkable sequence of images taken at Cranborne Manor in 1901, which also betray the influence of the mid-nineteenth-century photographer Julia Margaret Cameron).

Then there is the enthusiasm for old hedges and topiary in myriad forms, which became almost an obsession for *Country Life*, as well as all kinds of architectural detail: flights of crumbling steps and gate piers were particularly fetishised, and sundials, iron grilles, secret doorways, ivy-clad urns and terraces all feature repeatedly. The eigh-

teenth-century landscape parks were out of fashion at this point, with 'Capability' Brown in particular routinely vilified for supposedly destroying England's formal gardens single-handedly, but suitably overgrown eighteenth-century examples, such as Chiswick House, were admitted to the *Country Life* pantheon of approved old-fashionedness. Claremont, for example, was praised for its 'air of careless beauty'. Even Victorian Italianate gardens were requisitioned for the cause, with gardens at Holland House, Hughenden and Brockenhurst Park shown in a sympathetic light.

While this antiquarian rescue of Old England is primarily a matter of tone rather than content in the gardens of the early years of the century, it was being robustly put into practice in some quarters through the purchase and restoration, or re-creation, of decrepit manor houses (a subject covered in Chapter 3). Finally, the cottage

● *Country Cottages.* Country Life *illustrated the extremes of dilapidation* (left) *and renovation* (below). The Country Life Book of Cottages *(1913) was written by Lawrence Weaver, architectural editor of the magazine from 1910–1916.*

cult found a new outlet in *Country Life*, with numerous articles depicting picturesque villages such as Codford, Walberswick, Crowhurst and that of Bibury Court. It all started in 1901 with an approving article on 'the rustic cottage', the beginnings of *Country Life*'s near monopoly on advice about buying a country cottage, at its height between 1910 and 1920. Perhaps surprisingly, some of the images used in the magazine show cottages in a poor state of repair and without gardens. But there was no enlightened social commentary – rural poverty was probably viewed as an unavoidable fact of country life.

Let us end this opening chapter with an argument.

Incidental to J. D. Sedding's and Reginald Blomfield's more architectural conception of gardening was a suspicion of horticulture as an end in itself – a notion that superficially appeared to be personified in the extremely large target that William Robinson had made of himself. In their respective books of the 1890s, both Sedding and Blomfield implicitly traduced the role of the gardener as the prime artist of the garden. Sedding's was the more philosophical stance – 'Man's imitation of Nature is bound to be unlike Nature' – and more in tune with the Arts and Crafts ideal of unity among the arts: 'The art of gardening is not intended to supersede Nature … There is an unerring rightness both in rude Nature and in garden grace, in the chartered liberty of the one, and the unchartered freedom of unadjusted things in the other. Blessed be both!'

Blomfield, on the other hand, did not want to bless both, and he appears keen to demote the role of gardener to that of maintenance man, using as his ammunition the skewed example of the eighteenth-century landscape gardener, who was at that time the universal garden bogeyman. The aggressive conclusion to Blomfield's book targets a caricature of an idiot landscape gardener, whom Robinson, quite understandably, took to be representative of himself. He thundered back a retort in print, accusing Blomfield of historical inaccuracy (on decidedly shaky grounds) and horticultural ineptitude, and the spat has been celebrated ever since as an example of the old 'nature versus formality' debate. This interpretation is not correct. Every modern commentator who has read the material has recognised that, in reality, Blomfield and Robinson were almost entirely in agreement. Both parties insisted on the importance of structure in garden design; Blomfield did not denigrate plants, and Robinson did not dismiss architecture. Their argument was really a non-event; it was the aggressive way it was conducted that made it news.

It should also be remembered that both Robinson and Blomfield were professionals and public figures with reputations to enhance and sustain. Robinson was a journalist by profession, and the equally pugnacious Blomfield, later president of the Royal Institute of British Architects (RIBA), saw himself as a spokesman for architects. The pair were not publicity shy, and this public spat did neither of them any lasting harm. Throughout the history of twentieth-century gardening, many – if not most – of the key figures have been journalists or authors as well as gardeners or designers. In terms of posterity, the stark fact is that garden writing is usually more important than garden creating; it is obviously less ephemeral.

One regrettable by-product of the Blomfield–Robinson non-argument is that Gertrude Jekyll has been characterised as the sensible woman who steered the middle path. She herself said as much. The highly original gardens Jekyll made with Edwin Lutyens are not some superlative compromise between horticulture and architecture; this does a disservice to the work. Jekyll and Lutyens' gardens were the apogee of a whole new genre of garden design.

Country Cottages. Country Life published a number of articles illustrating genuine cottages and their vernacular charm, as with the steeply pitched thatched roof (above) *and* the topiary display (below).

2 · 'A little peace and some surprises' – Gertrude Jekyll

In William Nicholson's celebrated portrait, Gertrude Jekyll sits in half profile, a silver-haired woman approaching old age, dressed entirely in black and with tiny spectacles above a jowly expanse of cheek and a fixed expression. She has her hands raised in front of her almost at chin level, with her fingers but not her palms touching – a gesture of impatience, it seems, suggesting she is eager to rise from her chair and achieve something more useful and less vainglorious with her day than sitting for a portrait. This Jekyll looks a little like Whistler's mother, a little like Queen Victoria and a little like some stereotypical Mother Superior. What she does not look like is an artist.

The idea of Jekyll as essentially a dedicated, serious-minded amateur plantswoman has remained with us since

her death in 1932, and it is reinforced by the portrait and her own literary output. The practical usefulness of Jekyll's writings, coupled with the fact that most of her gardens have disappeared in their detail, has conspired to create the impression of a horticultural guru rather than a visionary artist who happened to be using the medium of plants. If Jekyll had been concerned about her artistic reputation in posterity – which she patently and impressively was not – she might have hesitated before introducing in her books the implicit idea that her style could be reproduced by anyone else, for this has served to diminish her artistic status. Jekyll's planting philosophy was summed up in her practical gardening books, but that does not mean to say the true spirit of her designs can be copied successfully. Indeed, the belief that Jekyll's ideas can be replicated might be described as the greatest misconception of twentieth-century English gardening.

Jekyll's writings are full of pointers to the type of practical gardener she was, but what of her artistic identity? Her work is generally bracketed with the Arts and Crafts movement, which was flourishing when her gardening career was getting underway in the 1880s, but Jekyll had been immersed in England's artistic life for two decades before that. It could be that by labelling Jekyll an Arts and Crafts designer and leaving it at that, we are telling only a part of the story.

It suited her, professionally and even socially, to be categorised as Arts and Crafts; no one likes to be thought of as old-fashioned. It is true that she went to meet William Morris and John Ruskin, but the William who was Jekyll's guide was Robinson, not Morris, and the wellspring of her

artistic philosophy was not 1880s Arts and Crafts but the burgeoning Aesthetic Movement of the 1860s and 1870s, with its emphasis on pictorial decoration and quasi-scientific experimentation with colour. This represented the real artistic excitement of Jekyll's youth.

Although Arts and Crafts itself grew out of Aestheticism, there were some crucial distinctions; Jekyll did not suddenly 'sign up' to Arts and Crafts when she was in her

mid-forties, jettisoning her entire artistic education to date. The gentlemen of the Arts and Crafts movement did not allow women into their various societies, and so Jekyll always operated on its margins. She took some of its key tenets to heart – in particular the idealisation of vernacular architecture and local building materials, as well as a certain asceticism – while passing by many of the others: the movement's progressive social dimension, its medievalism, its male clubbability, its anti-commercialism, the uniformly cellular structure of its gardens, and its suspicion of superfluous decoration and 'prettiness'.

In fact, there is more evidence of Jekyll's work mitigating against Arts and Crafts theory and practice than there is of her consciously aspiring to it; she simply took on those aspects which appealed to her. Jekyll has nevertheless been appropriated as 'a one-woman Arts and Crafts garden movement', to use Jane Ridley's phrase; the problem with this label is that Jekyll's ideas about gardening and garden design simply do not tally with those of a true Arts and Crafts believer.

But that is an argument about categories and labels. Let us move on to the facts of Jekyll's life and education and

● *Munstead Wood, Surrey (c.1912).*

(left): Euphorbia characias wulfenii *was one of Gertrude Jekyll's signature plants at Munstead, used to create dramatic punctuation in the mixed border or the general flow of the garden. Yuccas were another favourite. The autochrome photographs on these pages were taken in about 1912, most likely by Herbert Cowley, who was then gardens editor at* Country Life.

(below): *Looking towards the Spring Garden. The wooden gate at the break of the hedge was one of the vernacular-inspired elements designed by Edwin Lutyens.*

the artistic milieu in which she was nurtured. Jekyll was born in 1843, not in a West Surrey farmhouse, but in Grafton Street, in the vicinity of Cork Street, cheek by jowl with all the major private galleries in London's Mayfair. Now it would be an exceptionally harsh critic who found fault with a person for the location of their birth; the point here is rather that Jekyll was brought up by artistically inclined parents in a sophisticated and progressive atmosphere. The family moved to the country when she was four, but she could never be a true cottage-gardener: her native habitat was the London salon and picture gallery; her life-long relationship with the countryside was at heart a romantic affair.

Jekyll's affection for West Surrey, where she spent most of her childhood, has been well documented. It was here that she first became interested in gardening, as a small child (another fallacy is that Jeyll 'took up' gardening only when her sight began to fail in middle age), and it was here

that she was to spend most of her life, surrounded by the deep-cut, winding lanes and scattered villages that she came to love. Her education at the Government School of Design attached to the South Kensington Museum (later the Victoria and Albert Museum) from 1861 to 1863, when she was in her late teens, and her subsequent artistic life before gardening took over, have been less amply recorded.

The influence on Jekyll of the designer Christopher Dresser, one of her tutors at South Kensington, has perhaps been underestimated. Dresser is best remembered for his strikingly proto-Modernist geometric designs for tea-sets and other works in electroplate, as well as his early championing of Japanese art and design. The fact that Dresser also designed an extraordinary watering can (all bright-red angularity, its spout almost vertical) provides a clue to his other life: he started out as a professional botanist, and it was only when this career foundered that he turned decisively to the decorative arts.

As a pioneer of what he called 'art botany', Dresser epitomised the South Kensington School's policy of uniting science and art in its teaching. His *Popular Manual of Botany* (1860) is both a scientific and an aesthetic explication of flower anatomy. In his designs for textiles and other applied arts, Dresser encouraged his students to study plants from life and thus render them more naturalistically. This meant that Dresser was unafraid to juxtapose bright, even gaudy colours in his designs, since such colours occur in nature: an aesthetically controversial tenet that Jekyll was to follow in her planting designs. Dresser's large-scale lecture drawings – several of which survive – clearly illustrate the potential decorative applications of subjects such as the cross-sections of stems and the arrangements of inflorescences. His vivid floral motifs, jangling with colour, seem to have more in common with Jekyll's garden work than the more muted elegance of William Morris's graphic designs.

Dresser's *The Art of Decorative Design* was published in 1862, when Jekyll was an art student and he was a lecturer at the same institution, so it seems fair to speculate that she was probably familiar with the ideas espoused in the book (there are no surviving records pertaining to this at the V&A, and Jekyll's own autobiography disappeared after her death, and was reportedly burned). It contains a whole chapter on the use of plants as the inspiration for design in the applied arts, and the art botanist stresses the close appreciation of the form, texture and above all colour of plant life. Dresser suggests that a single flower might provide sustenance to the artist for a month, and – crucially for Jekyll – posits the idea that the world of living things might provide the basis for an artistic attitude: 'The formation of an intimacy with nature will be found most conducive, as it inevitably leads to the cultivation of taste … the wood, the garden, and the hedgerow will each form a suitable studio.' This must have chimed with Jekyll's own appreciation of nature, if we are to accept her comment about her own childhood forays into the garden: 'If you will take any flower you please, and look it over and turn it about and smell it and feel it and try to find out all its little secrets, not of flower only, but of leaf, bud and stem as well, you will discover many wonderful things.'

A little later, Jekyll turned her artistic connoisseur's eye on cottage gardens, as she recalled in her first book, *Wood and Garden* (1899): 'I was collecting hardy garden plants wherever I could find them, mostly from cottage gardens. Many of them were still unknown to me by name, but as the collection increased I began to compare and discriminate, and of various kinds of one plant to throw out the

worse and retain the better, and to train myself to see what made a good garden plant.' The idea of training oneself to look carefully was perhaps something she owed to Dresser and her art education.

Another tutor at South Kensington in Jekyll's time was Richard Redgrave, an enthusiastic promulgator of recent scientific theories about colour, as well as the author of an 1848 lecture series entitled 'The Importance of the Study of Botany to the Ornamentist', which must have encouraged Dresser in his art botany. The idea of primary and complementary colours, and the formulation of a colour wheel of graded tones as a practical aid to artists and designers, had been pioneered in the 1830s by Michel-Eugène Chevreul of the Gobelins tapestry works in Paris, where the minutiae of colour tones was obviously of prime importance, both artistically and commercially. His findings have been acknowledged for their influence on painting, particularly on the French Impressionists.

In Britain, Chevreul's work was translated in 1854 and his ideas were taken up by designers for decorative purposes, most notably by Owen Jones, author of the all-encompassing *The Grammar of Ornament* (1856), the most influential mid-century design manual – later vilified for its role in encouraging unbridled eclecticism. Jones was also concerned with laying down rules about colour harmonies. For example, in a Great Exhibition lecture on colour in 1851, Jones's Proposition 11 states: 'When two tones of the same colour are juxtaposed, the light colour will appear lighter, and the dark colour darker.' Half a century later, Jekyll was to make a similar point during a discussion of blue flowers in a mixed border.

Redgrave's own *Manual of Colour* (1853) constitutes a catechism of colour for aspiring designers: it is an extremely precise exploration of the effects of adjacent colours on each other, with numerical values assigned to the various tints. Later on, Jekyll was to appropriate the spirit, if not always the letter, of the theories of Redgrave and others (notably Claude Naudin, whose colour-based botanical treatises she owned) and apply them to garden plants used in an informal manner. This helps to explain the confidence and surety of Jekyll's pronouncements on colour arrangements: they were all based on 'scientific' precedent, remembered and practised since student days.

However, in 1895, Jekyll warned that adhering to 'the "laws" of colour laid out by writers on decoration is a waste of time', and she was to distance herself explicitly from Chevreul's colour charts in a letter of 1913. So it is important not to overstretch the point, and some will wish

▲ *Munstead Wood, Surrey (c.1912).*

(top left): *The September borders were a highlight of the Munstead year, with pale yellow snapdragons, rose pink sedums, blue heliotropes and plenty of asters.*

(top right): *The main border in the Spring Garden, with morello cherries on the high wall. Drifts of white arabis and yellow and white tulips give way to the stronger colours of crown imperials and tulips beyond.*

(middle left): *A blaze of salvias. A typically Jekyllian moment.*

(middle right): *The double borders of lupins and flag irises in June, with the loft beyond. Intermixed in the border are pink China roses and white pinks and pansies.*

(below left): *The hardy flower border, the garden's pièce de resistance, with red geraniums, Dahlia 'Fire King' and salvias backed by hollyhocks. By mid-century, this kind of boldness with colour was largely disregarded by Jekyll's self-styled disciples. While single-colour gardens remained perennially fashionable, they were almost always realised in gentler colours than this.*

(below right): *Clematis was one of Jekyll's preferred plants for ornamenting, but not obscuring, 'hard' features, such as drystone walls and more formal stonework.*

to take Jekyll entirely at her word and suppose that her ideas about colour were self-taught. But perhaps the garden artist protested a little too much about colour theory: there is a strong possibility that this way of looking at colour, if not the precise formulations of the theorists, did inform Jekyll's attitudes.

Redgrave was at pains to stress the importance of practical first-hand experience of all subject matter for designers. In his *Manual of Design* (1876), he describes the teaching methods at South Kensington: 'The pupil has natural foliage, fruit, and flowers placed before him; he is taught to imitate natural objects carefully, then to investigate the laws of their growth and development; and finally, as a step to invention, he is instructed how to arrange according to like geometrical laws and principles the unnumbered beautiful forms and varied colours with which nature supplies him.' With tutors such as Redgrave and Dresser, Jekyll could hardly emerge from her artistic training without a feeling for the study and appreciation of nature from life, with a particular emphasis on flowers and foliage and a scientific understanding of colour.

For Jekyll, however, discussions of colour would lead her in a new direction: to a critical reappraisal of contemporary planting in gardens. In 1924 she reminisced about the previous century: 'Formerly a border was planted according to the heights of plants only … and they were placed, not only without any regard to colour combination, but in single plants, so that the whole effect was like a patchwork of small pieces indiscriminately dotted about.' There was no 'unity in variety' (the title of another botanical treatise by Dresser).

When Jekyll began to apply her colour theories to gardening, she found she had opened a Pandora's box of horticultural possibilities. Chromatic exactitude was to remain a habitual trait in Jekyll: she was the epitome of the

aesthete in that she believed in the possibility of the objective description of colours, and her *bête noire* was the way terms such as 'gold' or 'azure' or 'true blue' were used in nurserymen's catalogues and by other garden writers to describe colours which were not quite of that hue, according to her 'scientific' precepts.

One can almost see Jekyll mixing up colours on a palette in her mind's eye, as in the case of her careful discussion of the leaves of tree peonies in *Wood and Garden* – 'Their colour is peculiar, being bluish, but pervaded with a suspicion of pink or pinkish-bronze' – or in her discovery of cold blues and golden greens in the yew hedges of Levens Hall in *Some English Gardens* (1904): 'The play of light and variety of colour of the green surfaces is a delight to the trained colour-eye.'

During the 1860s and 1870s, Jekyll moved among the artistic, literary and scholarly circles of London, as well as making extended painting forays and flower rambles to Greece, Italy, Spain, Algeria and the Alps with artistic friends. This period was the zenith of the Aesthetic Movement, a loose term which encapsulates the trends for, among much else, Japanese art and Oriental blue-and-white porcelain, Queen Anne architecture in red-orange brick with Portland stone facings, and the children's-book illustrations of Kate Greenaway. There was a penchant for the laying-down of rules for artistic appreciation and overall a heightened sense of professionalism in art. Perhaps most importantly for Jekyll, this was also a time when the domestic sphere came to be seen as a fit milieu for high art (hence the 'house beautiful' concept), and amateurism ceased to be derided as a matter of course – both of which factors clearly worked in favour of the female maker.

As well as painting watercolours, Jekyll followed Aesthetic Movement principles by practising a wide range of applied arts, from embroidery to woodcarving to silverwork. She soon became a minor but respected figure in the world of interior design, too, securing commissions from friends as well as from influential patrons who immediately saw quality in her work. Frederic, Lord Leighton, commissioned a tablecloth from her purely on the basis of seeing some of her needlework, and she also made embroidered panels for the Duke of Westminster at Eaton Hall.

The few photographs of Jekyll's painted decorations for walls and doors at this time reveal that she was working very much in the spirit and style of Dresser, producing decorative yet naturalistic depictions of foliage and flowers that look as if they have just been brought in from the garden. Botany, in the form of floral motifs for decoration,

LEFT:
◆ *Munstead Wood, Surrey (1900).* The square tank, sited at the point where the north court widens out to form an L-shape, was an early essay by Lutyens in formal geometry using stonework and in handling changes in levels and awkward angles. Jekyll's arrangement of box topiary balls indicates that she was not averse to a formal aspect in her designs.

RIGHT:
◆ *Orchards, Surrey (1901).*

(above): *View from the Dutch garden, with its distinctive curved stone seats, up to the loggia terrace. In this early work of 1897, Jekyll's planting can be seen to complement rather than 'soften' Lutyens' architecture. Indeed, a number of formal garden elements, such as the pots, bolster the architectonic rhythm of the design.*

(below): *The south loggia.*

as well as living plants, was the lifeblood of interior design at this time.

Embroidery was one of Jekyll's abiding artistic interests – it probably meant more to her than any other art form except gardening. So instead of stating that she was forced to give up painting to preserve her eyesight, we should perhaps say it was embroidery that she relinquished. (Jekyll herself referred to her thwarted 'artistic' ambitions, a remark that does not necessarily refer to painting alone.) Art embroidery, as it was known, was an applied art that was taken seriously in the 1870s and 1880s, although its artistic status, like that of gardening, has since plummeted. Yet, even more so than painting, embroidery forced Jekyll to learn about the anatomy of colours and their compatibility. Fine needlework demands not only exceptional finesse in colour matching, but also the ability to create one's own dyes – a process Jekyll enjoyed.

The opinions of John Ruskin, the wayward colossus of Victorian art criticism, could not be ignored by anyone with an interest in the arts at the time – including Jekyll, who attended his lectures and met him at least twice. It was Ruskin, as the champion of J. M. W. Turner, who reportedly inspired Jekyll to study Turner's use of colour, and she spent hours copying his works in the London galleries. From Turner, Jekyll learned how to use colour expressionistically rather than decoratively, in rhythmic surges which inspire emotion in the viewer; she must also have learned much from the artist about pictorial composition using colour alone. One of Jekyll's greatest friends, and her informal art tutor while on holiday, was Hercules Brabazon Brabazon, the English painter whom Ruskin praised as the inheritor of Turner's facility with colour. Brabazon has been much underestimated – his work can superficially appear to resemble a watery version of Impressionism – but his original use of colour and careful composition within an apparently free execution is comparable with Jekyll's gardening style.

Ruskin had a lot to say about flowers, but little that is specifically horticultural: he generally spoke of gardens and plants in symbolic terms, as a kind of antidote to industrialisation. He did, however, attack the Victorian obsession with hothouse flowers – 'pampered and bloated above their natural size, stewed and heated into diseased growth' – and went so far as to recommend that 'on the turf, the wild violet and pansy should be sown by chance, so that they may grow in undulations of colour, and should be relieved by a few primroses'. This is, however, essentially artistic rather than horticultural advice (the same is true of the essay 'Of Leaf Beauty' in *Modern Painters*); William

Robinson was to be far more influential on Gertrude Jekyll in this vein.

The influence of William Morris on Jekyll, and indeed on the gardens of the Arts and Crafts movement as a whole, is also problematic. There is little in Jekyll's work that can be directly attributed to Morris's example, and in terms of later Arts and Crafts designers, only a handful faithfully followed what might be interpreted as Morris's garden precepts (Edward Barnsley's Rodmarton Manor is the prime example). Taken as a whole, Morris's garden writings constitute slim pickings – certainly not a coherent philosophy of Arts and Crafts gardening, as has recently been suggested. Morris's specific writings about gardens are frustratingly vague and piecemeal, and his gardening by example does not seem to marry with his printed ideas. Morris envisaged the ideal garden as either a compartmented space echoing the style of the house to which it is attached, or else as an unadorned medieval greensward.

Like every other forward-looking designer of the late nineteenth century, Morris attacked the Victorian 'nightmare of "horticulture"', as he called it, and imagined instead a simple, unaffected plot where vegetables and fruit are grown alongside flowers: 'Large and small, it should look both orderly and rich. It should be well fenced from the outside world. It should by no means either imitate the willfulness or the wildness of nature, but should look like a thing never to be seen except near a house. It should in fact look like a part of the house.' In this passage from *Hopes and Fears for Art* (1882), Morris appears to be suggesting that the architectonic volumes of the house be echoed in plan form by the garden surrounding it – a complex architectural and horticultural idea, and one which designers since Bramante had wrestled with.

He slightly altered his ideas when writing in *The Quest* of 1895: 'The garden, divided by old clipped yew hedges, is quite unaffected and very pleasant, and looks in fact as if it were a part of the house, yet at least the clothes of it; which I think ought to be the aim of the layer-out of the garden.' This is still frustratingly vague, however: that a garden should be 'very pleasant' is not a particularly helpful injunction. Elsewhere, Morris seems to envisage the ideal garden as a flowery mead – this underpinned his pioneering vision of houses in a 'green belt' around a city, which he imagined as being situated in one huge meadow.

Lack of clarity underlies much of Arts and Crafts thought and writing on gardens. Morris's ideas were interpreted as a kind of formalism, imbued with nostalgia for old-fashioned gardens (like those discussed in the previous chapter). His own approach at Kelmscott Manor and Red House was sturdy, unsentimental and functional. Red House's garden in particular became an experimental laboratory designed to produce plant materials for his celebrated designs – a cross-fertilisation between garden and drawing board. The garden also functioned as a retreat and a source of food; it was not self-consciously decorative in the same way as his designs on paper and, crucially, the garden was not celebrated as an art form in itself.

As for planting, Morris seems to have been caught between the pleasures of horticulture (he apparently enjoyed gardening) and the ideal of unmediated nature – the conceit of the un-gardened garden again. In his lecture entitled 'Making the Best of It', Morris states: 'I think the best and safest plan is to mix up your flowers, and rather eschew great masses of colour – in combination I mean.' Morris is talking about gardening here, but he seems loath to admit it. For when faced with the idea of a garden, Morris was confronted with a moral problem. Is it right to treat the native flowers and other plants of the countryside as a kind of artistic palette, appropriating them and arranging them artfully in imitation of the fecund chaos of nature, as one might when thinking about a new textile design? Or is it better to leave plants to their own devices as far as possible, within a rigidly arranged formal structure? Morris, in his writings, opted for the second solution; a few years later, Jekyll, who was just nine years younger than him, decided on the first.

The garden at Kelmscott Manor was described by Georgina Burne-Jones as 'enchanting with flowers, one mass of them, and all kept in beautiful order', and Morris's last house, in Hammersmith, featured large terracotta pots on the terrace, a highly stylised design intervention. These contradictions must have been self-evident to the practical-minded Jekyll. She was to jettison Morris's incoherent ideas about gardens and replace them with a self-consciously artistic but more intellectually honest model for gardening – inspired by nature, informed by art, and celebrating rather than denying the idea of active creativity on the part of the gardener.

This does not mean to say that Jekyll was intellectually honest in every way. Her attitude to vernacular architecture – specifically cottages – on one level appears to bolster her Arts and Crafts credentials, since it appears to be part of an embrace of rural life in its totality. But in fact her interest is entirely aesthetic; the social dimension of the Arts and Crafts movement is absent.

In *Old West Surrey* (1904), Jekyll's pæan to her home locale, she is able to appreciate vernacular architecture and even engineering (there is a detailed chapter on gates and fences), but is uncomfortable when it comes to human beings, preferring to keep them at a distance by idealising them. 'Cottage folk are great lovers of flowers,' she writes, 'and their charming little gardens, in villages and by the roadside, are some of the most delightful incidents of road-travel in our southern counties.' Jekyll evidently viewed the rural poor as ornaments to the local architecture and the cottage gardens she admired so much. Her trenchant views on the importance of the conservation of cottages were not accompanied by a similar concern for the welfare of the people inside them, whereas a true Arts and Crafts disciple in the Morris mould would have recognised the poverty as well as the beauty.

Morris himself had suspicions about the vernacular authenticity of Surrey as more and more middle-class artists sought it out. 'For one thing it is very thinly inhabited,' he commented to Georgie Burne-Jones, 'and looks more than most countrysides as if it were kept for the pleasure of the rich, as indeed it is.' This kind of social criticism was not in Jekyll's line. However, in certain superficial aspects she seems to outdo the Arts and Crafts designers – while the male architects were holding

◂ *Little Thakeham, Sussex (1909). The great pergola which shoots off at a right angle from the house, designed by Lutyens in 1902–04, was the main garden feature. According to Lutyens, the owner Tom Blackburn originally planted it with massed hollyhocks.*

vociferous meetings in London followed by dinners at Gatti's restaurant on the Strand, Jekyll remained alone in Surrey, sleeping on a wooden bed on the bare brick floor of her 'hut' at Munstead Wood.

Jekyll was a pictorial sensualist, an evoker of ancient atmospheres, a true aesthete. Her appropriation of the

▲ Little Thakeham, Sussex (1909). The pergola (above) seems rather stark and unevenly weighted seen in context, but closer to the house, a formal water garden (below), next to the dining room, is a more successful interpolation.

cottage garden was essentially imaginative, and her garden assemblages were like nothing ever experienced by a humble cottage-owner, whatever she may have protested in print. In fact, Jekyll disparaged the old-fashioned florists' societies – which flourished in the north of England at this time and consisted almost entirely of working-class gardeners – because of what she saw as the artificiality of their techniques and the resultant blooms. So Jekyll rejected the urban and semi-urban working class as it actually existed in favour of lauding a romanticised rural working class whose gardens ostensibly chimed with her social and horticultural outlook.

Jekyll extolled simplicity in rural life and gardening, but her plantings were in fact extraordinarily complex and sophisticated constructions of colour and form, drawing on a wide range of plant material, much of it non-native. For Jekyll, the artistic imagination was paramount, as evinced by the fact that she visited relatively few of the sites for which she was to design gardens in the years leading up to the First World War, and hardly any after 1918. She would

Sullingstead (now High Hascombe), Surrey (1912). An early example (1896–97) of the Lutyens–Jekyll Surrey garden vernacular, with drystone walls, steps and shallow terraces leading to a half-timbered house. It was built at the same time as Gertrude Jekyll's nearby home, Munstead Wood. The music room, on the left, was added by Lutyens in 1903, and shows his success in juxtaposing contrasting architectural styles.

sit at her workshop table with perhaps a dozen photographs of the site, painting pictures with plants in her mind's eye and then sending off the plans in the post. There could be no consideration of the site's atmosphere, of the clients' personalities, of the quality of light or any of the other barely tangible variables so important to most other garden designers. Such a disconnection between art and life was anathema to authentic Arts and Crafts thinking. There is also a sense in Jekyll's later writings that she is going through the motions, as she trots out variations on the same old format of a month-by-month year in the flower garden, waymarked by scores of personal favourite plants.

But, setting these anomalies aside, Jekyll's skills were self-evident and her image of horticultural guru self-perpetuating: in the first quarter of the twentieth century, and on both sides of the Atlantic, Jekyll enjoyed a monopoly on

horticultural style akin to 'Capability' Brown's monopoly on landscape in the eighteenth century.

In spite of appearances, Jekyll was not so much the nun-like disciple of the morally edifying Arts and Crafts movement; she was more of a closet aesthete, an unbohemian bohemian, a child of 1860s and 1870s Aestheticism, obsessed by beauty in the form of her picture-making with living flowers and foliage and also steeped in the sensual, amoral pleasures the garden has to offer. Seen in this light, Jekyll has more in common with Oscar Wilde than William Morris – but not too much in common, since Wilde's backfiring exhibitionism forced 'respectable' artists such as Jekyll underground.

Jekyll's official gardening career began in 1868, with her first tentative steps at garden design for the family home at Wargrave. By the mid-1870s she was ready to begin contributing to horticultural periodicals and start designing in earnest (although only by the 1890s was she creating at a rate of six or seven gardens a year). Jekyll's earliest writings tend to be her most candid concerning her artistic intentions, though her very first contributions to *The Garden* concern the foliage plants, herbs and flowers she came across in Algiers and elsewhere (grey- and silver-leaved plants from warmer climes were to become part of the Jekyll signature), and she contributed a long series of articles on indoor plants in 1881–82.

Thereafter, most of her writings in the 1880s and 1890s were essays on individual plants and their qualities; she did not write a great deal about the overall garden scene. One exception was the essay 'Colour in the Flower Garden' in the 26 August 1882 issue of *The Garden*, a key early exposition of her ideas. Jekyll states: 'One of the most important points in the arrangement of a garden is the placing of the flowers with regard to their colour-effect, and it is one that has been greatly neglected … In setting a garden we are painting a picture, only it is a picture of hundreds of feet or yards instead of so many inches, painted with living flowers and seen by open daylight.' This sounds almost banal today, but it must have seemed radical at the time even to an audience used to reading the works of William Robinson, since his main emphasis was on naturalistic composition rather than colour arrangement. And with her reference to 'open daylight', Jekyll might perhaps also have been making reference to the Impressionist painters of the French avant-garde, who saw themselves above all as 'painters of light' rather than of colour itself.

Jekyll continued to set out her store unequivocally: 'One of the commonest faults in arrangement is a want of simplicity of intention, or an obvious absence of any

● *Deanery Garden, Berkshire (1903).*

(right): *Made by Luytens and Jekyll in 1901 for* Country Life's *founder, Edward Hudson, the layout of Deanery Garden comprised a series of long rectangles and squares, with a long lawn flanked by the main herbaceous border.*

(below): *In a bold move the lawn was bisected by a narrow iris channel featuring the typical Lutyens flourish of alternating square and circular pools. He later reworked this device at Hestercombe.*

definite plan of colouring'; she recommended large drifts of similar coloured flowers planted together, 'to follow each other in season of blooming'. Jekyll does not shy away from giving precise advice on colour-combining derived from her artistic training, but this incorporation of the dimension of time in her discussion of colour is what most sets Jekyll's ideas apart from conventional art theory.

In other early articles, Jekyll praised J. D. Sedding and Humphry Repton for their formal handling of the relationship between house and garden. Her design in collaboration with Lutyens for Munstead Wood, however, was to owe more to the Repton example of relaxed transition between formal areas by the house and the landscape

beyond than to Sedding's yew-hedged enclosures, inspired by the Morris example. Jekyll also sought to associate her planting palette with what was considered authentic and desirable – that is, old-fashioned gardens. Essays such as 'The English Garden 200 Years Ago' (1884) inject a horticultural antiquarianism into her garden recipe, as she praises simple yet neglected flowers mentioned by John Evelyn, such as the musk rose: 'A fine single white rambling rose, very little in cultivation, but well deserving a place in every garden.'

Jekyll also gave voice to her aesthetic agenda in a letter to Eleanor Vere Boyle of Huntercombe Manor, Buckinghamshire, quoted in the preface, dated 1885, to Boyle's *Seven Gardens and A Palace* (1900). This passage has been overlooked, but it shows Jekyll at her most relaxed and engaging, perhaps because it is (purportedly) a private letter. 'I wish to gain a knowledge of all garden flowers,' she writes, 'but only to see which can be used in a picturesque and beautiful way, and which had better be rejected and left alone. In gardening I try to paint living pictures with living flowers, paying attention to throwing them into groups both for form and colour, and so on.' She stresses that making pictures is indeed the whole point of her gardening style, and highlights two instances at Munstead: 'The Primrose Garden in its season is a river of gold and silver flowering through a copse of silver-stemmed young birch trees for a hundred yards or more. Another of this year's pictures that pleased me was a large isolated group of white foxgloves with bracken about their base, backed by a dusky wood of Scotch firs.' Unusually, Jekyll is here describing her garden in purely artistic language as a series of pictures, with none of the practical horticultural information she felt obliged to include in her writings.

The best way to understand Jekyll's approach to planting, however, is to read her published works: they are written with clarity, directness and economical style. Many observations have been made on the subject of what Jekyll said about plants in colour combination, and it is all too easy to get caught up and tumbled about in Jekyll's colour kaleidoscope, so perhaps we should briefly note what she omitted to mention but obviously practised in her own gardening.

When looking at contemporary photographs of Jekyll's gardens (these are chiefly of Munstead Wood), one is immediately struck by the fact that her plantings were as much sculptural as pictorial. Her border of Michaelmas daisies seems to be exploding out on to the path, but the volumes of flowers appear controlled; signature plants such as large euphorbias and yuccas are boldly placed as

dramatic punctuation marks in the mixed border, and not necessarily co-mingled and toned down by neighbouring plants; she betrays her liking for clarity in her picture-making with preferences for bergenias and hostas. Her planting is muscular, not wispy and ethereal; there are spaces in her borders, bright colours are used unashamedly, and unusual rhythms create surprises.

Graham Stuart Thomas, the plantsman and garden writer, noticed the structural aspect of her borders when he visited Jekyll towards the end of her life: 'What was so remarkable about the colourings in the main border – from cool to strong – and to cool again at the far end – was the solidity of the whole, bolstered by the shrubs and great clumps of *Yucca recurvifolia* and *Bergenia cordifolia* "Purpurea".' Jekyll rarely mentions this aspect of planting design in her writings, however, which are generally taken

Folly Farm, Berkshire (1922).

(opposite): *View from the pergola at Folly Farm, where Lutyens extended a Georgian farmhouse in two phases from 1906. In the wider garden, Jekyll designed several relatively unadorned areas to allow more formal features room to 'breathe', and supervised the complex irrigation works necessary for the canal and other features, which involved diverting a natural stream on the estate.*

(below): *Among the unusual aspects to Lutyens' design was the loggia with sleeping balcony above, prefaced here by Jekyll's mature planting.*

up with considerations of colour (nor is this factor observable in her one-dimensional planting plans). She tends to illustrate by example, advancing few general precepts beyond those concerning colour and the injunction to plant in drifts rather than blocks.

Jekyll's most concerted attempt to discuss this aspect of her work, in *Colour in the Flower Garden* (1908), is uncharacteristically inelegant and opaque, and she seems only too aware of the shortcomings of her prose: 'The shaping of every group of plants, to have the best effect, should not only be definitely intended but should be done with an absolute conviction by the hand that feels the drawing that the group must have in relation to what is near, or to the whole form of the clump or border or whatever the nature of the place may be. I am only too well aware that to many this statement may convey no idea whatever.'

Jekyll's decriptions of colour in the garden are masterly by comparison. Perhaps her clearest discussion of the construction of the long border at Munstead Wood was published in 1929: 'It begins with flowers of tender and cool colouring – palest pink, blue, white and palest yellow – followed by stronger yellow, and passing on to deep orange and rich mahogany, and so coming to a culminating glory of the strongest scarlet, tempered with rich but softer reds, and backed and intergrouped with flowers and foliage of dark claret colour. The progression of colour then recedes in the same general order, as in its approach to the midmost glory, till it comes near the further end to a quiet harmony of lavender and purple and tender pink, with a whole setting of grey and silvery foliage.' Her prose is so straightforward that it makes her painterly advice sound like a column of weekend gardening tips, as if it was simply a matter of painting by numbers (which is exactly what Jekyll's planting plans resemble).

A more visionary counterweight to this version of artistic endeavour can be found, once again, in the earlier works – in this case her first book, *Wood and Garden* (1899), in which Jekyll recalls an incident from her painting days when she studied a white horse from life: 'On looking up I was amazed by the sight of a blue horse with a large orange spot

Folly Farm, Berkshire (1922).

(above): *To one side of the house, Lutyens designed a series of intimate courts. The clump of bergenias to the left of the doorway is a typical structural device by Jekyll.*

(right above): *View from the end of the rose garden. The canal garden is over the hedge.*

(right below): *The canal garden was one of several formal features Lutyens incorporated into his design after 1911.*

on his flank. I never can forget the sudden shock of that strangely coloured apparition.' Jekyll's vision of a blue horse pre-dates the explosive chromatic revelations of Derain, Matisse and the Fauves – the Post-Impressionists, who gloried in colour above all else. Simply by virtue of the fact that she was able to see a horse that appeared blue and also realise the implications of this, we can see that Jekyll's artistic sensibility was truly ahead of its time; this is often obscured by the fact that she was a retiring, middle-aged lady living in Surrey who had no interest in cultivating an avant-garde image.

Jekyll's meeting with Edwin Lutyens is unlikely to have been an accident. In 1889, the independent-minded twenty-year-old architect had only just started out in private practice designing cottages, and he was visiting a client, Henry Mangles, a cultivated individual who was well known for his rhododendron breeding. Jekyll lived nearby and was at that time considering how to proceed with the wooded land across the road from her mother's house at Munstead, which she had acquired in 1882 and made into a garden. She could either find a cottage elsewhere in Surrey to move into, or build a small house in the wood-land at Munstead and keep the garden going. She even-tually opted for the latter solution and therefore needed an architect. The small house was to become The Hut; then, after the death of Jekyll's mother, Lutyens would start work on a full-sized house: Munstead Wood.

Presumably the tea party at Mangles' house in 1889 was engineered so that Jekyll could size up the young architect, having already seen his plans for the small house he was building for Mangles. According to Lutyens, Jekyll did not say a word to him until just as she was leaving, when she invited him to visit Munstead. But she had obviously discerned that in Lutyens she had found someone with whom she could work: after all, he had been born only seven miles from Munstead and was as enthusiastic about local buildings as she was. Lutyens remarked that when he visited Jekyll a few weeks later, she had been transformed from the stiff Victorian spinster of the tea party into the mischievous, rather eccentric artist he came to adore. (Jekyll was no old lady at this point, it should be noted: she was forty-five years old.)

Lutyens, like many Englishmen, communicated with the world essentially through the medium of jokes and attempts at wit, a philosophy of the absurd that led some architect colleagues to deride him as whimsical or lacking in seriousness. Jekyll, however, loved his manner, and despite their age difference the two formed a remarkable and fruitful partnership. Lutyens was always known as Ned

● Hestercombe, Somerset (1908). The great sunken plat with massed bergenias. The garden designed in 1906 by Lutyens and Jekyll was their most famous collaboration. Of Hestercombe, Christopher Hussey wrote, 'the design and texture of the garden seem to be inseparable, vegetation providing much of the design, and the architecture often affording texture'.

and Jekyll was the subject of various mock-heroic or childish nicknames, from Aunt Bumps to Oozal, Woozle or Swoozle. Ned and Bumps were to have some great adventures together, riding round the Surrey lanes in a gig looking at old buildings, or thrashing out a garden design over supper together at Munstead.

Lutyens' very early, pre-Jekyll work is steeped in the philosophy of the Arts and Crafts vernacular, with tiled roofs sweeping down in a low embrace of high gables, and leaded windows winking from half-timbered walls covered in climbing roses. Jekyll introduced him to the work of Philip Webb, who, as well as designing Morris's Red House, had renovated the derelict Great Tangley Manor in Surrey for Mr and Mrs Wickham Flower (mainly Mrs Flower, according to Lutyens) in an imaginative and original way, with well-cast decorative additions and extensions – notably a pleached-lime walk, a pergola, large rock

garden and a covered way and bridge across the re-dug moat. Jekyll had known Great Tangley since childhood, when she had been entranced by its romantic atmosphere, but she thoroughly approved of Webb's changes. She was no reactionary.

Great Tangley also transformed Lutyens' view of the possibilities of vernacular architecture. Lutyens formulated his own cool, modern version of the straightforward Surrey cottage style of his youth – inspired partly by Webb and in tandem with Jekyll – and then fitfully progressed towards a more romantic and formalised Classicism

It was natural that Jekyll should create some of her finest work in collaboration with an architect. She was never purely a plantswoman and was predisposed to the architectural treatment of gardens; during her career she collaborated with a number of architects, though mostly only by correspondence. Writing in *The Garden* in 1900, she came

▲ *Hestercombe, Somerset (1908).*

(right): *Small enclosed courts with circular pools terminate the 140ft long rills – which flanked the great plat.*

(below): *A corner of the great plat by the pergola, with underplanted steps.*

the closest she ever did to criticising her friend Robinson for his 'denunciations of all architectural accessories', praising in the process the gardens of the Italian Renaissance; elsewhere, she was at pains to stress the importance of built structure in gardens. Planted pots and urns, used architecturally, were an integral part of her design vocabulary from her very first garden at the family home at Wargrave, in Berkshire. Jekyll often returned to this theme of single-minded artistic expression lending strength to the whole, and this idea was echoed by Lutyens. Theirs was a conceptual approach to garden design.

The relationship between Jekyll's planting and architecture has been best summed up by Fenja Gunn in *Lost*

Gardens of Gertrude Jekyll (1991): 'Most of her gardens were based on a formal plan, with terracing, pools and the shaping of lawns and borders contributing to the formality of the layout. Within this disciplined structure, Jekyll's bold drifts of planting and ingenious use of colour would have appeared all the more rich and exuberant. Although apparently complex on paper, the actual effect that was achieved was never fussy. By planting in generous swathes and with a carefully controlled blend of colours, Jekyll harmonised plants with their setting.' It is this technique, and the careful ordering of garden spaces, that makes the photographs of Munstead Wood in the 8th December, 1900 issue of *Country Life* appear so radical.

In fact, if one looks through each issue of the magazine from its inception in 1897, many Jekyll – Lutyens collaborations seem revolutionary when they appear during the first decade of the century. Gardens such as Orchards (1901), Marsh Court (1903), Deanery Gardens (1903), Goddards (1904), and Hestercombe (1908) positively burst on to the scene, making everything else pale in comparison. Orchards and Goddards, particularly, seem to suggest both grandeur and humility at the same time – the Holy Grail for the English sensibility.

What was different about the work of Lutyens and Jekyll – beyond the genius of Lutyens' fearless geometry in his flights of steps and other details – was the way that the garden seemed to have been designed as all of a piece with the house. This is not apparent in the work even of brilliant contemporaries such as Voysey, Mallows, Baillie Scott and Webb, let alone the legions of less talented designers working in the Arts and Crafts milieu. It means that the Jekyll – Lutyens look seems able to fit with houses of any scale: the planting schemes expand and contract to fit the needs of the space. Perhaps part of Lutyens' recipe for success was the fact that he was not a

47

good technical draughtsman; he rarely sketched plans and elevations and designs would take shape in his head. This fluidity may have meant that he was able to conceive of designs where the formal divisions between house and garden are less important, in which their volumes segue into each other.

The biggest cliché about Jekyll's style is that her plantings somehow 'softened' the outlines of Lutyens' garden architecture, as if it was an answer to a problem (an idea reinforced by the gender stereotyping that is common in garden writing, which dictates that women like flowers and curves, and men like stone and straight lines). Jekyll did not soften anything; in fact, her plantings were often designed to enhance architectural form. Again and again it can be seen that Jekyll's plantings do not blur the edges of the architecture but instead bolster its impact in a way that Lutyens, too, must have envisaged. An example of this can be seen in the pair of long rills at Hestercombe House in Somerset, where Jekyll's plantings of irises, rising vertically from the water, accentuate their elegant length and satisfying narrowness. Similarly, her plantings on pergolas, in the crevices under steps and at the edges of paths all conspire with, rather than obscure, the architecture. Jekyll's sympathy with stonework can be found in her stern instruction that climbing plants – ivy, in particular – should never be allowed to smother architectural detail. So it is in every Lutyens and Jekyll design: they worked in a spirit of collaboration and mutual respect, never in opposition. While both designers had an idiosyncratic style, theirs was not a partnership that thrived on tension and disagreement. They indulged each other's eccentricities, and this was perhaps the key to their apparently unlikely friendship.

Towards the very end of her life, Jekyll was visited by the well-known garden writer Marion Cran, who recalled the occasion in *I Know a Garden* (1933): 'I do not know exactly what I expected, but I found a large old lady in Victorian dress wearing strong spectacles on half-blind eyes. She opened the door to me herself and welcomed me very sweetly, with a charm of other, statelier days than this – she had little active wonderful hands, and while we talked she began moving a large chair – quite strongly, and would not let me help. … When some other visitors came she flushed and trembled, asking me to take them through the grounds and pour out tea for them … "I have tried to make a little peace and some surprises," she said at parting.'

If we try to blot out the prevailing image of Jekyll as the kindly Queen Victoria of gardening, we might conclude that it was the surprises rather than the peace that Jekyll the artist valued the most.

◣ *Hestercombe, Somerset (1908). The great pergola is 230ft long, with alternating round and square pillars, and oak cross-beams. Clematis, Russian vine, and above all roses clothe it. The orangery can be seen in the distance.*

3 · Arts and Crafts Ascendant
1900–1939

LEFT:
● *Moor Close, Berkshire (1924).*
A relentless experimenter, Oliver Hill used the Arts and Crafts hallmark of a sunken garden in this early work, while the circular and rectangular pools joined by a rill and leading up to a fountain mask, betray the influence of Edwin Lutyens, to whom Hill was initially apprenticed.

ABOVE:
● *Kelmscott Manor, Oxfordshire (1921). Long after William Morris's death, the house and garden at Kelmscott continued to influence designers. Specific features such as the enclosed front garden and straight, rose-lined path seen here were appropriated for use in smaller-scale gardens.*

The late 1880s, when Edwin Lutyens was embarking on his career, was an exciting time to be an architect. The influence of Arts and Crafts was at its height and in flux, inspiring both established designers and new names to experiment with ideas drawn from vernacular architecture. There was no lack of opportunity for innovation, and there was enough money around to keep a healthy number of architectural practices thriving, both in London and the provinces. The upper echelons of Edwardian society had been augmented by industrialists and self-made men who were self-possessed enough to envisage building new houses that were modern in inspiration.

Another group of patrons, mostly from well-established upper-middle-class families, rallied to the cause of Old English manor houses and their gardens, buying up superlative examples that lay derelict, then restoring and modernising them in a creative spirit, usually with the help of professional architects. Whatever the situation, those individual owners and architects who made significant forays into garden design each produced their own idiosyncratic versions of the Arts and Crafts style, and sometimes changed their approach quite radically from commission to commission. What we now call Arts and Crafts garden design was in fact a rolling programme of restless experimentation in which each garden seems different but somehow of the same stamp. The style continued to develop and find new modes of expression right up to the Second World War.

Three main thrusts of Arts and Crafts garden design can be discerned. The first was short-lived, but is usually viewed as the most 'authentic', in that it was directly inspired by William Morris. This was the medievalised garden of yew enclosures and flowery bowers. The second type of garden described as Arts and Crafts is that associated with old houses, often restored manor houses or castles; it was usually more relaxed in structure than other gardens of the time and planned on a larger scale. The third category is the garden designed in tandem with a new house, almost always by a professional, where the theory was that exterior and interior should co-exist and complement each other in a holistic design embrace.

Although there were some spirited attempts at this synthesis, arguably it was Lutyens alone who achieved and sustained it in England.

The appeal of the medievalised Arts and Crafts garden was grounded in William Morris's ideals of Old England and a paradisiacal ruralism inherited from the Pre-Raphaelites – in artless craft, in local buildings that seem to grow out of the soil, and in ancient proletarian skills. The spirit of original or 'authentic' Arts and Crafts gardens could be found at Old English houses such as Montacute, Hardwick Hall, Penshurst Place and Groombridge, and in historical re-creations such as those of F. Inigo Thomas at Athelhampton and Barrow Court. Thomas successfully based his architectural method on antiquarianism, but most designers found the Old English prototype wanting when it came to gardens: it was too restrictive – it seemed to be informed by ideological dogma yet lacked specifics.

One professional group whose work consistently reflected Morris's principles was the Cotswolds collective: Sidney and Ernest Barnsley and Ernest Gimson. At his cottage in Sapperton, Gloucestershire, near the manor house of Daneway which he used as a workshop and showroom, Gimson lived a life of spartan simplicity in keeping with a medievalised vision of his vocation, inter-mixed with a thoroughly modern socialism. His fenced garden provided vegetables and was simply planted with cottage flowers. It was not a highly architectural compo-sition, but it was quite in the spirit of Morris.

In his book *The Edwardian Garden* (1989), David Ottewill also makes the case for the architects Ernest Newton, Mervyn Macartney and E. S. Prior (all ex-pupils of Richard Norman Shaw), who followed Sedding's ideas in creating a series of enclosures around the house. These designs, consisting of relatively large spaces and incorporating impressive vistas, do not display quite the intimacy and tight structure of most later Arts and Crafts gardens. In fact, many of the new houses and gardens built at this time were reactionary in essence.

In the last years of the nineteenth century and the first two decades of the twentieth century, professional archi-tects such as Sir Ernest George, Walter Cave, W. H. Romaine Walker, and Reginald Blomfield made large, solid, vaguely Classical or Neo-Georgian houses and gardens for a smart, transatlantic set of Edwardian socialites whose taste was for grandiose formal effects. There is a sense with some of these gardens – West Dean by Sir Ernest George was perhaps the apogee, where the Prince of Wales was a frequent visitor – that they were designed to be looked at from the terrace rather than

enjoyed sensually from within. As John Cornforth put it: 'Edwardian classicism has a marked tendency to coarse-ness and even vulgarity', which makes Lutyens' successful integration of Classical motifs into an Arts and Crafts milieu all the more remarkable. Forward-looking architects such as Charles Voysey, Halsey Ricardo, Leonard Stokes and E. Guy Dawber, designing on a smaller scale and in a more innovative vein, made essays on the Arts and Crafts garden, based on the principle of a terrace around the house that led to a series of enclosed gardens, with features such as sundials, lavender beds and pergolas.

Yet of all the architects designing in the spirit of Arts and Crafts from the 1880s and into the new century, relatively few consistently engaged with the garden as a medium in its own right – the revelations of vernacular architecture were perhaps exciting and challenging enough. Turn-of-the-century architectural plans show houses placed on platform-like terraces, surrounded by low balustrading or walls, with nondescript shrubs or vague prettifications below the windows and smooth green lawns spreading

● *Wardes, Kent (1919). Sir Louis Mallet was an influential figure among the renovators of old manor houses in the first three decades of the century. Rather than create a garden that was an historical pastiche for his fourteenth-century house, Mallet incorporated modern sculpture and a contemporary, crazy-paved layout.*

away on all sides. Sometimes yew hedges or trees are incorporated to suggest stability and permanence, and perhaps there might be an unruly flower border by the house, but all too often the garden is in effect a blank slate. This was symptomatic of a perennial problem in the history of building design: these architects had no experience of or sympathy with gardens, and they saw it as being against their interests either to collaborate with others or to compromise the quality of their architectural plans by producing what they knew might well be second-rate garden designs. That was why so many of them turned to Jekyll for garden designs and planting plans, and later to local nurseries or to one of the professional garden-design pattern books which had started to appear.

The cult of the Old English manor house and castle developed in the first decade of the twentieth century.

Among the best-known examples of restored manor houses of this era are Westwood Manor, Avebury Manor, and Great Chalfield Manor, all in Wiltshire, Lytes Cary Manor in Somerset, and Owlpen in Gloucestershire. The West Country and the Cotswolds were particularly rich in grand old Tudor or Elizabethan houses that had fallen on hard times, often used as farmhouses and left partially derelict, the gardens overgrown or stony and bare. Solutions ranged from the minimal to the outlandish, from the avowedly horticultural to the purely architectural – there was no generally accepted methodology, although many of those engaged in such restorations mixed with each other socially; it was a rather smart thing to do.

Wardes in Kent, a fourteenth-century 'yeoman's house' of modest proportions, was remade after 1905 by Sir Louis Mallet, an influential contemporary figure among those

● *Athelhampton Hall, Dorset (1899). Francis Inigo Thomas captured the period's veneration of the 'Old English' garden in his works of the 1890s, and pre-eminently in the formal gardens he laid out at Athelhampton. The pool garden was a cool counterpoint to the rich detailing of the adjoining garden enclosures.*

interested in the decorative arts and a confidant of Sir Philip Sassoon, owner of the extravagant Port Lympne and Trent Park (see page 98). Mallet was, like Sassoon, a diplomat, and the leading figure of a Foreign Office circle of cultivated colleagues interested in renewing old houses, among them Colonel Reggie Cooper of Cothay Manor and Harold Nicolson of Sissinghurst.

At Wardes, Mallet reconstituted the timber-framed house (it had been separated into cottages) and made a small formal garden to complement it. This garden was modern rather than antiquarian in spirit, featuring a swirling geometric arrangement of beds planted with tulips and various sculptures in Renaissance style (perhaps influenced by Harold Peto's Iford Manor). But there is something of the knot-garden tradition about the design, making it seem compatible with the house. Mallet's idiosyncratic design is typical of the ad hoc formulation of the Arts and Crafts garden.

Colonel Cooper used his retirement from the diplomatic service after the First World War to indulge his passion for

LEFT ABOVE:

● *Cothay Manor, Somerset (1927). Colonel Reggie Cooper acquired and remodelled this fine fifteenth-century manor house in the 1920s. His formal design of hedged garden rooms was perhaps more influential than has been appreciated – among his friends were Lawrence Johnston of Hidcote and Harold Nicolson of Sissinghurst.*

LEFT BELOW:

● *Nymans, Sussex (1932). A simple and elegant cruciform garden of lavender beds and clipped bay trees. The house was less than 100-years-old when Colonel and Mrs Leonard Messel moved in; they transformed it into what appeared to be a fifteenth-century manor house.*

RIGHT ABOVE:

● *Nether Lypiatt Manor, Gloucestershire (1934). Violet Gordon Woodhouse created the garden in a romantic spirit from 1923, with the aid of Percy Morley Horder. The long, double herbaceous border is proof that effusive plantings could complement an austerely formal, early-Georgian house.*

RIGHT BELOW:

● *Waterston Manor, Dorset (1916). The formal water garden leading to the great east gable was part of Horder's restoration programme of a previously derelict house, completed during the First World War.*

finding and restoring old manor houses. In relatively short order over a period of thirty years, he lived in and worked on four houses: Cold Ashton Manor in Gloucestershire (just two years there), Cothay in Somerset, Julians in Hertfordshire, and finally Knightstone in Somerset. Cooper was a dedicated gardener and a friend of such garden taste-formers as Norah Lindsay of Sutton Courtenay, Lawrence Johnston of Hidcote Manor, Sir Louis Mallet and Sybil Colefax. At Cothay, the fifteenth-century house where he lived from 1925 to 1936, Cooper introduced the geometri-cally planned layout of box-hedged compartments, in a style also practised by professional architects such as W. H. Romaine Walker, who created a formal garden of hedges at Great Fosters in Surrey.

The garden areas near the remodelled house at Nymans in Sussex were treated in a similarly elegant fashion, with cool lavender beds offsetting the paved paths, plats of lawn, clipped bay trees, dovecote, and sculptural fragments with an Italian Renaissance feel. Nymans is today one of the most celebrated of the surviving gardens dating from this period, and its popularity derives both from its romantic atmosphere (much of the house burned down in 1947 and its ruin remains) and from its plantings. It was perhaps the most horticulturally ambitious of the 'old' manor-house gardens. The wider garden had been planned from the outset with a plantsman's eye and was packed with unusual azaleas, rhododendrons and other recently discovered Himalayan plants, as well as a pinetum and a walled garden for the tenderest subjects. But somehow the prevailing Arts and Crafts atmosphere of Nymans, a sense of dreamy antiquity that is established by the house and the formal part of the garden, seems to pervade even the farthest reaches of the estate.

Coleton Fishacre, a house and garden made by Oswald Milne for the D'Oyly Cartes, set in a steep-sided Devon combe, is another unusual example of an Arts and Crafts garden designed specifically with serious horticulture in mind, since the owners were enthusiastic and know-ledgeable gardeners. Milne's terraces and pool are perfectly weighted in relation to the house and were always intended to harbour unusual shrubs.

Old castles tended to attract American buyers, who generally opted for a more monumental tone in their gardens (see Chapter 5), but in a few cases a castle provided the backdrop for a garden in the Arts and Crafts spirit. Herstmonceux Castle in Sussex is a prime example, restored by Colonel Claude Lowther from 1911 and after his death in 1929 by Sir Paul Latham. Here, a new garden was made at a distance from the north façade of the castle,

on the site of an old orchard. From a sturdy doorway a straight grass path took the visitor north across a bridge over the dry moat, between white standard roses and up to a flight of rose-embowered steps which led on to a statue of Mercury, the centrepiece of the upper garden where the long borders were situated. The whole effect was redolent of the sense of discovery and mystery so potent in gardens of the period; to roam the castle grounds must have been a truly Tennysonian experience.

There is a celebrated instance of a First World War officer serving in France writing home to say that his regular shipments of *Country Life* provided him with escapist solace and also reminded him of what he was fighting for. Charles Paget Wade was another serving

officer, and the story goes that towards the end of the war he saw an advertisement for the near-derelict Snowshill Manor at Broadway in Gloucestershire and resolved to buy it. On a small scale, Wade was to achieve the Arts and Crafts ideal of creating a new garden that looked as if it had been there for centuries.

At Snowshill, the descending axis of small, stone-walled garden courts also took advantage of the steepness of the site, with the uppermost Armillary Court leading down via flagged paths flanked by columnar yews to the Well Court and then on to the kitchen garden. Special emphasis was placed on the importance of surprises and different moods, and Wade played down the importance of flowers. It was an entirely architectural conception – apparently achieved with some assistance from the architect Mackay Hugh Baillie Scott, who had a special interest in garden design. Snowshill illustrates the adaptability of the Arts and Crafts garden: here, it is made to fit into a small, awkwardly shaped and sited space, but seems entirely felicitous.

The adaptability of the Arts and Crafts garden is demonstrated again at Nether Lypiatt Manor in Gloucestershire, where a long double herbaceous border, flanked by yew

compartments, complemented the austere, symmetrical south front of the house of 1705, with its pavilion-like wings. From 1923 Violet Gordon Woodhouse transformed the garden with the assistance of the architect Percy Morley Horder, who also worked at Waterston Manor in Dorset. In *Noble Essences* (1950), Osbert Sitwell poetically recalled the garden's 'high yew hedges and stone walls, with its exquisite dark-toned flowers' and how it seemed to overflow into the house, so that 'among the pieces of solid 1790 or 1800 mahogany and well-worn carpets and chairs, had strayed baskets of apples and pears, shallow wicker trays of walnuts, even, occasionally, vegetables – a turnip or a carrot – roots of flowers, a piece of bass [bark], so that by the contents of the room … you could judge of the season outside'. This fusion of house and garden, amid an atmosphere of faded grandeur and faux rural simplicity, was an Arts and Crafts domestic ideal of the 1920s and 1930s that fed into Bloomsbury chic.

Madresfield Court in Worcestershire was one of the earliest and most unusual experiments in Arts and Crafts garden design made to complement an existing house – in this case another Tudor manor, but one that had already

ABOVE:
▲ *Snowshill, Manor, Gloucestershire (1927). The adaptability of the Arts and Crafts approach is perfectly illustrated here: the steeply sloping, relatively small site turned to advantage by the owner Charles Wade and the architect M. H. Baillie Scott. Each garden room contains its own surprise.*

RIGHT:
▲ *Herstmonceux Castle, Sussex (1918). Old castles were an attractive proposition for those with the means to take them on. Colonel Claude Lowther began restoring Herstmonceux from 1911, and beyond the dry moat he created a garden in the new 'old-fashioned' style. The statue of Mercury was the centrepiece of this new garden.*

undergone a phase of comprehensive restoration. The seat of the Lygon family had been heavily restored between 1863 and 1888 for Lord and Lady Beauchamp. In 1903, they commissioned Thomas Mawson to create a raised parterre garden as a counterpart to the remarkable contemporary interiors, including the celebrated chapel. Mawson's low brick terraces and circular flights of steps were perfectly in keeping with the austere elegance of the existing garden.

Mawson was one of the few architects of this period to address the garden aspect of a design with the same seriousness as the house (Charles Mallows was another such exception). His work seems a little pedestrian and stiff today in comparison with that of Lutyens, but Mawson successfully gave expression to a highly architectural Arts and Crafts approach to gardens, with his expansive terraces, sunken gardens, sturdy pergolas, terraces and steps, short avenues of pleached trees, Classical detailing in wrought-iron gates and stone gate piers, clipped evergreens and tall cypresses. He was, above all, a master of levels, and his best work is seen in his terraces, as at Burton Manor, Cheshire, and at Rivington in Lancashire.

Mawson's architectural plans also show how much larger many Arts and Crafts gardens were compared with what we can see in photographs: small formal courts by the house may have been the most intense part of the design, but they did not take up much acreage. Beyond there were often vistas, woodland walks, rock gardens, kitchen gardens, lawns and meadows – chiming with the prevailing Reptonian notion that formality around the house should give way to a looser structure beyond. This stricture underpinned the shape of the majority of large gardens for the remainder of the century.

This attitude to structure also suited clients' practical needs. Just as architects were asked to build or remake houses that were modern, practical and glamorous, so the requirements of the motor car and of sporty young weekend guests were to be recognised in the form of garages, turning-circles in front of the house, tennis and croquet courts and even swimming pools (usually disguised as ornamental pools, and growing ever more popular, especially from the 1930s onwards). The decorative aspects of the garden had to co-exist with opportunities for leisure. This was lifestyle gardening.

Professional designers who earned commissions for new houses were faced with a thorny problem when it came to the garden. The very first words of Jekyll and Lawrence Weaver's influential *Gardens for Small Country Houses* (five editions of which were published between 1912 and 1924) are: 'It is upon the right relation of the garden to the house

OPPOSITE ABOVE:
Hilles, Gloucestershire (1940). Detmar Blow was among the first architects to move away from the Arts and Crafts concept of enclosure. Here, at his own house, he used wide, informally planted terraces with loose-fitting flags to create a feeling of space and lightness.

OPPOSITE BELOW:
Crowhurst Place, Surrey (1919). The straight path from the gateway, through the lawned gardens, up to the front door was a classic Arts and Crafts device.

BELOW:
Ashford Chace, Hampshire (1920). This Arts and Crafts design for a sunken garden by H. Inigo Triggs and W. F. Unsworth seems as redolent of the sun-baked Alhambra as the Surrey vernacular.

that its value and the enjoyment that is to be derived from it will largely depend.' Their book, a well-illustrated source-book of ideas rather than a visionary manifesto, was a response to a perceived stylistic vacuum, intended to help remedy the situation through good example. Professional designers had been left without a viable prototype for Arts and Crafts gardens, and while several of them simply turned to Gertrude Jekyll for planting plans, as the new century wore on it became common for architects to try their hand at garden design – and architects naturally tended to opt for an architectural solution.

The individualistic example of Lutyens led to an eclectic Arts and Crafts style that was broadly Classical or Italianate yet modern in tone, rather than medievalised and historicist in the Morris fashion. Within this modern sensibility, certain elements from 'authentic' Arts and Crafts

were retained, chiefly the ideal of formal enclosures within yew hedges, the desirability of changes in level (first conceived as the raised terraces of 'Stuart' gardens, but later realised as the Italianate sunken or Moorish rill garden), some evidence of the use of local materials, and exuberant 'old-fashioned' planting schemes and formal herb gardens. Great play was made of the use of different stone materials in paving design and for handbuilt walls and other structures such as pergolas, small pavilions, canals, reflecting pools and flights of steps.

The cellular structure of Arts and Crafts gardens – derived first from the idea of garden enclosures and later developed into the more intimate 'garden room' concept – provided designers with the ideal template for experimentation and owners with the opportunity of reworking sections of the garden if they wished. One important aspect

PRECEDING PAGES:

● *North Luffenham Hall, Rutland (1919).* Architectural eclecticism and horticultural exuberance were the watchwords of Arts and Crafts garden design. Here, the owner Guy Fenwick and his wife combined vernacular terraces, shaggy borders, an Italian-inspired sunken garden, and standard 'lollipop' bay trees against the backdrop of the early-eighteenth-century garden front of the house.

LEFT:

● *Little Boarhunt, Hampshire (1912).* Designer-owner Harry Inigo Triggs created a riot of architectural eclecticism, which somehow works, using classic Arts and Crafts features, such as the sunken plat, drystone walls with crevice plantings, garden pavilion, rose-covered pergola, canal pool, and Classically inflected statuary.

of the Arts and Crafts garden structure was that it was enjoyable to work with and adaptable enough for its discrete, self-enclosed areas to be developed at different speeds. A wide range of ornamental effects and different garden moods could be incorporated into a relatively small space, and the level of horticultural sophistication could be matched to the temperaments of the owners.

But this very flexibility and freedom led to its own problems, as Charles Thonger noticed as early as 1904 in *The Book of Garden Design*, one of the first Arts and Crafts garden-design manuals: 'So many people when seeking the assistance of the professional, impose upon him the necessity of giving them "a bit of everything" in the way of design. They must have a rose garden, a corner devoted to rock plants, a few square feet for carpet bedding, a place for water and bog plants, a pergola, and much else beside.' There is a sense with some of the less distinguished Arts and Crafts gardens that their constituent parts have been unpacked in kit form and then assembled to echo current fashions. One commonplace error was to introduce cellular

Arts and Crafts spaces but then leave them clinging rather desperately to the environs of the house, whereas a surer methodology would have been to plan house and garden in tandem.

On a smaller scale, Arts and Crafts gardens were sometimes reduced to set-pieces – a wishing well here, a pergola there, a herbaceous border, a rose arch, a pair of topiary peacocks, a brick terrace – and in such cases they quickly became irredeemably twee. A garden such as that at Ruckmans, in Surrey (an early house by Lutyens in 1894), provides a fascinating example of the two sides of Arts and Crafts garden style – indeed, it is a Janus-faced garden, made by the owners. At the front is a 'soft' romantic cottage garden, whereas behind the house is a panoply of Arts and Crafts 'hard' structural features, including a terrace, a sundial and a rose arch. Yet the whole thing is realised on an inappropriately small scale.

Horticulture was another bone of contention. The Jekyll – Lutyens partnership may have represented the ideal – but what was everyone else supposed to do? The landscape

▲ *Great Tangley Manor, Surrey (1905). The architect Philip Webb had made some decisive changes to the garden in the 1880s, including the covered bridge and walkway across the re-dug moat. The 'old-fashioned' tone of Webb's work pleased Jekyll and influenced Lutyens.*

painter Alfred Parsons, who settled at Broadway in Gloucestershire in the late 1890s, was a rare example of a specialist Arts and Crafts professional plantsman. He designed several exuberant cottage-style gardens for Cotswolds houses, such as The Court Farm at Broadway, and at Wightwick Manor in Staffordshire, where his plantings complemented Mawson's garden architecture.

Among the architects, there was ambivalence about gardening as opposed to garden design – that perennial simmering hostility between those who believe a garden is intended for growing plants, and those who think that plants are one of the materials of garden design. It was the amateur garden owners, often acting on informal advice and collaboration, who tended to achieve most in terms of horticulture in the Arts and Crafts garden.

In England for about a decade-and-a-half from 1900,

hundreds of gardens were designed in tandem with new, medium-sized houses, and certain architects responded to the challenge with verve and originality. Their work betrayed the influence not just of Sedding, Lutyens, Webb and other Arts and Crafts exemplars, but also of a panoply of historical styles, from Moorish to Dutch to the ever-present Italianate (a style described in its own right in Chapter 5). One well-known example of the eclectic approach was the architect Thackeray Turner's garden at Westbrook, Surrey, which was admired by near-neighbour Gertrude Jekyll and receives a chapter all to itself in *Gardens for Small Country Houses*. Unlike most of his architectural colleagues, Turner was an accomplished plantsman, and the numerous small hedged gardens at Westbrook featured herbaceous borders inspired by Jekyll's experiments in colour progression.

The architect Charles Edward Mallows was one of the first and most successful Arts and Crafts garden designers. Working in partnership with George Grocock and informally with Mawson, Mallows produced geometrically arranged gardens consisting of square and rectangular beds in hedged or low-walled enclosures. There were long vistas and even a certain monumentality – as at Tirley Garth in Cheshire, his major work. Yet he reconciled this formality with a delicate sense of Arts and Crafts intimacy and seclusion in the garden's discrete spaces.

Robert Weir Schultz was another architect who became adept at designing Arts and Crafts gardens on a large scale, with yew-enclosed gardens, long borders and a diverse range of architectural detailing. But for his own house – The Barn, in Hampshire – Schultz created a much simpler garden in the Morris vein, with numerous small box-hedged compartments, topiary and hardy perennials packing the borders and a sundial at the centre.

The architect Detmar Blow made some grand gardens for some grand clients. At his own house, Hilles, in Gloucestershire, he created a feeling of great lightness and space with generous terraces of loose-fitting flags and beds of rosemary and alyssum, complementing expansive views over the Severn Valley. Like Lutyens and a number of other Arts and Crafts designers, Blow would turn more and more frequently to Classicism in later life.

Also situated in Gloucestershire is Rodmarton, perhaps the most authentically Arts and Crafts garden of all, where the ideals of both patron and designer were entirely in sympathy, and where every detail of house and garden conspires to create the sense of a rare unity of intention. Ernest Barnsley designed this wide, narrow arc of a house in 1909 for stockbroker and Arts and Crafts true-believer Claud Biddulph and his gardening wife; it was not completed until 1929. At the level of detail, the house design is obsessively authentic in its adherence to the Cotswolds vernacular, even if the house as it was built is thoroughly idiosyncratic. The garden is also quintessentially Arts and Crafts in that it is an imaginative re-casting of pseudo-medieval themes in a rigid cellular structure, with some degree of horticultural innovation, such as the all-white border (William Scrubey, the head gardener, was a rare find). Unlike later gardens made up of 'rooms', Rodmarton closely follows Morris's injunction to make the garden an extension of the house, in the intense arrangement of yew hedges on the terrace which gives directly on to the house.

The garden structure at Rodmarton is also curious in that it is much wider than it is deep (echoing the shape of the

OPPOSITE ABOVE:

● *Coleton Fishacre, Devon (1930).*
Garden buildings, pavilions and
arbours were incorporated into many
Arts and Crafts gardens. The rustic
lookout at Oswald Milne's master-
piece originally commanded open
views of the combe. Today, trees and
shrubs have grown up to enclose it.

OPPOSITE BELOW:

● *Rodmarton, Gloucestershire*
(1931). This is the garden realised in
closest sympathy with William Morris's
ideals. The photograph shows the
original scale of the great double
borders. Mature topiary now obscures
the view to the pavilion.

ABOVE:

● *Ashford Chace, Hampshire*
(1920). A garden with the character
of an architectural experiment.
The Classical dining loggia looks out
to the magnificent woods, while just
around the corner, lies the deep
sunken garden with Italian and
Moorish influences at work
(see page 59).

house), with the main double herbaceous border sited a little way to the west, secreted inside one of a series of carefully ordered and relatively spacious garden enclosures. The garden is highly architectural in conception, but feels unusually connected with the surrounding landscape, since meadows come right up to the box-hedged terrace garden, which is itself hard by the walls of the house, so that the building feels almost as if it is set in the fields.

Rodmarton Manor is one of those designs that cannot be captured well in photographs – it tends to look clichéd – but it is an exceptional garden; Hidcote and Sissinghurst may have emerged as indisputably the most influential English gardens of the twentieth century (see Chapter 6), but perhaps Rodmarton should be up there with them. Hidcote has its unique 'otherness', Sissinghurst its irresistible biographical appeal, but Rodmarton is possessed of an intense and sequestered atmosphere that is all its own, and even now retains a strong sense of its original integrity. It is still owned and gardened by the Biddulph family.

Harry Inigo Triggs was one of the chief proselytisers for

formality in garden design during the early years of the century. His taste ran from Inigo Jones to the Italian Renaissance to André Le Nôtre, and he wrote about all his favourite designers in a series of lavishly produced books. His sophisticated, cosmopolitan attitude was the polar opposite to the cultish ruralism of Rodmarton, but both are aptly labelled Arts and Crafts. Triggs's scholarship and first-hand experience of gardens throughout Europe led to a certain stylistic panache, and this is perhaps exercised most dramatically in his own garden at Little Boarhunt in Hampshire, where a sunken rose garden and pergola (Italianate in essence), surrounded by a low, crevice-planted wall dignified by a tiled pavilion (English vernacular), contains a formal canal (Moorish meets Dutch), out of which erupts a fluted column (Classical), surmounted by a sprightly *putto* or Cupid (Italian Renaissance). The planting is alpine. The extraordinary thing is that although Triggs's design sounds like a mess, it is so well focused (on the *putto*) and so well balanced structurally, that it seems rich and glamorous rather than disorientating.

The historical discrepancies prevalent in many Arts and Crafts gardens in fact help to create a sense of transcendent escapism: Moorish or Byzantine or French flourishes introduce a frisson of exoticism, but the old-fashioned plantings reassure us that we are safely in Albion. At Ashford Chace, also in Hampshire, which Triggs realised with his partner W. F. Unsworth (of garden suburb fame), there is an extraordinary sunken garden – much deeper than is usual – which incorporates some outlandishly Moorish elements, such as a curlicue rill and tile-lined pool. However, the house's principal vista, which shoots away into the surrounding countryside on the other side of the house, is deeply vernacular in inspiration, celebrating the mysterious hanging woods of the hills beyond.

Oliver Hill was one of the most intriguing, talented and prolific designers of the early twentieth century; he had been apprenticed to Lutyens, as a friend of the family. Hill is notoriously difficult to categorise because he seemed to change his stylistic affiliation by the week; it seems that the only constants of his work are originality and quality. His multi-levelled formal garden for Moor Close, Berkshire, is typical of his exuberance and unpredictability as a designer, featuring a series of interlocking garden courts of different shapes and sizes, surmounted by a pergola, and a riotous variety of stone paving, marble, brickwork and pebbles. This design represents perhaps the extreme of eclectic architectural experimentation in Arts and Crafts gardens. At Valewood Farm, his country cottage in Surrey, Hill enlivened the cottagey plantings with sculptural objects, blue-glazed pots, avians of various kinds, a loggia-like converted farm building, and a perfectly oval swimming pool. Valewood was the apogee of the designer weekend country cottage.

Baillie Scott's was also a distinctive architectural voice, not only for his modest yet elegant houses, but also because

ABOVE:
● *Barrow Court, Somerset (1902).*
The sunken iris pond, set within enclosed courts, was one of several features designed by F. Inigo Thomas in the 1890s to complement the Jacobean house. Elsewhere in this garden, Thomas's work is Neo-Baroque and certainly not in tune with Jekyll's ideas about the 'purity' of English Italianate.

RIGHT:
● *Moor Close, Berkshire (1924).*
Arts and Crafts design of the 1920s and 1930s could veer towards ostentation and monumentality. Oliver Hill's extraordinary, multi-levelled design, which included twin gazebos linked by a pergola, is a supreme example of this tendency.

he was particularly interested in the possibilities for small gardens. In his book *Houses and Gardens* (1906), Baillie Scott made some radical suggestions: ornamental vegetable gardening as a theme, and for the medium-sized country house a completely wild garden based on the idea of the woodland copse. For the suburban garden, he recommends a basically formal yet 'rough and homely treatment', with perennial plants overflowing from the borders and a few annuals. He also discusses the desirability of a lawn, a flower garden in two parts (one for roses, one for perennials), straight paths, a pergola, yew or box hedges, sundials, garden seats at the ends of views, pots on terraces, and even a wishing well. Here we have the vocabulary of the suburban garden clearly delineated.

Perhaps more than any other designer (including Webb), Baillie Scott's style was plundered by speculative housebuilders – first by the garden-suburb movement, with which Baillie Scott himself was involved (in 1912 he provided a prototype for the suburban house and garden at 48 Storeys Way in Cambridge, although in print he states that the garden was designed by the owner), and then by the creators of Metroland – the new commuter suburbs of the 1920s and 1930s. The inter-war period saw some four million new houses built. What Baillie Scott envisaged was a scaled-down version of the Arts and Crafts garden, and that is what was created millions of times over, effectively setting the tone for the domestic garden in England for the rest of the twentieth century.

The beginnings of this process can also be seen in the pages of *Country Life*: in the gardens of smaller country houses, formal Arts and Crafts gardens were sometimes writ small, with sunken gardens, terraces, rills and pergolas shrunk to fit the space available. By the mid-1920s in *Country Life*, garden after garden represents a scaled-down version of Arts and Crafts style, with an unvarying recipe of long double borders (often leading up to a gable end of the house), enclosing hedges, a lawn, low brick terraces, clipped box balls, brick paths, paved areas, sundials, pergolas and roses. In semi-rural situations, the country-cottage look was as popular as the more ornamental style, with an emphasis on a sense of profusion along the garden path, around the porch, and under the windows.

The idea of the Arts and Crafts garden was also appropriated wholesale by the publishing industry, forming the basis for garden-design manuals aimed at new homeowners. Early examples tended to be written by garden-owners rather than professionals. *A Garden in the Suburbs* (1901) by Mrs Leslie Williams is a pæan to her 'oblong' and its proliferation of lilies, while the descriptively entitled *My*

Old World Garden and How I Made It In A London Suburb (1910) by George Hillyard Swinstead does exactly what it says on the cover, describing a garden of bijou charm, with a wooden trellis for climbing plants, a low wall with crevices, a sundial and even a topiary bird. There were a few voices dissenting from the surge in popularity of Arts and Crafts ornament: Walter P. Wright, horticultural superintendent for Kent County Council, grotesquely satirised design and designers in *The Perfect Garden* (1908), and called for a garden made of plants alone, yet formal in layout.

Despite Wright's proselytising for simplicity in design, there was to be no stemming of the tide of unbridled ornamentation, which was positively encouraged by most garden-design commentators. *Garden Architecture* (1926) by Geoffrey Henslow is an Arts and Crafts sourcebook of off-the-peg garden solutions for the man in the street, even including the names and addresses of contractors who could provide a Tudor garden, a Dutch garden or a Stuart garden. Ralph Hancock's glamorous roof garden for Derry and Tom's department store on Kensington High Street (1938) was perhaps the high-water mark of this type of eclecticism, with Moorish and Tudor influences jostling with the celebrated flamingos. But in domestic gardens, there is little evidence of there being much interest in total makeovers – gardens were created in piecemeal fashion, according to precepts outlined in books such as *Garden Making by Example* (1932) by G. C. Taylor (*Country Life*'s

Valewood Farm, Surrey (1929).

(left and above): *At his weekend house, Oliver Hill created a sophisticated version of the country cottage with an oval swimming pool, blue-glazed pots, sculptural vernacular artefacts placed in the open-sided farm buildings, and Jekyllian plantings.*

gardens editor), which would be reprinted in new editions well into the mid-1950s.

Taylor's book is testament to the popularity of small circular lily pools, crazy-paved paths, sunken gardens, birdbaths, pedestal sculptures, planted urns, standard roses, diminutive rockeries, wishing wells (perverted versions of the very first one, at Morris's Red House), and sundials. (Sundials were the sole subject of several lavish books at this time.) It was a new kind of eclecticism, and the nursery trade enthusiastically responded with any number of variations on standard ornamental features, while also offering to plant up whole gardens for customers using plants from stock. George Dillistone was one of the few notable garden designers employed by a nursery; he also created large-scale gardens such as that at Hallingbury Place in Essex.

As Richard Sudell noted in *Landscape Gardening* (1933): 'We have had too much material, we have had many ideas. Our gardens suffer from a surfeit of good and indifferent things. Craftsmen give us a wealth of material in the form of garden ornaments, seats, furniture and elaborate pergolas. Builders provide us with coloured tiles and bricks, and gardeners offer us hundreds of plants, which they have

collected from every corner of the earth. We are thus involved in complexity, and this, in a nut-shell, is the reason for the need of careful design.' Sudell's advice was not to be heeded for most of the ensuing century. The ideals of Baillie Scott and the genius of Lutyens had been misappropriated and miniaturised to fit the scale of suburban gardens. This was the national garden style that prevailed through most of the twentieth century.

● *Smaller Arts and Crafts Houses. The double herbaceous border was de rigueur at many new houses in the 1920s and 1930s and was typically focused on a back door, as at Orchards Farm* (above) *or a gable end, as at Beaumonts* (below).

RIGHT:
● *The Yews, Cumbria. The long herbaceous border in a garden where both Thomas Mawson and H. Avray Tipping had a hand. Unusually, the border runs parallel to the house frontage.*

4 · Border Cultists
1900–1939

◣ *Hascombe Court, Surrey (1936). The 1930s was a high point for border planting. This kind of surging fullness with no 'flowerless gaps' was the aim. The prescription was for large groupings of single species, flowers from spring to late summer, and height variety created by tall flowers, such as delphiniums or lupins.*

ABOVE:

◣ *Littlecote Manor, Wiltshire (1927). The great border, 500ft long and 20ft deep, facing the canal in one of the compartmentalised areas at this Tudor manor house. In his article for Country Life, H. Avray Tipping described 'masses of phlox and* thalictrum, *of salvia and* gaillardia *flowering side by side with introductions such as sweet pea and snapdragon'.*

It was owner-gardeners – amateurs – who were to have the most decisive influence on horticultural style in the period leading up to the Second World War. The structure of Arts and Crafts gardens had been created predominantly by architects, while the profession of garden design was only just becoming established. Gertrude Jekyll had not only united horticulture with architecture though her work with Lutyens, she had also managed to bridge the divide between amateurism and professionalism through her design consultancy and thriving plants nursery – but it was an example others found difficult to emulate. It took time for garden design to become truly professionalised, particularly from a female perspective.

Through the popularity of her writings and garden designs, Jekyll had helped transform gardening into a pastime which could be practised by a middle-class lady of the house – and perhaps even be turned to professional

advantage. By 1910, there were seven ladies' gardening colleges in England; for single middle-class women lacking independent means and seeking a vocation, gardening had become as respectable an option as nursing, teaching or becoming a governess. Yet once they had qualified, professional women gardeners tended to go into market gardening or the nursery trade – the more artistic end of gardening remained the preserve of owner-gardeners, amateur advisors or head gardeners (always male).

Thomas Mawson paved the way for the modern profession of landscape architecture by setting up the Institute of Landscape Architects in 1929, but professional horticulture provided on a consultancy basis – that is, above the traditional artisan level of gardeners and head gardeners – remained largely an informal, word-of-mouth affair until after the war. This meant that in many cases, even where a client had paid for a designed Arts and Crafts garden, once the architect and his builders had gone, it was left to the client to find a gardener to fill in the spaces with plants – with predictably varied results. It was only in the 1930s that professionals like Percy Cane emerged (often from the nursery trade), calling themselves garden designers rather than architects, and specialising in planting as well as planning. Ralph Hancock was a particularly successful professional garden designer, who unlike most contemporaries offered a 'design-and-build' service rather than just a design on paper, made after an afternoon visit and sent off in the post with a bill. Hancock worked in a wide variety of styles, from Tudor knot to high Modernist, and was a fixture at the Chelsea Flower Show and the Ideal Home Exhibition through the 1930s and 1940s. (At this

time, it was common for designers to be commissioned to re-create their show gardens, or something like it, for clients who had visited the show to choose a garden 'off the shelf'.)

Creative horticultural advice was largely provided by respected amateur plantsmen and women, whose reputations and ideas were disseminated quite informally through the example of their own gardens, through visits to the gardens of friends and friends of friends, and in conversational (not overtly technical) books and magazine articles. The gardener with this kind of status – operating somewhere between professional and amateur, but often of high social class, even aristocratic – has been a resilient component of twentieth-century English gardening and is still an important part of the scene today.

What kind of planting schemes were favoured by these garden-makers? Arts and Crafts planting at the beginning of the century can be broadly defined as a profusion of old English flowers, or flowers that appear English, intermixed with artful abandon to create an impression of accidental beauty and natural healthiness. The mixed border should appear unplanned: gaps or spaces are to be avoided, as are strict progressions of height or palpably organised blocks of colour. Plants intermix and grow through each other (although a 'skirt' of low-growing plants at first persists at the front of borders), and where colour theming is encouraged – and it was by no means universal – the emphasis is on drifts of colour rather than on clumps. Exotics are perfectly acceptable, but they are never placed in the border self-consciously as 'specimen' plants to be singled out and admired; rather, they are absorbed into the whole scheme. Foliage is admired, particularly if it is dramatically large-leaved, variegated or spiky, but the main emphasis is on colour derived from flowers – on the whole, the idea of the garden as synonymous with the 'flower garden' has persisted. Finally, the mixed border should ideally be a source of delight and of surprises, with its own internal rhythm created by colour and structure.

Away from the borders, there is avid enthusiasm for horticultural specialisation, with rhododendrons and other flowering shrubs newly imported from China and Japan, rock-garden plants arrayed on artifical scree slopes or rockeries, lily ponds, and single-species areas for lupins, delphiniums, pinks, sweet peas, or one of the other obsessions of the time. To sum up: from the turn of the century until the Second World War, planting style evolved from vague notions of 'cottage planting' and ideas gleaned from the wild-gardening precepts of William Robinson into an ever more sophisticated appreciation of plants for their own sake (something which came to be known as plants-

● *Arley Hall, Cheshire (1904).*
The borders at Arley were among
the first to be replanted in an
informal, romantic style in accordance
with the writings of Gertrude Jekyll,
Eleanor Vere Boyle and others.
The topiarised hedging, a legacy of
the Victorian era, remained the same;
only the planting changed.

OPPOSITE BELOW:
● *Harleyford Manor,*
Buckinghamshire (1910). The
borders were described in Country
Life *as 'Old English', which to the*
magazine meant in the vanguard of
fashion. The colour-themed flower
groupings have been designed
with a painterly eye.

BELOW:
● *Packwood House, Warwickshire*
(1902). Herbaceous borders in
transition between the orderliness
of High Victorian and the looser Arts
and Crafts look.

manship) and an artistic engagement with the mixed border, in the manner of Gertrude Jekyll. If it all sounds rather familiar, that is because the basic template for horticulture in England did not diverge significantly from this model for the rest of the century.

The pioneers of the new look in planting before the turn of the twentieth century tended to be owners of larger, more established gardens, where the Arts and Crafts horticultural sensibility began to be absorbed into the garden's existing structure. So the long formal flowerbeds of strictly organised Victorian flower schemes were gradually replaced by herbaceous borders, areas of carpet bedding were overhauled and simplified or laid to grass, and climbing plants were encouraged to colonise steps, terraces and other architectural features. In many ways, the High Victorian version of Italianate, found in so many gardens of the period, was well suited to an Arts and Crafts treatment. The revolution, therefore, was relatively painless: existing

hedge systems were retained, and trees, terraces, fountains and so on could remain in situ, albeit coaxed into a certain dilapidation.

The long double border at Arley Hall, for example (which Jekyll praised in 1904 as just about the best example of planting in England), was contained within the sub-divided, topiarised hedging system that had previously seen some of the best horticulture in the High Victorian manner. In retrospect, this structure seems tailor-made for the herbaceous border – an episode conceived as complete in itself rather than as groups of plants and specimens, contained and offset by dark hedges – as does the hedging system at another prototype Arts and Crafts garden: Brickwall in Sussex, which Dante Gabriel Rossetti had 'discovered' in the previous century. At Packwood House, Warwickshire, herbaceous borders in the new style were juxtaposed with the garden's glorious arrangement of clipped yews on smooth grass, with no apparent incongruity. But the tone of

these gardens was nevertheless changed dramatically by the new planting style, since it introduced a much more relaxed and romantic atmosphere.

In terms of the detail of the planting itself, changes were not usually made overnight, or in a single season – rather, the order of Victorian borders was compromised and relaxed gradually, a transition that can be seen in several gardens in the first years of the century (at Hampton Court, Herefordshire, for example, featured in *Country Life* in 1901, or later at Harleyford Manor, Buckinghamshire, illustrated in 1910). When wholesale changes to the planting were made it could go very wrong, which is what seems to have happened at Kildwick Hall, Yorkshire, where the dignity of a fine old terrace was spoiled by some fashionable planting.

At some places, of course, the Victorian way of doing things remained imperiously unaffected by the revolutions described in the gardening literature – Borde Hill in Sussex

is a good example, as is Ashridge Park, Hertfordshire, or the extravaganza at Hewell Grange, Worcestershire, where the serried ranks of exotic plants stretching into the distance seem to provide a metaphor for Victorian imperialist conquest.

Even where the new ideas were being integrated, to judge by contemporary photographs the first experiments with the new planting style were often carried out in the kitchen garden or in a peripheral area – 'over the wall' as it were – leaving the rest of the garden intact, at least initially. At a garden such as Sturry Court, Kent, the herbaceous borders and topiary appear segregated, placed to one side of the lawn, and at Puslinch in Devon they seem to be hidden behind a high wall. In some places, the Arts and Crafts herbaceous border was to explode out of the kitchen garden to colonise the rest of the space.

There were, however, aesthetic benefits to 'imprisoning' the new garden look. The imagery of Frances Hodgson

▪ Compton End, Hampshire (1919). A cottage for the connoisseur: the architect George Kitchin created a sophisticated reworking of the Edwardian country-cottage garden. The sculptural shapes of branches, topiary, stonework and ornaments are in harmony with the interior decoration of the house.

◆ *Saighton Grange, Cheshire (1908). Hollyhocks and old-fashioned flowers complement the stately towers beyond. In the early years of the century, romantic borders were often sited at some distance from the house, behind hedges or walls, while areas closer to the house were still kept pristine in the Victorian manner.*

Burnett's *The Secret Garden* (1911) was to be influential in this respect, since it introduced the idea of a garden that might be discovered by the visitor almost by accident or even as an act of transgression. The Edwardian penchant for great swags of rambling roses on walls, pergolas, gloriettas and on chains certainly owes something to *The Secret Garden*. Indeed, the book became a cult in its own right – Celia, Lady Scarbrough, made a 'secret garden' at Sandbeck in Yorkshire immediately after reading it, and even nicknamed her son Dickon after one of the characters – and the potent image of the secret garden has been remarkably resilient in the popular imagination. *The Secret Garden* has also informed the romantic idea of 'rescuing' a garden (something Dickon terms 'wakenin' up a garden'), which has been another key twentieth-century horticultural preoccupation, enhancing the emotional appeal of restored gardens from Sissinghurst to Heligan.

Certainly the First World War had a drastic effect on the economy and manning of gardens – as it did everywhere else – but the most dramatic alterations to gardens brought about by economic and social change occurred after the Second World War, not the First. In fact, country gardens in the inter-war years continued to employ significant numbers of men (at a ratio of one gardener per acre, according to Graham Thomas's oft-quoted estimation), and in some cases extras were taken on during the Depression to help ease unemployment. There was also a good deal of new design work commissioned from architects.

Notwithstanding the sophistication of Jekyll's colour-themed borders, the romantic ideal of the cottage garden formed the basis of many planting schemes, and on an appropriately small scale the cottage idyll informed the whole tone of the garden. The look of the cottage garden has been well summarised by Stephen Lacey, describing Margery Fish's later interpretation of it at East Lambrook Manor in Somerset: 'Uneven, winding paths, littered with seedlings and prostrate herbs, twist their way through beds crammed with double primroses and hellebores, hollyhocks and astrantias, pulmonarias, pinks and campanulas;

culinary herbs rub shoulders with aristocratic shrubs and common native plants with eastern rarities; roses and honeysuckles tumble out of apple trees; curious wallflowers and miniature irises sprout from cracks and crevices; and the house and barn are engulfed in foliage. There are no views or vistas in such a garden: the interest is always in the foreground with the plants themselves.'

This type of gardening is not quite the same as gardening for colour effect in the herbaceous or mixed border, where the mid-range view is so important and the gardener revels in artistic control rather than an impression of a degree of abandonment. Many a garden-owner must have laid down Jekyll's doughty, technically prescriptive volumes and turned with relief to books such as *Garden of England* (1908) by E. T. Cook, with romantic illustrations by Beatrice Parsons, which simply equates cottage gardening with a 'love of flowers'. There are few rules here: plants newly introduced from China by the great plant collector E. H. Wilson are enthusiastically recommended for planting cheek by jowl with hollyhocks, campanulas and honesty, and simple beds of lavender and rosemary serve as the horticultural mainstay.

At Compton End in Hampshire, the Winchester-based architect George Herbert Kitchin, a friend of both Jekyll's and H. Avray Tipping's, made perhaps the quintessential Edwardian country-cottage garden. Having restored the modest thatched cottage in the 1890s, over the next twenty years he set about making a country garden with formal inflections. Straight brick paths led to the principal rooms of the cottage, and the geometric flowerbeds were filled with delphiniums, roses, verbascums, phlox and other cottagey plants. There were clipped yew hedges, topiary peacocks and box balls at the edges of borders, as well as a rectangular lily pool, terracotta urns and a sundial. Like Oliver Hill's Valewood Farm in Sussex, and Harold Falkner's Cobbetts in Surrey, Compton End was a sophisticated reworking of traditional cottage themes: pretty, rambling and a little tumbledown, but perfectly controlled and with crucial formalist interventions.

This kind of knowing appropriation of the cottage vernacular can be seen many times in gardens of the period: at Millmead, for example, a garden originally designed by Jekyll, or at St Nicholas in Yorkshire, where the Hon. Robert James became famous for his massed plantings (often of single species) within formal enclosures. Mark Fenwick of Abbotswood (a Lutyens house) was also celebrated for his panache as a plantsman; he entertained many gardening visitors who went away with new ideas.

The cottage look was deemed appropriate for almost any situation, whatever the scale, which led to anomalies, such as cottage borders at places like the monumental Allington Castle, enthusiastically restored by Martin Conway, with a garden by Philip Tilden, or West Bitchfield, where a cottagey garden path flanked by exuberant flowers leads the eye towards a crenellated tower. Jekyll was well aware of the potential for such incongruity, and in her commentary on Hardwick Hall in *Some English Gardens* (1904) she remarks with customary perspicacity upon 'some excellent gardening in a long flower-border outside the forecourt wall. Here the size of the house is no longer oppressive, and it comes into proper scale.' This also helps to explain why herbaceous borders were often secreted away at this time; today's gardeners are now so used to seeing the Arts and Crafts border in almost any situation that any impression of incongruity in such a situation has been lost.

West Bitchfield, Northumberland (1940). By the time of the Second World War, the romantic Arts and Crafts border was so entrenched that it could be used in almost any situation. A contrast between architecture and planting such as this would have appeared jarring a few decades earlier.

▲ *St Nicholas, Yorkshire (1936).*
The cottage garden, with many
different species of lilies planted
alongside old shrub roses, was one of
the many horticultural attractions of
Robert 'Bobby' James's seven-acre
garden. Discrete garden rooms,
enclosed by walls and evergreen
hedges, contained a dazzling display
of plant rarities, from rhododendrons
to alpines and unusual tender shrubs.

Jekyll was the most respected gardener of her time, but not many gardeners were able to follow her precepts to the letter, and there were several other eminent voices to heed. Robinson still loomed large as the conscience of modern horticulture, and his creed of wild gardening never fell from favour (he even outlived Jekyll). A book such as *The Summer Garden of Pleasure* (1908) by Mrs Stephen Batson eschews discussion of the fashionable colour-themed border and opens instead with a chapter on the wild garden, extolling the virtues of bulbs naturalised in grass, and shade-loving plants such as Solomon's seal, lily of the valley, aconites and hellebores. (It reads curiously like a late-1990s planting manual.)

Ellen Willmott of Warley Place in Essex was a contemporary of Jekyll, and Russell Page and others have sought to place her on a par with Robinson and Jekyll in terms of influence. Willmott gardened on a grand scale from the mid-1870s, following Robinsonian precepts in her garden perhaps even more closely than Robinson himself, with a sense of artful abandon and wildness amid exemplary horticulture. Willmott's great love was roses, but she also made a celebrated rock garden. Money seemed to be no object (until it ran out, and she was forced to sell everything).

G. F. Wilson was another influential disciple of Robinson's, and in gardens in Surrey – Heatherbank, Oakwood and Wisley – he gardened assiduously in the 'wild' style. The widely respected Canon Ellacombe seemed to straddle the Victorian and Edwardian eras, and through his example many garden owners were encouraged to opt for much greater informality in planting. His work remained an influential template for those who liked to

BELOW:
● *The Manor House,
Sutton Courtenay, Berkshire (1931).
Norah Lindsay's own garden was the
epitome of effortless style, and she
was in great demand as an informal
garden designer. The look of her
gardens was more carefree and
blowsy than Jekyll's who had more
definite ideas about structure.*

OPPOSITE:
● *Port Lympne, Kent (1933).
'The deepest and longest herbaceous
borders, the most colossal beds of
blue delphinium', was how Kenneth
Clark described the great double
borders at Philip Sassoon's coastal
extravaganza, where Norah Lindsay
had advised.*

read Gertrude Jekyll but perhaps felt a little daunted by her artistic prescriptions.

Perhaps because of the opportunities it presented for individuality and originality, the herbaceous border became and was to remain the national horticultural obsession. The usual caveat must be made at this point: strictly speaking, most herbaceous borders were 'mixed', in that they contained shrubs, bulbs and some annuals, as well as herbaceous perennials. Every serious garden had at least one long, deep border (preferably double – meaning on both sides of a path) as its climax, in which the creative force of the garden sought to make an impression. Then, as now, the herbaceous border was a horticultural laboratory in which any combination of plants could be attempted, and it remains the pre-eminent showcase for the gardener's skill.

The doyenne of amateur garden stylists at this period was Norah Lindsay, evidently an entertaining person. Mrs Lindsay possessed in spades the one attribute that Jekyll signally lacked: glamour. And in the 1920s and 1930s, glamour was not something to be taken lightly. Russell Page provided a pen portrait of her in *Education of a Gardener* (1962): 'Norah Lindsay, so typical of the English lady who gardens, even her hats an offering of fruit or flowers, had a special talent for handling gardens of herbaceous plants. Between the wars she moved from one country house to the next, gardening and keeping everybody amused and entertained. She rushed from garden to garden, leaving long and brilliant reports as to what should be done and what planted, all pencilled out in a large flowing writing on endless sheets of flimsy paper … She lifted her herbaceous planting into a poetic category and gave it an air of rapture and spontaneity. I think she visualised very surely, added the unexpected species whose form and colour would shake a group of plants out of the commonplace, and then she would be on her way, leaving the rest to nature and the astonished gardener.'

Lindsay worked at Port Lympne in Kent for Philip Sassoon, helping to plan the August borders which were the estate's most palatable glory; at Cliveden for Nancy Astor; and at Godmersham for the Trittons. She replanned a parterre at Blickling in Norfolk (a planting scheme still maintained by the National Trust); and she was a close friend of Lawrence Johnston of Hidcote, where her contribution is difficult to gauge but may well have been substantial. These are simply the better-known examples of her influence. Lindsay's frothy, spontaneous planting style was lent structure by the architectural forms of favoured plants such as cardoon thistles and her signature columnar Irish yews. The best sources of information about her unique style are the article she wrote about her own garden at Sutton Courtenay, in Berkshire, for *Country Life* in 1931 and her detailed description of her planting for Philip Sassoon in the 1929 *Country Life* article on Trent Park, Hertfordshire.

The main point about herbaceous planting style is that it always reflects the personality of the designer or gardener and that no two gardens ever feel quite the same for this reason as much as any other (which makes a mockery of modern attempts to restore gardens in the style of their long-dead owners). This has always led to great tonal variety in gardens. The Du Cane sisters, Ella and Florence, are a good example of the individualistic nature of herbaceous gardening, since the look of their gardens at Mountains and Beacon Hill, both in Essex, is far more

controlled in terms of structure and pictorial awareness than the effusive, fluid plantings of Lindsay and others at this time.

The Du Cane sisters travelled widely in the first two decades of the century and produced a series of books, most of them written by Florence and all of them with water-colour illustrations by Ella. By far their most successful and popular work was *Flowers and Gardens of Japan* (1908), and

it was this trip that was to have the most decisive influence on their garden design which is distinguished by a poised prettiness. The Du Canes did not create copies of Japanese gardens, but echoed the pictorial composition of the Classical gardens of Kyoto and Tokyo, using masses of bright tulips, introducing thatched pavilions, lines of cherry trees, and spreading cut-leaved acers. At Mountains, their interest in Japanese plants was reflected in a densely planted woodland dell, with azaleas, primulas, irises, and more maples.

Another gardening original was H. Avray Tipping of *Country Life*, who perhaps more than anyone else continued to work in the spirit of his friend Gertrude Jekyll. At a succession of three houses in Monmouthshire, between 1890 and 1925, Tipping made gardens with strong struc-tural bones but where the atmosphere was defined princi-pally by plants. Tipping gardened in a relaxed manner, but it was not the kind of artful informality practised by Norah Lindsay, with hundreds of plants and flowers clam-bering over each other in a tapestry of fecund profusion – it was more akin to the Jekyll approach, in which gaps in beds were tolerated, subtle rhythms were introduced by

▲ Crowhurst Place, Surrey (1919). George Crawley designed some modern interpolations for this moated house: the sunken 'Dutch' water garden (above), with a bridge doubling as a terrace, was placed to one side of a stone-roofed Elizabethan barn, and was clearly inspired by Lutyens. Nearby, a characterful fountain marks a crossroads in the grassy walks and deep herbaceous borders (left).

repetition, and architectural plants and flowers were combined in strong structural drifts where colour combinations were statements of intent rather than the result of happy accident.

Mathern Place was Tipping's first garden, and here he introduced a complex of yew-hedged enclosures, topiary and grass allées. Tipping was circumspect about the use of such formal features – like many writers of discernment, he was critical of the popular fashion for pergolas, which seemed to be introduced to every garden regardless of their suitability. Topiary was also particularly prone to a descent into cliché, and Tipping was critical of the obsessions of Nathaniel Lloyd of Great Dixter, whose garden and 1925 treatise represented the apogee of Arts and Crafts topiary.

In Tipping's other Monmouthshire gardens, Mounton and High Glanau, as well as in his commissioned work – including Wyndcliffe Court and the terrace at Chequers – he displayed a confident handling of formal features such as terraces and enclosed rose gardens, allowing them to segue together with more informal elements of the garden.

Only a designer with a sure understanding of both the planting and structural aspects of gardens could have achieved this.

Away from the gardens of the innovators, the *leitmotif* of popular planting in the 1910s and through the 1920s was a growing preference for grey and silver-grey foliage plants in combination with purple, blue or dusty-pink flowers. It was basically a simplified version of Jekyll's signature look, which, according to Jason Hill at the time of writing in 1936, had 'degenerated rather timidly into grey and blue borders'. Gradually, the notion that muted pastel colours were preferable to (and not as vulgar as) brightly coloured flowers took hold, until by mid-century the Jekyll style had become associated with a muted, subtle colour scheme that did not burn too brightly at either end of the colour spectrum. The era of the pastel-shaded garden had arrived. The fact that Jekyll had devoted an entire section of her own garden to brightly coloured pansies and revelled in hot colours where appropriate had been disregarded. But this prejudice against supposed gaudiness was deep-rooted,

83

dating back to the wholesale rejection of carpet bedding that had begun by 1900.

As the influential plantsman E. A. Bowles of Myddelton House in Enfield noted in *My Garden in Summer* (1914): 'It is fashionable nowadays to affect a horror of bedding plants. People say they must allow a few to please the gardener, just as they say they eat entrées and savouries to please the cook.' This equation between outmoded proletarian attitudes in kitchen and garden highlights an area of key social change at this period. The class stratification of garden style, in terms of plants and ornament, became ever more important as fewer and fewer homeowners could afford to employ their own gardeners and were faced with the same gardening dilemmas as those farther down the social scale. The idea that gaudy annuals are low-class is still with us, and it is regularly exploited and made fun of by Christopher Lloyd at Great Dixter, for example, where a sudden eruption of a mass of eye-scorching calceolarias might make the visitor laugh out loud.

One of the most popular garden writers and broadcasters of the 1920s and 1930s was Marion Cran, whose mischievous, flighty, gossipy writing – together with a penchant for including in her books photographs of herself and her dogs larking about – was an antidote to some of the more serious-minded horticultural writing. Cran wholeheartedly advocated the cottage-garden look for its lack of pretension and planning; indeed, her best-known book is called *The Garden of Ignorance* (1924), in which her herbaceous border is dubbed a 'muddle bed' of 'snapdragons, Canterbury bells, pinks, phloxes, sweet williams, all the other indispensables'. Cran must have detected a certain weariness in readers dazzled by multiple meditations on border style: 'A very large proportion of nearly every garden book is devoted to the scientific discussion of the construction of herbaceous borders.' Single-colour gardens have always been a controversial area of planting design, falling in and out of fashion rapidly, but the straightforwardness of the theme appealed to Cran – her yellow border contained golden pansies, yellow flag irises, roses, sulphurous tree lupins, heleniums and dahlias. This bold choice was intended as an antidote to what Cran viewed as contemporary garden clichés, mainly featuring purple or deep blue, such as 'a bed of white pinks edged with mauve violas, or a bed of purple blue Canterbury bells with yellow violas'.

As is perennially the case with horticulture, enthusiastic gardeners had been feeling for some years that ideas about design and colour theming of borders were taking away from the simple pleasures of growing plants and appreciating them on their own merits. This attitude coincided neatly with the old Morris fallacy that artless gardening was possible, that a garden could be a kind of annex of nature. Eleanor Vere Boyle, writing in *Peacock's Pleasaunce* in 1908, captures this spirit: 'In how many gardens of the day is evident an almost painful striving for effect! To achieve "masses of colour", "wonderful effects", is a chief aim; whilst the endless lovely forms of individual leaf and flower are unnoticed and unthought of.' There seems to be an implicit rebuke of Jekyll here, notwithstanding the fact that Jekyll's whole philosophy was supposed to be based on close appreciation of nature. But not everyone liked (or likes) the idea of the gardener as artist, and that is what was being attacked.

Plantsmen and -women also began to question why they should spend time thinking about the layout and overall appearance of their gardens, when all that really interested them was the plants. A plant-obsessed iconoclast such as the rock-garden guru and plant collector Reginald Farrer could feel confident enough in 1914 to question the very basis of Robinson's and Jekyll's style: 'It is now not so very long since carpet-bedding went out of fashion with a roar of contemptuous execration; and for a short period we were all for a return to what we spoke of as "Nature", but what was merely wobbly anarchy reduced to a high art.'

To the delight of gardeners such as Farrer, the first decades of the century (particularly the 1920s) saw a surge

in the number of new species and varieties made available in the nursery trade, either collected abroad or developed at home through crossing and hybridisation. As if to herald the new century, three new iris species appeared in 1900, and thereafter ever-taller and ever-bluer delphiniums (at first from the French nursery Lemoine of Nancy) and even more colourful lupins were added to the gardener's palette (lupins were far more popular than they are today, even before the celebrated Russell strains were launched in 1937). Daylilies (exotic fare at first) and gladioli became fashionable, alongside traditional favourites such as phlox, poppies, daffodils, tulips and peonies. New strains and varieties of all of these were sought out above all, in a quest for novelty that has never been abandoned by serious horticulturists. In the world of roses, hybrid teas and perpetuals, vigorous ramblers and dwarf polyanthas became nurs-

erymen's staples, and roses first began to be integrated into borders (rather than grown in isolation, perhaps underplanted with lavender) during the 1920s.

Rhododendrons first, then azaleas, camellias, fuchsias (always in and out of fashion), magnolias, Asiatic primulas and all the other Chinese and Japanese varieties were particular objects of obsession, and the delicate charms of alpine plants inspired gardeners to create mini Matterhorns of their own (the most famous example was at Friar Park near Henley, widely viewed as being in excruciatingly bad taste – not that its plantaholic owner was aware of this). A rock garden became an integral part of many gardens, both large and small. This was the period when names such as Loder of Leonardslee, Holford of Westonbirt, Rothschild of Exbury and J. C. Williams of Caerhays became legendary in gardening circles for their plant collections and new crosses (the Loderi rhododendrons, to take just one example).

In the midst of all this garden variety, however, gardeners were struggling to keep up with the nurserymen: in the new 1934 edition of *The Herbaceous Garden* Alice Martineau explains, 'So many new plants have been discovered, and new varieties of old plants introduced, that in justice to my readers I have found a complete revision necessary'. She adds that since the arrival of the Himalayan blue poppy (*Meconopsis betonicifolia*) in 1926, and then the bluer *sino-ornata*, 'our gardens have taken on quite a different aspect regarding colour'. Faced with so much choice and apparently possessed of a voracious appetite for novelty, which the nurseries fed and encouraged, many gardeners began trying to cram as much as they could into their gardens.

In *The Contemplative Gardener* (1939), Jason Hill discerns that, 'The general practice of gardening is so steadily towards filling up and putting in that there is something almost unnatural in making empty spaces and leaving them bare … It is in small gardens (and most of us have small gardens) that the need for space is most strongly felt, yet it is tempting to overcrowd them in order to make the most of every available inch.' It was a warning note that went unheeded in the media and in the nursery trade, where the emphasis has always relentlessly been on increased diversity (and profits), in the guise of a love of plants.

Gardeners had always visited each other, admired plants, talked about plants and swapped plants, but as gardening became more popular the social networks expanded and became ever more sophisticated and partisan. The plantsman or plantswoman became as important a figure in the English garden scene from the 1930s as

the artistic creator of herbaceous borders had been earlier in the century (when a more relaxed attitude to botanical innovation prevailed), and these two dimensions of creative gardening often overlapped. Norah Lindsay's daughter, Nancy, epitomised this development, in that instead of following her mother's example and becoming a *grande dame* garden consultant, she concentrated on the botanical aspects of gardening, seeking out new plants herself and quietly building up a remarkable collection at Sutton Courtenay in Berkshire.

Jason Hill (real name Anthony Hampton) was in the vanguard of this shifting social milieu of horticulturists with an aesthetic, connoisseurial eye. His classic text, *The Curious Gardener* (1932), set the standard for the new attitude: it is an almanac of good taste, in which Hill recommends plants such as then-disregarded shrub roses and climbing roses as 'Madame Alfred Carrière' (twenty years before Graham Thomas championed them), and includes chapters on delicate subjects such as green flowers and fastigiate trees. Perhaps the most fastidious meditation is that on scent, in which he compares the odour of phlox flowers with that of a live pig, and makes the following extraordinary observation: 'The scent of dying strawberry leaves is nearly matched by the fragrance which *Veronica cupressoides* gives off in damp weather or when it is wet with dew; but here the note of cedar wood predominates, and the effect is almost exactly that of Vetivert or Khus-khus, the grass-root which they weave into mats in India.'

Jason Hill was a friend of the artist John Nash, who gardened knowledgeably and enthusiastically at Lane End House, Buckinghamshire, and then at Bottengoms Farm, Essex. Nash was an accomplished botanical illustrator, and his sinuously elegant line drawings dignify books by Hill and others as well as his own writings.

ABOVE:
 Lees Court, Kent (1922). Long rectangular herbaceous beds were secreted behind yew hedges by Thomas Mawson in the 1920s remodelling of this garden. He combined a seventeenth-century style parterre garden, in the spirit of the Inigo Jones façade of the house, with Arts and Crafts inflections such as the borders.

RIGHT:
Sudeley Castle, Gloucestershire (1909). Roses and lavender became a classic Arts and Crafts planting combination. Here it melds perfectly with the scale and decorum of the stately topiary.

LEFT:

● *High Glanau, Monmouthshire (1929). H. Avray Tipping called this his 'ribbon border' on account of its narrowness. More than any other gardener, he had the confidence and the skill (and the background in Aestheticism) to carry the mantle of Jekyll's planting ideas.*

BELOW:

● *Little Paddocks, Berkshire (1934). The borders at this garden – also known for its rhododendrons – were praised in* Country Life *as epitomising the fuller, modern style of planting. In the middle part of the century, the herbaceous material of mixed borders was gradually allowed to mix more freely.*

Perhaps the most concerted experiment in artist-gardening was conducted by Cedric Morris at Benton End in Suffolk, home of the bohemian East Anglian School of Painting and Drawing, founded in 1937, which Morris ran with his partner Arthur Lett-Haines. Lucian Freud and Maggi Hambling attended this unconventional establishment, and it also attracted numerous other interesting people including cookery writer Elizabeth David, composer Benjamin Britten, and author and illustrator Kathleen Hale. It was a gardening version of the twentieth-century artists' colony.

Morris was an ardent plantsman and iris-grower, and he used the garden consistently as his inspiration. Among his gardening friends were Vita Sackville-West, Tony Venison (gardens editor at *Country Life* from 1979 to 1994) and Beth Chatto, who recalled Benton End in the early 1950s: 'Dotted here and there were pillars of old-fashioned roses and several huge clumps of sword-leafed Yucca gloriosa. The rest was a bewildering, mind-stretching, eye-widening canvas of colour, texture and shapes, created primarily with bulbous and herbaceous plants. Later I came to realise it was probably the finest collection of such plants in the country.'

Within a very few years, a taste for connoisseurial plantsmanship was well within the orbit of the average gardener, and horticulture in general became fixated either on appreciation of individual plants (plantsmanship) or a polite version of the Jekyllian herbaceous border, set in a miniaturised, highly ornamented version of the Arts and Crafts garden.

RIGHT:

● *Mounton House, Monmouthshire (1915). A typically naturalistic planting by H. Avray Tipping, which seems decidedly ahead of its time. This was just one facet of his interest – elsewhere at Mounton, he created a large rock garden, a pergola garden, a garden loggia similar to Peto's at Wayford Manor, and a parterre garden of roses and stone flags.*

5 · Monumentality
1900–1939

LEFT:
◀ *Iford Manor, Wiltshire (1907).*
Harold Peto's garden on a steep
hillside is packed with architectural
fragments and statuary – most of it
from Italy. The earnestness of this
amateur antiquarian is well tempered
in the garden by a playful succession
of surprises.

ABOVE:
◀ *Port Lympne, Kent (1923).*
Philip Sassoon and Philip Tilden's
1920s design for a formal garden
was both grandiloquent and
architecturally eclectic. The multi-
levelled fountain pool seen here
doubled as a swimming pool.

In the last years of the nineteenth century, architects such as Reginald Blomfield and F. Inigo Thomas had been working very much in the 'Old English' spirit, creating gardens with Tudor, Elizabethan, Jacobean and even Caroline inflections. (Blomfield's work was nicknamed 'Wrennaissance'.) The international 'Beaux Arts' look – a kind of romanticised, eclectic Classicism – had also become fashionable, although it did not translate specifically to gardens. With the new century, England's romantic affinities with Italy began to be expressed outside in features such as small loggias for alfresco dining, pergolas of every kind, fountains and troughs decorated with grotesque masks, sunken gardens focused on rectangular pools, and antique statuary framed against dark yew hedges.

Country Life made an important contribution to designers' knowledge by consistently featuring Italian gardens in its pages – with articles illustrated by photo-graphs, rather than the watercolours still favoured by book publishers at this time. Edwin Lutyens, Oliver Hill and others drew heavily on this design vocabulary and elabo-rated from it imaginatively (Lutyens' Ammerdown is a fine small-scale essay in this vein). A few designers, such as Leonard Rome Guthrie – whose major works are Townhill Park, Hampshire, and Chelwood Vetchery, Sussex – made Italianate references the basis for all their design work, but Harold Peto was pre-eminent in this respect.

Peto had been in partnership with the architect Sir Ernest George until 1892, when he struck out on his own and forged an international reputation as a first-class garden designer capable of working in a variety of styles. He is most associated, however, with the ultra-romantic Italian-ate style exemplified by his own garden at Iford Manor in Wiltshire, which he began in 1899. Here, Peto introduced Renaissance and medieval architectural fragments and statues to a steeply sloping terraced site, where each level forms a vista punctuated by sculpture, the whole clothed in cypress, yew and acanthus and somehow absorbed into the wooded hillside. A number of other features, including a loggia and a circular lily pool with Tuscan colonnade on the top terrace, help create an atmosphere of almost monastic aesthetic sanctity.

Iford is a little bit too precious and mannered for some – palpably a self-conscious invention – but Peto was able to turn his hand to all kinds of situations and clients, and many of his other designs seem perfectly poised between Old English and Old Italian, between architecture and horticulture. At Wayford Manor, Somerset, he constructed for his sister a series of descending garden rooms of different shapes that interlock and complement each other, each one with a different atmosphere and planting style. Peto's great skill was to inject a palpable note of mythic fantasy into his gardens, like a latter-day William Kent. The lily-covered canal at Hartham Park in Wiltshire and the architecturally eclectic pavilion at its head were flanked by wide paved walks edged with herbs and other crevice plants, very much in the manner of a Jekyll – Lutyens garden. It is clear that, like his friend Tipping and unlike many of his architect contemporaries, Peto was comfortable with plants.

Buscot Park in Oxfordshire is a water garden dignified by a brick-edged water channel running through woodland towards the lake, with several pools and statue-lined garden rooms along the way. The chunky stone staircase seems satisfyingly caught between English vernacular and Italianate poise. And at Bridge House in Surrey, Peto introduced a truly exotic, otherworldly aura with his delicate casita, perched at the top of a T-shaped formal pool. This transcendent quality is repeated at West Dean, Sussex, where Peto made perhaps the finest pergola in England – a self-contained feature positioned halfway up a hillside.

The glamorous Italianate look epitomised in Peto's work was intensely fashionable in the first two decades of the twentieth century: Buckhurst Park, Sussex, was among several gardens given the full treatment in imitation of Peto, while at other places, such as Balls Park in Hertford, or Tusmore House, Oxford (by Angell and Imrie), a new sunken garden was made as a nod to contemporary fashion. It was not just an English phenomenon – in the United States, Dumbarton Oaks and Vizcaya were created in this mode, and in Italy itself, in the hills around Florence, the expatriate community were constructing gardens that reflected an idealisation of Renaissance villa life. Arthur Acton's La Pietra on the via Bolognese was perhaps the most influential here – Vita Sackville-West, Lawrence Johnston, Diego Suarez (of Vizcaya) and Ralph Dutton (of Hinton Ampner) were among the many visitors to this terraced extravaganza of statues and garden rooms. So, too, was English designer Cecil Pinsent, who in the 1920s developed a thriving practice making Neo-Renaissance Italian gardens for non-Italian (mainly American) clients, such as Bernard Berenson at Villa I Tatti.

Peto's own work on the Italian and French Rivieras for English and American clients has been rather forgotten, but his experiences there appear to have influenced his style back in England. Rose Standish Nichols' *Italian Pleasure Gardens* (1929) describes two of his gardens at Cap Ferrat,

LEFT:
▲ *Hartham Park, Wiltshire (1909).* Harold Peto's Italianate designs, always tinged with an element of fantasy, were intensely fashionable in the pre-war period. Every garden he made was distinctive: here, the lengthy, lily-covered pool terminates at a tall pavilion.

BELOW:
▲ *Gledstone Hall, Yorkshire (1935).* Typically imaginative attention to paving detail by Lutyens in the twin loggias at this new Classical house, designed in 1923. The massive scale of the loggias was continued in the great sunken canal garden, for which Jekyll provided the planting plans.

Villa Rosemary and Villa Sylvia, which are replete with loggias, terraces, pergolas and exuberant plantings, as well as his spectacular Villa Maryland, which was lavishly illustrated in *Country Life* too. Indeed, it might be argued that by the late 1920s the fashion for an Italianate look had mutated into a Riviera style of more generalised 'Continental' features (*Country Life*'s series on Riviera gardens ran from 1927 to 1929).

Edith Wharton's *Italian Villas and their Gardens* (1904) was the most famous of a clutch of influential pæans to Italian gardens published around the turn of the century. Wharton's most telling contribution was her insistence on following the spirit of Italian gardens rather than seeking to recreate an authentic copy. Perhaps the most fervent homage to Renaissance Italy was Sir George Sitwell's *An Essay On The Making of Gardens* (1909), a philosophical – aesthetic treatise on large-scale garden making. 'These old Italian gardens,' Sitwell writes, 'with their air of neglect, desolation, and solitude, in spite of the melancholy of the weed-grown alleys, the weary dropping of the fern-fringed fountains, the fluteless Pans and headless nymphs and armless Apollos, have a beauty which is indescribable.' Indescribable, perhaps, but Sitwell came closer to identifying their spirit than anyone else. Its seemingly unedited stream-of-consciousness notwithstanding, Sitwell's description of Italian gardens is unmatched for its sensitivity, vigour and poetic accuracy – he is able to capture the atmosphere of, for example, the 'intensely solemn loveliness' of the Giardino Giusti in Verona.

Sitwell attempted to re-create this essence in his own garden at Renishaw Hall in Derbyshire, where a severely geometric arrangement of yew hedges, shallow stone terraces and pools is enlivened by white statuary against dark yew. Sitwell engaged Gertrude Jekyll to draw up a planting scheme, but this appears not to have been implemented. As his son Osbert observed, Sir George disliked flowers, and later planting interventions at Renishaw perhaps detracted from his vision. In fact, Renishaw does not have the feel of an authentic Italian garden at all – how could it, when the battlemented seventeenth-century house looks so English? It is likely that F. Inigo Thomas, a first cousin of Sir George, advised on the system of massive yew

The Hill, London (1918). The covered terrace, designed by Thomas Mawson for Lord Leverhulme, his principal client. It led on to a formal water garden and then to a massively scaled but rather charmless pergola with thrilling views.

hedges, which owes more to Old English precedent than Old Italian.

Thomas Mawson's work in an Italianate manner is characteristically muscular and energetic, making use of the natural qualities of the topography and surrounding landscape – his gardens seem expansive and semi-public, whereas Peto's are introspective and fantastical. Mawson's most extreme essay in Classicism is his garden at The Hill, Hampstead, made for Lord Leverhulme, his most important client. This is a highly architectural design of pools and terraces that gently descend to a massive pergola crowning a monumental bastion with thrilling views. It is not a particularly charming garden experience and is in no way redolent of actual Italian gardens, as Harold Peto's work was, but one cannot help but be impressed – which was perhaps the point.

Even more impressive is Hever Castle in Kent, remodelled from 1903 by William Waldorf Astor. Here, Astor's exceptional collection of statuary and architectural fragments, gathered while he was American Minister in Rome, is arrayed along a series of monumental covered walkways and pergolas that lead to a massive manmade lake (famously shallow, and reportedly created in part as a way of easing local unemployment). In one sense, the garden has the atmosphere of an open-air gallery, but in its disorderliness, in its clothing of climbing plants and in its architectural monumentality, the garden also produces an antiquarian sensation, the feeling that one might just be roaming an authentic Roman ruin such as Hadrian's Villa at Tivoli.

Lord Fairhaven produced quite a different atmosphere in the sculpture garden he made at Anglesey Abbey, near Cambridge. Here, a loose and unwieldy overall structure is a help rather than a hindrance, since each garden area or vista is an episode in its own right, in the eighteenth-century manner. Superlative statuary and architectural fragments are sensitively arranged amid a landscape of interesting trees, great lawns, green hedges and long allées. This is a garden in which the nostalgic savour of Italy has been replaced by a more abstract appreciation of forms and volumes and the potentialities of scale.

Clough Williams-Ellis, like Oliver Hill, is an awkward character to categorise, and like Hill he should perhaps be celebrated for this rather than marginalised. Williams-Ellis's Italianate extravaganza at Portmeirion in Wales is well known, and he worked in similarly idiosyncratic Classical mode at Garsington Manor and Cornwell Manor (both in Oxfordshire), among other places. But it was in his own garden at Plas Brondanw, which he inherited in 1902 at the age of nineteen, that he found fullest expression in his garden-making. The structure is typical Arts and Crafts in that it is a succession of great yew-hedged enclosures, with clipped topiary and sculptural episodes, but in the unorthodox use of the sky-blue and gold estate colours for the metalwork and in the garden's insistent focus on distant Snowdon – not to mention jokey aspects such as the statue of a 'fireboy' wearing a helmet and squirting water – it triumphantly transcends categorisation.

At Bodnant, North Wales, the 2nd Lord Aberconway was constructing the Italianate terraces that would provide the setting for one of the most important twentieth-century gardens. Made over the course of the first half of the century, it is utterly unique. This is a garden that has every-thing, yet seems to hold it all in balance: a fine collection of Asiatic shrubs, formal terraces and an Arts and Crafts Italianate hedge system with statuary and herbaceous borders in Jekyllian mode, together with numerous botanical rarities and exotics. It is an exceptionally rich and varied garden, but its scale and careful pacing make it appear effortlessly harmonious. There are no rules to be followed in a garden of this ambition; instinct is the key.

Perhaps the most ostentatious expressions of monumen-talist taste in gardens, however, were made at the behest of Philip Sassoon of Port Lympne in Kent and Trent Park in Hertfordshire. Like most of those who had a taste for the grand gesture in gardens at this time, Sassoon was a millionaire – several times over (his mother was a Rothschild). Secretary to General Haig during the First World War, Sassoon went on to fill a number of important positions in the civil service – including permanent private secretary to Lloyd George – although there was a sense at his death that for one so rich and well connected, he had rather underachieved.

Sassoon is an intriguing and enigmatic figure. The view of his friend (and ex-fag at Eton) Osbert Sitwell that he was 'always unlike anyone else' was the generally held opinion; Harold Nicolson called him 'the most unreal creature I have known', which must have been saying something. It was not his Jewishness or his presumed homosexuality that made Sassoon an outsider – neither quality was necessarily problematic for English high society, especially if the person in question was rich and hosted extravagant parties – it was his whole demeanour and personality. Sassoon made no attempt to 'blend in'. In his two country houses he sought to create a culturally vibrant, internationalised version of the English country-house weekend, where political, artistic, sporting and social grandees could meet and exchange views – at least, that was the idea. Winston

Churchill was a regular guest, and George Bernard Shaw, John Singer Sargent and Charlie Chaplin were among the diverse figures who accepted Sassoon's fabled hospitality – 'he frankly loved success', according to his friend Robert Boothby, the politician.

Trent Park, set amid woodland on the northern fringes of the capital, was conveniently situated for London guests, while Port Lympne, overlooking the Channel at its narrowest point, was ideal for European visitors. There were airfields at both houses (Sassoon was a keen aviator) and myriad sporting facilities, including an eighteen-hole golf-course with resident professionals at Trent, which Sassoon would regularly tackle at breakneck speed. Operatic stars and chamber orchestras were engaged as after-dinner entertainment, and there were often acrobatic displays and fly-pasts from Sassoon's fleet of aircraft. Yet the art historian Kenneth Clark maintained that while Sassoon's weekend parties were never boring, nothing of any interest was ever said.

Given the decorative excesses inside his houses – Sassoon had a weakness for luxurious fittings, gilded French furniture and painted ceilings and walls – for many visitors, Sassoon's gardens were his saving grace in aesthetic terms. Clark, for one, was quite relieved when his host took him into the gardens at Lympne, away from the 'hideous' interiors and towards 'the deepest and longest herbaceous borders, the most colossal beds of blue

delphinium'. Boothby maintained: 'Here his natural gifts found full scope … No one who has seen the great border at Lympne, stretching from the house to the Marsh in the height of its glory during August and September, can ever forget it.' Norah Lindsay had advised on the planting of these great borders from 1919, which were designed to be at their height in August when Sassoon held his parties. He once joked to a visitor that, 'At twelve noon on the first of August each year, I give a nod to the head gardener who rings his bell and all the flowers pop up.' These borders do indeed appear to have been perhaps the deepest (if not the longest) in the country, a surging sea of bright colours in broad, bold swathes that descend the steep hillside, so that the visitor has the impression of diving into them.

Sassoon's gardening exploits at Trent Park were also noteworthy. There was a long pergola of wisteria, masses of naturalised daffodils along the entrance drive, an ornamental bathing pool of rectangular form (a feature that was to become ever more popular, even into the late 1940s), an orangery designed by Reggie Cooper, and, of course, sumptuous long borders, in which lemon and white flowers gave way to deep blues and purples and then hot scarlets and oranges. This colour scheme does not surge and recede in the Jekyllian manner – it simply surges. The lemon-meringue-pie theme for the start of the border is particularly strident. Sassoon was known for his habit of introducing a complete new bedding scheme overnight, to the amazement of his guests (a trick copied from the Rothschilds); and melons and other fruits from Trent would be sent by air to Port Lympne when required. Airborne melons were not the last of it: Sassoon gilded the horns of his parkland deer, and his flamingos (part of a large waterfowl collection at Trent) were fed dried shrimps to enhance their pinkness.

But more ambitious and extravagant than all of this was Sassoon's monumental plan for the gardens at Port

Lympne. The H-plan house, dramatically sited on a steep hillside overlooking the Channel and Romney Marsh, had been designed by Sir Herbert Baker in the Cape Dutch mode that he had employed for Groote Schuur, Cecil Rhodes's house in South Africa. On one level, Baker's great twin gables seem incongruous here – not least because the architect was himself a native of Kent – but there is something of the Arts and Crafts vernacular about the design, with its tiled roof, ornamental brickwork and twin loggias.

The view from the house created a sensation Sassoon described in a letter of 1918: 'I am on the lip of the world and gaze over the wide Pontine marshes that reflect the passing clouds like a mirror. The sea is just far enough off to be always smooth and blue – and everywhere the acute stillness that comes from great distances.' Sassoon's

instincts with regard to the site seem to have been well founded, since the system of great buttressed terraces and fountains that he introduced enhances the sense of exhilaration at this landscape. The versatile architect Philip Tilden was engaged by Sassoon to alter parts of the house and help design the garden from 1918, and something of the appeal of this kind of monumentalism can be felt in his remark that: 'Here at Lympne all was to be new and forceful, pulsing with the vitality of new blood.'

The rationale for the garden's structure is somewhat confused, however. In terms of its scale and its emphasis on food production (there is a vineyard and a fig yard), the great terrace system echoes fifteenth-century Italian precedents such as the Villa Medici at Fiesole; it also brings to mind images of the Hanging Gardens of Babylon. Some of the paving detail is pure Arts and Crafts, and the lettered balustrading is Stuart in theme. The great fountain and multi-levelled swimming pool of the second terrace, and

the massive pergolas that flank it, owe something to sixteenth-century Italian gardens such as the Villa d'Este at Tivoli, and perhaps even to Le Nôtre and Versailles. There is an Art Deco quality to the geometric parterres on the pool terrace. And in the central well of the house there is a Moorish patio of delicate marble columns and rills, while the entrance forecourt is ringed by caryatids in yew niches, in the eighteenth-century English manner (the statues came from Stowe).

According to Tilden in *True Remembrances* (1954), however, the core of the design was none of these things: it was in fact Romano-British. The name Port Lympne was derived from the Roman station of Porta Lemanis, which had been in the vicinity of the site, and – said Tilden – the garden's 'majestic scale, cypress hedges and classical plinths recall the ancient splendours of Roman Britain'. The great flight of steps that ascends the steep hill behind the house, clothed in smooth walls of cupressus, with

PRECEDING PAGES:
● *Port Lympne, Kent (1923).* View from one of the twin loggias on to the main terrace, with the monumental bathing pool beyond. Winston Churchill, a regular guest, enjoyed painting this view.

BELOW:
● *Ditchley Park, Oxfordshire (1934).* The parterre designed by Geoffrey Jellicoe in 1933 for Ronald and Nancy Tree. The scale and proportion of Italian Renaissance gardens was an inspiration for Jellicoe and other Modernists. The pool at the far end doubled as a swimming pool, the fountain jets screening it from the house.

▲ *Gledstone Hall, Yorkshire (1935). Here in his last major commission, Lutyens used the Arts and Crafts vocabulary – on a larger scale than usual – of a pergola, a sunken garden with retaining walls, stone steps, and a formal canal and terminating pool.*

colour-themed gardens at each level and twin octagon pavilions at the summit, was designed 'to lead from the smooth lawns below to a world of new delight to be, high above the house'. This was not a case of purposeless monumentality: Sassoon envisaged a transcendent, futuristic dreamland, a Kentish Valhalla for the dinner-jacketed denizens of Belgravia.

Despite its stylistic incongruities, the garden at Port Lympne was well integrated with the surrounding landscape. But the same cannot be said for its relationship with the house. Baker felt that Tilden's and Sassoon's monumental interpolations in the garden unbalanced the more domestic, cottagey feel of the house – which seems a fair assessment. In their excitement at creating these massive terraces, Sassoon and Tilden made the basic error of not relating garden to house.

Tilden received a wide variety of commissions on different scales, and castle design was well within his capabilities. Castles were not only popular subjects for large-scale restoration – Herstmonceux, Hever and Allington have already been mentioned; others included Leeds, Saltwood, Skibo, St Donat's (owned by William Randolph

Hearst), Lindisfarne and Lambay (these last two were by Lutyens) – but a few new 'castles' were also being made. Tilden provided designs for Gordon Selfridge's massive, unrealised Highcliffe Castle, opposite the Isle of Wight (where Mawson was to have created the formal gardens). In 1919 Lutyens made the monumental granite buildings of Castle Drogo, in Devon, where the terraced formal gardens by George Dillistone echoed Lutyens' gravitation towards a still romantic but occasionally monumental Classicism – the beginnings of which can be identified in the sunken pool garden at Marsh Court (1901) and which culminated in his design for the Viceroy's House in Delhi (1913–29).

Lutyens' later work is often monumental in scale and dazzlingly multiplicitous in terms of identifiable influences, while still somehow retaining a lightness of touch. At Tyringham in Buckinghamshire, for example, a late-eighteenth-century house by Soane, Lutyens made a pool more than twice the length and width of the one he designed for Gledstone Hall, Yorkshire, so that it took on the character of a reflecting sheet of water rather than a canal. The masterstroke here was Lutyens' addition of a pair of Tuscan columns just over halfway along the length of the

pool: a minimal way of creating a vertical accent to complement the perfectly flat landscape beyond.

In the 1920s and 1930s, a new strand of large-scale garden design sporadically emerged: the beginnings of the trend for 'authentic' historical restoration or re-creation which was to become such an important part of the English garden scene later in the twentieth century. Arts and Crafts revivalism had sometimes bordered on this more academic mode of historicism – the formal parterres by Romaine-Walker at Great Fosters in Surrey, for example – but the new spirit was open-handed, expansive and gregarious, and more undisciplined. Architects began to be commissioned to create formal gardens that were not informed by

ABOVE:
● *Ammerdown, Somerset (1929).* An unusual commission for Lutyens, this 1902 design is focused on a large yew enclosure, at some distance from the house, peopled with white Italianate statues set against dark foliage.

LEFT:
● *Bodnant, Denbighshire (1920).* The canal terrace. The architectural possibilities of clipped evergreens and statuary were explored at many leading gardens. Lord Aberconway used Italianate terraces as a setting for his horticultural extravaganza.

ideology but simply seemed historically appropriate to the architecture of great houses. They were also glamorous and extravagant in a way that was anathema to the disciples of the Arts and Crafts movement.

The first glimmerings of this new attitude can be seen at Eaton Hall in Cheshire, where in 1911 Detmar Blow was commissioned by the Duke of Westminster to create a new parterre garden to replace a detailed scheme by W. A. Nesfield, doyen of Victorian parterre designers. Blow designed box-hedged enclosures in the Arts and Crafts manner, and with a much simplified bedding scheme – but these enclosures were focused on a pair of Baroque statue groups and flanked a rectangular piece of water unabashedly French seventeenth-century in inspiration. This Continental emphasis was in itself a departure: Arts and Crafts stylistic internationalism (principally Italianate) was always acknowledged as an evocation, mediated in some way by English precedent, whereas here it was being presented more or less as a straightforward quotation.

By the early 1920s, there had emerged a new kind of appreciation of the English formal gardens of the seventeenth century. Sir Thomas Fermor-Hesketh imaginatively

created a garden in Baroque spirit to complement the façade of the Hawksmoor house of Easton Neston, Northamptonshire: it featured a massive terrace and a circular reflecting basin surrounded by statuary and flanked by box-hedged enclosures. A few years later, the Duke of Marlborough commissioned Achille Dûchene to design a water parterre next to Blenheim Palace, Oxfordshire. This overwhelmingly betrays the influence of Le Nôtre, although some of the sculptural detail is Italianate, at the Duke's behest.

Not all historicist design of this period was conducted on the ducal scale, however. Gardens such as Kemsing St Clere, Kent and Lowesby Hall, Leicestershire, incorporated new terraces and sequences of steps in this historicist spirit. At the The Pleasance, Gullane, a suburban garden in Lothian, a knot garden was integrated into a rather stiff interpretation of Arts and Crafts planting – small knots and herb gardens remained perennial favourites. Something similar was created by that singular designer Ralph Hancock for the 1937 Chelsea Flower Show: a formal Tudor-style garden of knots which appeared to be evoking a glamorous vision of historical authenticity. The sunken

Cheney Court, Wiltshire. Existing architectural features were often exploited for their romantic qualities: this garden also contained a large amount of new stonework in an Arts and Crafts spirit .

parterre garden that Lutyens had created at Hestercombe inspired several others – including those at The Platts and Island, Steep, both in Hampshire.

All the while, gardens that were essentially Victorian in mode were still being kept up in the old way, years after they had fallen out of fashion (as was the case with interiors). Among those featured in *Country Life* at this time were Old Buckhurst, Sussex (1919), Rowehurst (1920), and Brownsea Castle, Dorset (1921).

Perhaps the most successful experiment in design in an avowedly historicist milieu was Ralph Dutton's reinterpretation, begun in 1936, of the garden at Hinton Ampner, Hampshire. Dutton's published description of his garden in *A Hampshire Manor* (1938) is rather pedestrian, but his design on the ground is anything but. Behind the redbrick Neo-Georgian house (rebuilt in 1960), a wide paved terrace gives way to a long rectangle of lawn and then brick steps down to a central sunken garden that is dignified by topiarised yew mushrooms. The gentle changes of level and the relaxed, low-key ambience are a wholly successful complement to the expansive prospect over the country-

side from the wide, low-slung terraces. The garden's spaces seem to flow into each other and propel the visitor along through gentle changes in level, revealing vistas and intimate spaces episodically, just as Dutton intended. It is like an eighteenth-century landscape park on a domestic scale.

There is no single precedent for Hinton Ampner: it combines simplicity and modesty of tone with an uncompromising architectural attitude – Dutton was a historian who produced books on the English country house and garden in the 1930s. Brent Elliott has usefully compared Dutton's reductionist ideas with the stylelessness that was one of the avowed aims of Modernism, quoting Dutton in

The English Garden (1937): 'Only with the present century, so one likes to think, has that just alliance of interesting detail, coupled with broad and simple lines, untrammelled by particular style or fashion, been achieved.'

A Modernist vein in historicist gardens can be detected more easily at Ditchley Park in Oxfordshire, where in 1933 an inexperienced Geoffrey Jellicoe was asked by Ronald and Nancy Tree to design a formal garden. The result was a rectangular parterre garden flanked by yew pyramids and avenues of pleached limes, culminating in a circular pool (which doubled as a swimming pool) with perimeter fountains placed to form a water curtain so that bathers could not be seen from the house. The garden was not quite Italian and not quite French in inspiration; it was really a little too bijou to be either.

Writing in 1982, Jellicoe described it as 'neo-historicist', which is a good non-specific term for a deliberately non-specific approach. Jellicoe thought it strange that an avowed Modernist such as himself should be asked to undertake this commission, but Italian Renaissance garden design was as influential to the English Modernists for spatial reasons as it had been to Arts and Crafts designers such as Peto for decorative and atmospheric reasons. Indeed, Jellicoe and J. C. Shepherd had produced *Italian Gardens of the Renaissance* in 1925, a pioneering work filled with plans of Italy's great gardens, and this must have been what Edward Hudson had in mind when he recommended the young landscape architect to the Trees, who were modern-minded people.

Almost fifty years later, Jellicoe recalled his anachronistic design for the gardens at Ditchley: 'If they lack the psyche for which the mind of modern man is searching, they can certainly remind him of some of the qualities of history he may be passing by.' Which is one way of reconciling the discrepancy. Jellicoe also noted that in the 1930s there were seventeen servants at Ditchley. The Second World War was to mark the end not just of that way of life, and of ostentatious monumental and historicist gardens in the Ditchley mould – it was to be the death knell, for a decade at least, of meaningful garden design of any sort.

ABOVE:
▲ *Trent Park, Hertfordshire (1929). The reflecting pool lifted Philip Sassoon's London house well above the ordinary, just as he would have wished. The borders, designed by Norah Lindsay, and in their pomp from May to July, were almost as admired at those at Port Lympne.*

RIGHT:
▲ *Cornwell Manor, Oxfordshire (1941). The old courtyard and the view out beneath the galleried corridor leading to a new ballroom, all designed in singular style and on an appropriate scale by Clough Williams-Ellis just before the Second World War. This was a garden of broadly defined outlines and interlocking shapes.*

6 · Sissinghurst and Hidcote

Indisputably the two giants among twentieth-century English gardens are Sissinghurst, in Kent, and Hidcote, in Gloucestershire. They are often mentioned in the same breath, as if they have somehow become conjoined (perhaps we should call this 'The Sissingcote Effect'). Their pre-eminence is taken for granted and it is difficult to talk about them in the context of other examples because they seem somehow to be set apart.

How have Sissinghurst and Hidcote attained this iconic status? Of course, both gardens have intrinsic qualities that appeal to a wide number of visitors and they have always been maintained to a high standard, but there are historical reasons, too, for their exalted position. Their fame became entrenched in the second half of the century, and for most of that period they were both in the care of the National Trust. Hidcote was in fact the first property to be taken on by the Trust principally on the merit of the

garden rather than the house (in 1948), and Sissinghurst was another early addition to the Trust's garden portfolio (in 1967).

Sissinghurst was well-known before the Trust took it on, as a result of the *Observer* gardening column written by Victoria 'Vita' Sackville-West, while Hidcote was much celebrated and visited by the cognoscenti during the lifetime of its owner, Lawrence Johnston. Under the National Trust, however, the *raison d'être* of both gardens abruptly shifted away from private pleasure ground and realm of horticultural and design experimentation, and moved towards a new role as a visitor attraction and shrine to the lives and work of the previous incumbents. At an early stage in the development of the twentieth-century heritage industry, the two sites became public spaces in a way that Rodmarton, for example – a garden of comparable stature – never did. Sissinghurst and Hidcote not only had a head start on other key gardens opened to the public in the twentieth century, they were also backed up by the organisational and (later) marketing expertise of the National Trust, and as a result they became the unchallenged flagship gardens of England.

The very structure of both Sissinghurst and Hidcote appears in retrospect to have been designed with mass appeal in mind (although neither were actually conceived in this spirit). The 'garden room' idea, while hardly original, found an appreciative audience, who detected a certain democratisation in the business of parcelling-up large tracts of land into manageable enclosures. Hidcote and Sissinghurst were also inspirational, because they appeared to showcase small-scale gardening, and plants-

men and -women always found intriguing new ideas there. Conversely, neither garden alienated those visitors who had little interest in horticulture, because a strong structure, elements of surprise and an episodic narrative are stimulating in themselves.

Hidcote continued to appeal more to the cognoscenti, while Sissinghurst became by far the most influential full-scale model for garden-making, not just in England but worldwide. Its romantic atmosphere has been emulated in every country where gardening is valued, regardless of climate, not just in terms of overall tone but in specific details – the White Garden, the use of terracotta urns as focal points, plants spilling on to paths, roses around old doorways. Of course, this imagery was already entrenched in English gardening style – Sackville-West never

pretended it was original – but general ideas about England's cottage-style or old-fashioned gardens became associated in the minds of the international gardening public with this one specific garden in the Kentish Weald.

The emotional appeal of Sissinghurst and Hidcote must not be overlooked either. Both gardens have a tangible atmosphere of intimacy; at Hidcote at least, on a quiet day visitors can still have the sense that they might be trespassing on private property. At Sissinghurst, the biographical element is particularly strong – indeed, it is arguably this that is the garden's principal attraction – while at Hidcote, even if the personality of Lawrence Johnston remains elusive, there is also the feeling of a single directing force or character at work. Visitors are aware that both owners created – or, in the case of

Sissinghurst Castle, Kent (1942). In the age of the hybrid tea and floribunda, old shrub roses were the horticultural leitmotif of Sissinghurst and Vita Sackville-West was an authority on them. Sissinghurst, she wrote in Country Life *in 1942, 'lent itself to their untidy, lavish habit; there was space in plenty, with the walls to frame their exuberance, and consequently they could be found foaming in an unorthodox way in the midst of flower borders'.*

Sissinghurst, 'rescued' – their gardens from scratch with some difficulty, and this ideal of adversity overcome has proved a potent psychological draw. The fact that the owners of these two gardens were amateurs has also appealed to visitors, inspiring them to make something of their own plots.

Both Sissinghurst and Hidcote have been lauded consistently in late-twentieth-century gardening literature, by designers, horticulturists, authors and journalists alike. The genteel background to gardening on this scale and the importance of social connections has meant that it has been taboo to attack another garden in print (although a lot was said in private, of course). This void in the place of garden criticism has reflected and perpetuated the generally low status of gardens in the hierarchy of the arts.

In the case of Sissinghurst, the physical appeal of the garden has been eclipsed by the personality of Vita Sackville-West. The role of her husband, Harold Nicolson, has faded into the background, even though it was he who laid out the loose formal structure of the gardens, on the site of a dilapidated, part-demolished medieval and Elizabethan castle. Sissinghurst was the couple's second garden. At their first, the fourteenth-century Kentish cottage of Long Barn, which they enlarged substantially, Lutyens himself had assisted Nicolson in the laying-out of raised, brick-edged flowerbeds to help make what Nicolson called 'a garden in a series of lawns and walled terraces … sunny, pretty, romantic and comfortable'. The principal feature was a line of stately clipped yews standing sentinel behind the house.

At Sissinghurst, which the couple acquired in 1930, Nicolson enlisted the help of Reggie Cooper, and in a letter of 12 September that year he observed: 'Our general line is to keep the whole thing as green and quiet and simple as we can.' Seven years later, Nicolson was able to write to his wife, 'We have got what we wanted to get – a perfect proportion between the classic and the romantic, between the element of expectation and the element of surprise.'

Sissinghurst is often described as a garden of rooms, but while it does contain discrete spaces, Nicolson's design was quite loosely structured and is deliberately illogical and unpredictable: his was not the dead hand of geometry and symmetry. (In this regard, Cooper's Cothay was perhaps more of an influence than has been acknowledged.) There

◆ *Sissinghurst Castle, Kent (1942). The purple border was one of several areas reserved for a planting scheme realised in a single colour.*

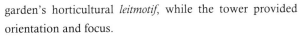

• *Sissinghurst Castle, Kent (1942).*

(left): *The tower stands sentinel over the whole garden, striking a note of harmony and unity amid the complexity and artful illogicality of Nicolson's cellular layout. The buildings contribute a great deal to the atmosphere and pacing of the garden.*

(below): *If Sissinghurst is a cult garden, then the White Garden is a cult within a cult. Although this photograph shows the garden before it was planted as a 'pale garden' in 1950, many of the elements seen here were retained, such as the grey Ming Dynasty vase and the canopy of plum and almond trees.*

is more statuary and ornament in the garden than is sometimes remembered: most of those narrow brick paths, encroached upon by plants and defined by yew walls, lead to some formal focus, whether it is the shallow, thyme-filled bowl and lion statue of the herb garden, the raised grass dais at the castle end of the rose garden (a clever late addition by Nicolson) or the four columnar yews which anchor the ramshackle cottage garden. These formal elements enrich rather than stultify.

Ten separate garden spaces were laid out and their content or theme changed quite radically over time. Some of them were seasonally organised (the orchard, nuttery and spring gardens), some were species-based (the rose and herb gardens), and some were of one colour (the purple border, the White Garden). From the 1930s, roses and climbing plants flourished profusely throughout as the

garden's horticultural *leitmotif*, while the tower provided orientation and focus.

Yet although the garden was organised into enclosed or semi-enclosed spaces, the edges between these areas were often blurred and there were many openings in hedges and walls offering new vistas: these gardens never feel quite like 'rooms', either in the sense of interior spaces or as the cellular compartments of a layout such as Rodmarton. The prevailing tone was shabby chic: a kind of gardening version of the aristo-bohemianism of Bloomsbury – a super-relaxed rendition of Arts and Crafts planting in a loose formal structure, a structure which itself feels organically grown. Sackville-West reacted against the artful, pictorial compositions of Jekyll and in the process made a garden more in tune with Eleanor Vere Boyle's poetic romanticism. Nicolson affectionately described Sissinghurst as a 'ramshackle farm-tumble', which sums up its appeal for visitors in his time (in comparison, the garden today looks positively manicured).

The development of planting ideas at Sissinghurst has been described many times and in considerable detail – even more minutely than Munstead Wood – but perhaps the main reason for the garden's extraordinary popularity lies not in its planting but in the character and writings of Sackville-West herself. For while it is correct to give Harold Nicolson the credit for Sissinghurst's structure – without which, the garden would be lost – there can be no doubt that it was principally Sackville-West's personality and taste that gave the place its distinctive atmosphere.

From the very first time she visited the derelict Sissinghurst with one of her sons, the romantic, emotionally charged nature of Sackville-West's relationship with the garden was defined. 'We had picked our way between the old bedsteads, matted wire and broken-down earth-closets,' Nigel Nicolson recalled, 'climbed the tower staircase and found the rooms open to the weather and the birds, whose droppings made it almost impossible to cross the floor. Then we walked through an archway into the cabbage-patch where the rose garden now lies, and up the path towards the south end of the Tudor range. Nowhere else at Sissinghurst does the pink brick glow more mellow than on this flat, gabled surface, and at that moment the late-afternoon sun came out from behind the clouds and seemed to set the brick on fire. My mother turned to me. "I think we shall be happy in this place," she said.' Who could fail to be a little moved by such a story? The notion of rescuing a grand old house – and perhaps its garden too – reverberates deeply in the English breast.

Sackville-West's project at Sissinghurst was documented

LEFT:
● *Hidcote Manor, Gloucestershire (1930).* The White Garden, formerly the Phlox Garden, one of the hedged compartments at Hidcote. The white flowers included roses (notably 'Gruss an Aachen'), campanulas and crambe. The topiary birds were deliberately made unsymmetrical (note their tails).

obliquely in her conversational gardening column for *The Observer*, which ran weekly from 1947 to 1961. It was a natural successor to the kind of confessional, usually female vein in garden writing that had first found real commercial success in 1898 with the surprise bestseller *Elizabeth and Her German Garden* by Countess von Armin. An Englishwoman living in Bavaria, she wrote with disarming candour about her gardening failures, seguing effortlessly from discussions of soil composition to the marital problems of her neighbours. (One cannot dislike a writer who observes: 'The longer I live the greater is my respect and affection for manure in all its forms.')

In Sackville-West's column, Sissinghurst is rarely referred to by name or as the source of particular examples, but despite this seemly reticence her readers knew very well she was talking about her own garden. Throughout her writing career, Sackville-West never lost her good humour, freshness of style and knack for summing up sentiments that every gardener feels on occasion. She was a natural columnist, irresistibly starting a 1953 piece with the words, 'May I put in a good word for dill?', and observing of the plant-failure rate in gardens of novices, 'Infant mortality in

the Middle Ages is the only approximate comparison.' Sackville-West was a consummate journalist, even though she would have much preferred to have been a consummate poet – which she was not.

As for her gardening style, it was romantic yet practical, experimental but traditional, and in this her approach seemed to chime with that of thousands of others. Just like Jekyll and Robinson before her, Sackville-West gloried in the fantasy of a secret lore among cottage gardeners, but she was also at pains to offer advice aimed at the contemporary gardener working on a small scale. She relentlessly recommends informal gardening in town situations – the same curious mix of humility and lavishness that can be detected in middle-class cottage gardens earlier in the century – and she notes Johnston's technique (Hidcote was probably her primary influence) of not massing clumps of single species together but creating a tapestry effect that takes advantage of the forms and colours of many different varieties in a small space. To achieve success with this approach is of course an extraordinarily complex feat, but, like Jekyll, Sackville-West generally refrains from giving useful (yet potentially vulgar) advice about design in

OPPOSITE:
● *Hidcote Manor, Gloucestershire (1930).*

(above): *The view from the cedar lawn through to the stilt garden. This is the principal vista at Hidcote.*

(below): *The view in the other direction, taken from the gates just inside The Circle – a cool grass roundel – and past the borders of the Old Garden, where the colour scheme was predominantly blues, whites, pinks and mauves.*

general, in favour of assessing the qualities of particular plants. She was influential in all sorts of other ways, however, from her promotion of old roses and her campaign for plants which flower in August and September, to her dislike of pergolas ('they drip').

As with so many media personalities, Sackville-West's readers came to feel they knew her personally, and so naturally they were curious about her own garden at Sissinghurst. After her death in 1962 a more intimate picture emerged, and the garden came to be seen as the emotional autobiography of a poet – a living portrait of a marriage. The war years seemed particularly poignant, with Sissinghurst in stasis as the bombers and rockets threatened overhead: Sackville-West's stoicism constituted a kind of horticultural Blitz spirit. Her literary and intellectual status as a Bloomsbury satellite has also legitimised the garden (and to an extent, gardens in general) for some. Overall, it is the biographical aspect, rather than the garden's physical qualities, that remains the key to Sissinghurst's popularity. It is an important garden – indeed a great garden – but it is also perhaps the most overrated of gardens.

In place of the genial, aristocratic unruliness of Sissinghurst, Hidcote offers clarity of design and uncompromising originality. It is generally considered by commentators to be a better-balanced and more innovative garden than Sissinghurst, although it is unlikely that it will ever match Sackville-West's garden for popular appeal: Johnston is too enigmatic a figure.

In 1907, on an unpromising, windswept hilltop site on the northern edge of the Cotswolds, this thirty-six-year-old Anglophile American soldier-aesthete set about creating a new kind of formal garden, more modest in spirit than the architectural extravaganzas of Lutyens and other Arts and Crafts designers. In its formal structure, of a wide corridor of grass bounded by yew hedges which gives on to a variety of small, contrasting, colour-themed enclosures and expansive lawns and vistas, Hidcote is perhaps more than anything an English-Italian Arts and Crafts garden. Johnston's visit to Arthur Acton's garden at La Pietra in Florence, as well as other Italian gardens (he was a close friend of Edith Wharton's), may have been more important than has been appreciated. And Lutyens was perhaps more of an influence than has been acknowledged, because although there is relatively little stonework in the garden, there is evident pleasure taken in the garden's geometrically inventive plan of interlocking circles, squares and rectangles. Yet Hidcote amounts to much more than this. In their un-grandiloquent intensity, the set-piece effects

seem to eclipse those in every other contemporary garden, including those of Lutyens and Jekyll. The remarkable double row of pleached hornbeams, boxily clipped, might not have been the first stilt hedge ever made (there was one at Great Tangley, for example), but its integration with the celebrated twin pavilions and searing red borders below is quite original. And the wide, empty Long Walk at a right angle to the main allée, which suddenly frees up the heart of the garden, is well timed: a shaft of pure void that seems to shoot up from the surrounding landscape, through the heart of the garden and the open doors of the pavilions.

The pool garden, in which the great dark round almost completely fills the space, has always drawn admiration from designers, and Russell Page for one noticed its transcendent power: 'One is free to accept this little scene as intensely real; the pool becomes like a sea which reflects the sky and floating leaf … time and space change scale.' Johnston's garden does indeed seem caught in a moment between space and time, displaying various cosmopolitan inferences yet being not quite like anything else. It is dreamily, intimately engaging – a surreal space.

Johnston was much more of a plantsman than is reflected in the garden's current incarnation. Recently discovered garden books covering the years 1927 to 1932, compiled by Johnston himself, list more than a thousand different plants in addition to those growing in the garden now. Within closely confined spaces and against dark yew, Johnston experimented with dazzlingly complex combinations of plants growing in artful profusion, exotic rarities entwined with commonplace subjects. Looking at photographs of the garden in Johnston's time, one can see that it is less the precise contents of the borders that are important – although one would always expect that flowerbeds at Hidcote would abound in rarities, some of them from Johnston's equally important French Riviera garden, Serre de la Madone – but more the achievement of a beautiful balance in terms of scale and unity of tone. It is a quality that cannot be described (or emulated) easily, but it is tangibly present.

In his planting, Johnston was abetted significantly from the 1920s by his close friend Norah Lindsay, although the precise extent of her involvement is not known (he had hoped she might take on the garden after his death, but she predeceased him). A shy man but no recluse, Johnston travelled widely, played a great deal of tennis and entertained hosts of gardening guests, including the Aberconways of Bodnant, Mark Fenwick of Abbotswood, Louis Mallet of Wardes, Robert James of St Nicholas, and, of course, the Muirs of neighbouring Kiftsgate.

In her celebrated account of Johnston's garden, Sackville-West described Hidcote as a succession of little cottage gardens and a 'combination of botanical knowledge and aesthetic taste'. The idea of Hidcote as basically an agglomeration of cottage gardens clearly reflected Sackville-West's own preoccupations (it is an accurate enough description of Sissinghurst) and is perhaps what she found most useful about the garden. But it fails to take account of the sophisticated episodic nature of Hidcote, its many vistas, and its structural interest.

The genius of Hidcote lies in part in Johnston's subversion of expectations, chiefly through surprising anomalies in scale: the outsized topiary birds; the bathing pool that takes up almost the whole of its enclosure; the sudden width of the Long Walk. Through the alternation of enclosure and vista, Hidcote is a garden that seems to expand and contract in synchronicity with our emotions. Yet instead of engaging critically with the garden – 'I cannot hope to describe it in words,' she says – Sackville-West attempts to appropriate Hidcote for the cause of effortless, unintellectual cottage-gardening. For this daughter of Knole, the secrets of garden beauty must remain locked in the hearts of the gentlefolk of the English shires, unfit for public consumption. Yet Hidcote, made by an outsider, a green palace of dreams all parcelled up, has a strong claim to be the greatest garden made on English soil in the twentieth century.

▲ Hidcote Manor, Gloucestershire (1930).

(above): The Pillar Garden. Perhaps the hand of Lawrence Johnston's friend Norah Lindsay can be discerned here, as the flowers drift and surge in peaks beneath the slender evergreen pillars, which have grown more substantial today.

(right): The Stream Garden to the south bisects the formal plan at Hidcote, introducing quite another tone – a naturalistic streamside walk under trees with spring bulbs and autumn tints for colour.

7 · The Modernist Garden
1920–1999

LEFT:
▲ *Cray Clearing, Oxfordshire (1967).
Completed in 1964 to the design of
Francis Pollen, this flat-roofed modern
house incorporated three courts as
'outdoor rooms'. With the figurative
statue in its pool, this space makes
reference to Mies van der Rohe's
seminal Barcelona Pavilion.*

ABOVE:
▲ *High and Over, Buckinghamshire
(1931). Amyas Connell's design was
the first major modern house in
England. Unlike many later Modernist
houses, it included a design for a
triangular garden, with roses and a
Classical pergola. The roof terrace
draws on Le Corbusier's Villa Savoie
and on the Modernist ideal of the
health-giving qualities of sunbathing.*

The death of the Modernist garden in England has been greatly exaggerated and should not be confused with the dearth of Modernist gardens. While it is true that the Modernist architectural aesthetic defined by Le Corbusier, Mies van der Rohe, Adolf Loos, Walter Gropius and the other Modernist polemicists never translated satisfactorily to the garden scene, a number of garden designs of lasting value, inspired or informed by the Modernist creed, were nevertheless completed – and not only in the 1930s.

These successes range from the early experiments of Christopher Tunnard, Serge Chermayeff and Oliver Hill, to the communal landscapes of the Span architectural practice from the 1960s, John Brookes's pioneering 'room outside' concept, right up to the explicitly Modernist gardens of Christopher Bradley-Hole in the 1990s and beyond. A Modernist agenda for garden design surfaced periodically throughout the century – with high points during the 1930s,

1960s and 1990s – and it has never gone away entirely. In fact, Modernist gardens have been made in England in every decade since the movement first materialised on our shores, which makes it an unusually long-lived phenomenon in gardening terms. For this reason, this chapter is treated thematically rather than chronologically.

The central problem for Modernist garden designers was common to all garden design in the twentieth century: how to make a garden that related to the architecture of the house but was also relevant to the practical and leisure requirements of the people living there. If one is to judge early-twentieth-century Modernism by its own harsh criteria, then it undoubtedly failed to achieve a coherent garden aesthetic and, as a result, also failed to gain widespread popularity. But its influence has been far greater than might at first seem apparent – by the 1990s, while country gardens delved ever deeper into richly conceived eco-fantasies, urban garden design was seeking a balance between Modernist and Arts and Crafts ideals (see Chapter 10).

The unavoidable paradox of Modernism in garden design has been that the proselytisers for the functionalist garden, in which beauty arises naturally from forms designed to be useable, insist that it is not a unitary style with specific features that might be repeated in different situations. In practice, in the case of buildings, the practical necessities of the 'machine for living' and the application of new materials automatically led to the deployment of specific modes of construction and architectural forms. This determined the development of an instantly recognisable architectural 'style'.

When it came to the garden, however, there was little practical, theoretical or even polemical guidance from architecturally minded Modernist gurus: outdoors, designers and owners enthused by the tenets of Modernism essentially had to make it up as they went along. As we shall see, some of these individualistic experiments worked well, and during the course of the century certain modes of expression were developed piecemeal: chiefly, the idea of the house on a green platform; the house set in its landscape; the house in woodland; and the house with a 'modern' garden. As Alan Powers' *The Twentieth Century House in Britain* (2004) has shown, there was considerable overlap between Modernism and more traditional modes of architecture in England in the twentieth century. The same could be said of the garden: while there was no garden equivalent of the 'white-cube' house, Modernist tenets such as the principle of subtraction, asymmetry and the importance of function can be seen to have altered the course of garden design.

The first convincingly Modernist house had been constructed in England in 1925, and a few years later Geoffrey Jellicoe made a modernistic display garden with rubberised paths for the Ideal Home Exhibition; but the earliest experiments in full-scale Modernist garden design did not appear until the early 1930s. As Brent Elliott has pointed out, these early designs were rather confused – a house such as Woodfalls in Hampshire by Darcy Bradell (1930) is an uneasy mix of Cape Dutch and Spanish colonial influences, while the garden appears to have been a pared-down version of the more exotic end of the Arts and Crafts vocabulary.

The 1925 Paris Expo had been an important influence on forward-thinking designers, introducing them to the work not only of Le Corbusier, but also a school of designers working in France at this time whose work could best be

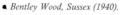
● *Bentley Wood, Sussex (1940).*

(above): *The modern house set in woodland: Christopher Tunnard worked with architect Serge Chermayeff at Bentley, thinning the birch woodland and planting drifts of daffodils.*

(right): *The projecting terrace terminated in a framing device, which calls in the landscape conceptually and physically. The plinth by the steps originally boasted a Henry Moore sculpture, now in Tate Britain.*

▲ *The Homewood, Surrey (1993).*

(left): *Architect Patrick Gwynne built this house for his own family in 1938, and it features a number of architectural devices which blur the distinction between inside and outside, such as full-height windows, decked terraces and an external staircase.*

(above): *The piloti, or stilt legs, of the house echo the verticals of the pine trees surrounding the building.*

described as Art Deco. One of these designers, Gabriel Guévrékian, was particularly admired for his exciting triangular gardens and use of materials such as metal, concrete, glass, and coloured gravels. His major work was the triangular garden made for the Vicomte de Noailles at Hyères in Provence, which still exists. This inspired the triangular rose garden at High and Over (1931) by Amyas Connell, the first major Modernist house in England; and in the early 1930s Ralph Hancock was making gardens in a kind of geometric-Italianate Art Deco style: zigzagging raised beds, sunken gardens, clipped box hedging, sculpture and fountains. These designs were showcased in Hancock's grandiosely styled book, *When I Make A Garden* (1936). But even as more and more architects became enthused by Modernism through the 1930s, there was far less interest in the movement among the garden-design profession and an accordingly less coherent development of design.

In most cases, there was no garden to speak of at new Modernist houses in the 1930s: the entrance front consisted either of a large, curving asphalt area for car parking, or else grass running up to the house with small groups of trees or a fringe of shrubs, while the rear garden was generally laid to lawn, again right up to the house. Favoured trees were pines or birches – perhaps an unconscious homage to the natural landscapes of Scandinavia or Germany, whence Modernism came – although apple or pear trees were also popular by mid-century, often because new houses were built on redundant orchard plots. Where

a garden had been consciously designed, it was often inspired by the form of the house and to some extent by the surrounding topography – it is notable that so many Modernist houses echo the landscape milieu in their names, containing words such as 'hill', 'view', 'high', 'wood', 'sea', 'orchard', or the names of specific trees such as 'beech' or 'pine'. The concept of leaving the landscape alone was sanctioned by Le Corbusier himself in his writings and in the example of the Villa Savoie, Poissy, France (1928–31), where views into the surrounding woodland were conceived as an extension of the architecture (although this perhaps over-generous reading of the architect's intentions has been challenged recently).

Innovative garden-making has always been a bourgeois preoccupation, and this would have stifled interest among politically leftist architects; paradoxically, Mies van der Rohe's own attempts at ornamental garden design for his villas are in several cases notably staid versions of conventional rose gardens. F. R. S. Yorke's *The Modern House in England* (1937) illustrates a house at Wimbledon by Kaufmann and Benjamin that features a ludicrously bijou flowerbed skirting the building, and even Oliver Hill's Modernist houses at Frinton-on-Sea boast front and back gardens which ape suburban pseudo-Arts and Crafts models to dispiriting effect. As with many of the Arts and Crafts architects, most Modernist architects realised they did not have the technical knowledge to work effectively in the garden environment (the main exceptions to this on the international scene were Adolf Loos, Irving Gill and Frank Lloyd Wright).

The development of *piloti*, or stilt legs, for Modernist buildings provided not just a practical solution to car parking and other utility issues (perhaps echoing Palladio) – it also allowed the surrounding landscape to invade the building space so that the two became indivisible. Living rooms became landscape-viewing areas. In fact, outdoor living elements were often contained within the dimensions of the house, in the form of roof terraces (one benefit of the Modernist flat roof) and balconies, which also afforded the necessary privacy for sun-worshippers. The front cover of F. R. S. Yorke's seminal *The Modern House* (1934) showed a couple enjoying outdoor living in deckchairs on the roof terrace of their Modernist house, complete with external staircase. And, of course, a green platform meant that the building's clean-lined beauty could be shown off to advantage; aesthetically, the architecture of the house was overwhelmingly the dominant element. But away from the immediate vicinity of the house, architects and theorists were less sure: the ideal of the unmediated landscape meant

that many Modernist houses appear to have been beamed down into the landscape from another planet.

Christopher Tunnard led the attempt to create a Modernist garden-design ethos. Tunnard was a Canadian of English parentage who came to London when he was nineteen, trained in horticulture at Wisley and then studied building construction. In the early 1930s he moved in key British Modernist circles, and in 1932 he was briefly articled as a landscape architect to Percy Cane. Tunnard's period of influence in Britain was short, however, spanning the years 1936 to 1939, and he completed just half-a-dozen commissions in that time. But this blond-haired, shy, softly spoken young man was also angry – enraged by what he saw as the romantic trivialisation of garden design. He vented his spleen in a polemical book, *Gardens in the Modern Landscape* (1938), which was influential for decades to come, particularly in the United States.

In Tunnard's opinion, 'The present day garden, with the sixpenny novelette, is a last stronghold of romanticism.' He goes on the offensive against supporters of both the wild garden and Arts and Crafts gardens, accusing the media and retail industries of pandering to the most basic preju-

dices of the public and eliminating the artist from the garden: 'The most ephemeral of garden styles, the apotheosis of naturalism, offers all the charms of escape for those who pursue this policy in their waking lives – the type … which prefers animal to human society and deplores the advance of science and civilisation. In the wild garden they are in fairyland.' Tunnard called instead for a garden design that eschewed decoration, sentimentality and links with past styles in favour of a crisp, pleasing functionalism that catered to the needs of the owners and employed modern materials such as concrete and glass.

Tunnard's most successful design was for the landscape around Bentley Wood in Sussex (1935–38), a timber-framed Modernist house designed by Serge Chermayeff, where the surrounding woodland was thinned and replanted to naturalistic effect with drifts of daffodils. A Henry Moore sculpture was placed at the end of a terrace positioned at right angles to the house, and this terrace was bounded by a high wall to provide privacy. The use of a paved terrace near the house, large sliding windows blurring the distinction between inside and out, and minimal intervention in the landscape were all

● *No. 16 Kevock Road, Lasswade, Midlothian (1960). The house in its landscape: as well as woodland settings, another successful Modernist landscape device was to site a house on a promontory with thrilling views.*

prototype features of the Modernist approach to gardens at this time.

At St Ann's Hill, Surrey (1936–38), where Tunnard himself lived with the owner in a new Modernist house by Raymond McGrath, he designed formal terraces to radiate out from the circular building, as well as a curved swimming pool by a clump of rhododendrons some distance away. The designed garden area is placed within a parkland setting. The tone of Tunnard's large-scale designs is not dominated by smooth-edged austerity, in the same mode as much of the architecture, but is really quite romantic – often a celebration of the surrounding English countryside. Tunnard himself described the Bentley Wood design as 'a subjective and essentially picturesque scheme'. It feels relaxed, but is nevertheless crisply arranged to complement the house – very much like the English landscape style of the eighteenth century, in fact. The marriage between the Modernist house and the Georgian landscape proved to be a surprisingly happy one.

Modernist architecture was to be blighted by its association with the second wave of tower blocks of the 1960s and 1970s, but it is worth noting that the eminent critic Sir

John Summerson described Bentley Wood as 'the most aristocratic English building of the decade'. Tunnard's prescription for the Modernist garden amounted to a return to the landscape tradition of the eighteenth century as the setting for a house, combined with telling formal interpolations. In this sense, Tunnard broke with Le Corbusier, who could not justify an aestheticised conception of landscape. In contrast, the opening words of Tunnard's *Gardens in the*

ABOVE:

● *High Sunderland, Borders (1960).* A modern house sited for its prospect view. As might be expected, almost the whole valley-facing side of the house is glassed, uniting interior and exterior.

RIGHT:

● *Sir Eric Geddes' Penthouse (1935).* The concept of indoor-outdoor living was slowly becoming popular in the 1930s. Here, the whole wall is made of glass doors that opened on to a semicircular balcony.

Modern Landscape are: 'A garden is a work of art. It is also a number of other things, such as a place for rest and recreation, and for the pursuit of horticulture, but to be a garden in the true sense it must first be an aesthetic composition.'

Tunnard's executed commissions were for rich, enthusiastic patrons of Modernism; on a smaller scale, his most revealing design is for the All-Europe House, a prototype for social housing devised for the 1939 Ideal Home Exhibition. Functional, simple, yet attractive, the design is the embodiment of his theories: zigzag, back-to-back rows of small, box-like houses are each apportioned a rectangular garden about 35 feet long. 'The right style for the twentieth century is no style at all,' he wrote, 'but a new conception of planning the human environment. In the modern garden an attempt is made to let space flow by breaking down divisions between useable areas, and incidentally increasing their usability.' Tunnard's identikit gardens are half lawn (sometimes with a tree), a quarter vegetables and a quarter decorative plants, with a smart terrace of concrete paving stones by the house and a paved path up the side of the lawn which then goes on to bisect the planted beds. There is a shed at the bottom of the garden and a gate leading on to a rectangular communal area of grass, trees and shrubs. This productive aspect of gardening was honoured by Tunnard in his large-scale designs too, such as that for Land's End, a house designed by McGrath at Galby in Leicestershire (1938), which features a gridded plot behind the house, bounded by a low hedge, and a park of pasture and tree clumps at the front.

Tunnard's pleas for a new approach to gardens fell on deaf ears, and in 1939 he accepted an invitation to teach at the Graduate School of Design at Harvard University. He never returned to Britain. Gardens in a Modernist milieu were left to evolve unfettered by ideology, or, indeed, by design advice of any kind. How different it was in the USA, where a new generation of Modernist landscape designers, led by Thomas Church and Dan Kiley, were able to create an impressive body of work. Looking at photographs of newly built Modernist houses in England (they were generally recorded by *Country Life* when they were new), it is easy to come to the conclusion that the gardens remained relatively blank spaces. In practice, of course, owners made gardens to suit themselves and their own vision of what a garden for a modern house should be.

LEFT:
▲ *Gribloch, Stirlingshire (1951).*
The landscape as a platform for architecture: many architects believed that the best way of showcasing their building was to site it on smooth grassland, as seen here. The historical precedent was the eighteenth-century landscapes of Capability Brown, in which pasture would come right up to the walls of the Classical house.

RIGHT:
▲ *Charters, Berkshire (1944).*
High Modernism meets the Georgian landscape: 'Regency' dolphins form the fountain centrepiece of a columned enclosure at the entrance front of this house completed in 1938 by Adie, Button and Partners. Prostrate junipers and other evergreens, stark against the white stone, strike a Classical note.

In their house designs, Modernist architects often tried to unite interior with exterior, chiefly through the use of large glass windows, which might slide back to open house to garden, and in balconies, roof terraces and external staircases (Hyver Hill in Hertfordshire by Jane Drew is a notable essay in this mode). *Country Life* had been in the vanguard of publications promoting Modernism (from 1928), and in 1935 the magazine featured Eric Geddes' penthouse ('a useful new term from America') in which one whole wall was a series of sliding glass doors that opened up on to a semicircular balcony. One of the most successful early Modernist experiments in exterior design in England was the 1938 swimming pool and leisure area designed by Berthold Lubetkin and the Tecton Group for a communal household near Regent's Park, where the residents' penchant for all-weather swimming and alfresco dining had to be taken into account: the Penguin Pool at London Zoo. House plants were another area of burgeoning popularity:

as early as 1932, in *The Curious Gardener*, the stylist Jason Hill had equated a fancy for cactus with an interest in Le Corbusier, and Tunnard had also enthusiastically promoted the decorative potential of plants. In 1952 the Modernist designer Frank Clark published *Indoor Plants and Gardens*.

On the ground plane, paved areas next to the house provided sitting areas or connected the house to features such as swimming pools and courtyards – Patrick Gwynne's The Homewood, Surrey (1938), was notable in this respect. A terrace also provided the most subtle and minimal way of relating the house to its garden or landscape setting, and in many cases it remained the only serious outdoor intervention.

The idea of the house secreted into its landscape and connected with it remained the most potent ideal for Modernist landscaping in the post-war years – the late 1950s and 1960s saw a vogue for modern house-building –

◆ *Serenity, Surrey (1958). The house set in woodland was a key Modernist approach. The cedar boarding and buff brickwork harmonise with the sandy soil and surrounding two acres of birch and conifer plantation.*

with emphasis placed on unimpeded views from the rooms and hallways of the house. Indeed, the landscape setting began to define the look of the house in some cases: at Lasswade, near Edinburgh, built in 1960, and at High Sunderland, in the Scottish Borders, completed in 1957 by Peter Womersley, the houses were perched dramatically on top of escarpments (perhaps following the precedent of

ABOVE:
● *Heathbrow, London (1963). The geometric lines of the house sit happily amid the trees that were left exactly as they were. An untouched landscape proved to be an effective setting for a number of Modernist buildings.*

RIGHT:
● *Upper Wolves Copse, West Sussex (1958). Built for his family as a rural bolt-hole, Kenneth Capon's house is raised above the woodland under-growth on concrete posts.*

Mies' acclaimed Tugendhat House of 1930), while at North Landing, by Tayler and Green, it is the views from the pasture setting that give the space its character. This was a positive development of the pre-war notion of the Modernist garden as a platform for the house, as can be seen at Charters, Berkshire (1938) by Adie Button and Partners, in its simplified parkland setting, and at Basil Spence's Gribloch in Stirlingshire of the same period.

The house set amid woodland emerged as another key Modernist treatment of exterior space. At 1930s houses such as The Homewood and Hamstone House in Surrey, Ashcombe Tower, Devon, and of course Bentley Wood, trees and lawns defined the areas around the house, adding a certain sense of mystery and glamour. The tradition continued in the 1950s, betraying also the influence of Frank Lloyd Wright, at houses such as Heathbrow in Hampstead, by Hal Higgins and Reyner Ney; Serenity in Surrey, by Leslie Gooday; Wildwood in Perth & Kinross; and Upper Wolves Copse, Sussex, by Kenneth Capon, where the building's *piloti* give it an appealing frisson of the treehouse.

131

In the 1960s, several of the Span housing schemes were conceived in terms of houses sited amid woodland and pasture (see Chapter 8). In many cases, the wildness of the woods was offset by more formal compartments near the house, as at Cock Rock, Devon, although these more 'designed' areas took on many forms. The ornamental garden as envisaged for the Modernist house was in some cases simply transplanted from more conventional settings. At Witley Park, Surrey, the 'white-cube' Modern house is complemented by lavender and roses in geometric beds – this works extremely well – while at Buttersteep House, Berkshire (1938–39), by Francis Lorne, there is a double herbaceous border of considerable scale and depth.

Modernist gardens are most successful when the exterior spaces are shaped and scaled to complement the existing topography, the architecture of the house and the wider landscape. A good example of this is New England, Surrey, designed by Derek Lovejoy and Partners, where the entrance front to the small, one-storey brick house is approached via a stairway through gently sloping grass verges, and where the rear of the house is dignified by full-length windows and a grid of paving stones set in the grass.

Courtyard gardens became very popular in Modernist houses of the 1960s, especially following revelations about

LEFT ABOVE:
• *Olantigh, Kent (1969).* In 1960, the architect John Stammers dramatically updated the saloon of this Neo-Georgian house of 1912, cladding one end entirely in glass to create a garden room looking out to the swimming pool.

LEFT BELOW:
• *Joldwynds, Surrey (1934).* The west loggia looking across the L-shaped terrace – simply a piece of grass and a piece of water – at Oliver Hill's white-rendered Modernist house. Christopher Hussey described the terraces as 'a raft ... above the luxuriant boscage of the wild garden'.

ABOVE:
• *Buttersteep House, Berkshire (1942).* An ambitious garden was envisaged for this house built in 1938–39, at a moment when English horticulture was on a high note. It shows that the traditional double border can work in a Modernist context if realised on the correct scale.

the potential of concrete made in the Cement and Concrete Association's marketing campaign, for which they enlisted the support of Geoffrey Jellicoe and Sylvia Crowe. Arne Jacobsen's design for St Catherine's College, Oxford (1960–64), is comprised of such interlocking spaces. At High Sunderland, Selkirk, the courtyard featured a rectangular pool with sculpture and complementary areas of planting and paving. Reference to Mies van der Rohe's seminal pavilion at Barcelona was made more explicit at Cray Clearing, Oxfordshire (1962), by Francis Pollen, where the dining room looked on to a pool with a figurative statue. This enthusiasm for enclosure outside can be set against the vogue for 'open-plan' inside. Peter Aldington's development of Turn End and two other houses at Haddenham in Buckinghamshire featured courtyards as well as substantial communal areas for more serious horticultural endeavour. An interest in plants has been by no means anathema to Modernist designers.

In *Room Outside* (1969), his breakthough publication, John Brookes allied the values of functionalism with the idea of intimacy with nature seen in so much Modernist design to date: 'As working life becomes more and more hectic and communal pleasures more varied, it seems more than ever essential that the individual and his family should have some place into which they can retreat; somewhere quiet where they have time to think, and can enjoy and refresh themselves by re-establishing contact with nature.' This ideal became less important to those trying to envisage gardens for people living in urban areas, where woodland settings and extensive prospects were not available (see Chapter 8).

In the 1980s and 1990s, designers such as Jill Billington and Preben Jakobsen have reconciled with no difficulty the formal strictures of Modernist design with an abiding interest in plants. As Jakobsen put it: 'Despite being an avowed European Modernist, I have often been known to use pinks, mauves and lavenders in borders ...'. His borders looked modern because of their careful weighting and the complementary use of devices such as paved, geometric, asymmetrical edges to the borders.

Nevertheless, it has been difficult to reconcile garden design with more mainstream Modernist genres such as architecture and interiors: the use of colour has been a problem (too much of it), as has been the issue of artistic

control (not enough of it); this has forced Modernist designers into either monumental austerity or exuberant conceptualism. However in the 1990s, Christopher Bradley-Hole successfully created perhaps the most successful incarnation of Modernist garden design seen to date by fusing authentic Modernist tenets with thoughtful planting inspired by the New Perennials movement (see Chapter 10).

There are two ironies related to Modernist garden design in England, however. The first is that the idea of the house in its landscape – without a garden, in other words – actually worked extremely well in many cases. In the case of several classic Modernist houses (such as Mies' Farnsworth House in Illinois), the organic relationship between house and nature is intimate and effective, but it is uninterventionist – almost an abstract relationship. A garden has no place here. In this sense, a handbook to the ideal Modernist garden would be a slim pamphlet indeed. The second irony is that for all its ambitions to be a popular international style, Modernism never spread itself widely enough or thinly enough to become accepted as the equivalent of a vernacular tradition by any nation. That honour fell to the garden style that so enraged Modernists like Tunnard: the English cottage garden, which conquered the world with apparently effortless ease.

Geoffrey Jellicoe was one of the overarching figures of the English landscape and garden scene of the twentieth century. Trained as an architect, he started out researching and writing about the gardens of the Italian Renaissance before embarking on a career as a Modernist designer which nevertheless saw him engaging in various projects informed by history above all. In later years he moved away from the functionalist doctrines of Modernism and towards an idiosyncratic Jungian conception of the universe and mankind's place in it.

◄ *New England, Surrey (1961).* One of the best examples of small-scale Modernist garden design by an architect. Derek Lovejoy and Partners set this small house on undulating grass (above), with a grid of concrete pavers defining the area to the rear of the house (right).

At Shute House in Dorset, Jellicoe made a garden of episodes incorporating a celebrated water staircase that emits musical tones, but his unfinished masterpiece was Sutton Place in Surrey, the garden he made for his American patron, Stanley Seager, between 1980 and 1986. Jellicoe's design was entwined with existing historical elements and romantic features, such as the long borders along the south side of the house, originally planted by Gertrude Jekyll.

One of the great lessons of Sutton Place is the power of letting things alone: the great double row of yew pillars that leads to the south front of the house is one of the most memorable parts of the garden – but it was originally planted in 1904 and left in place by Jellicoe (who planned a

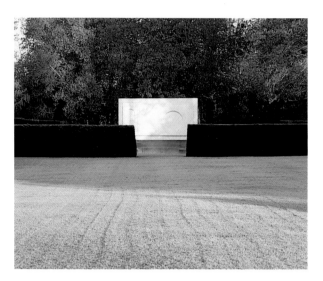

▲ *Sutton Place, Surrey (1996). Geoffrey Jellicoe's use of a massively enlarged version of a relief by Ben Nicholson (left) is the sculptural climax of the garden and an icon of twentieth-century design. The Paradise Garden (right) is reached via modernistic stepping stones across the lily pond.*

BELOW:
▲ *Hamblyn's Coombe, Devon (2001). In her garden, Bridget McCrum's sculptures are sympathetically sited, with the surrounding lawns, trees and hedges all maintained to intensify the effect.*

FAR LEFT:
● *Antony House, Cornwall (2001).
William Pye emerged as the leading
garden sculptor of the 1990s,
spawning several imitators. This
commissioned piece works well in its
formal context, echoing the
surrounding clipped yew cones.*

LEFT:
● *The Manor House, Bledlow,
Buckinghamshire (1996). 'Three
Fruit' (1986) by Peter Randall Page,
sensitively sited in a garden
landscaped by Robert Adams.*

cascade to run through it). The garden is an allegory of human existence. It begins with Creation, represented by a fish-shaped lake, overlooked by three hillocks representing Man, Woman and Child, north of the early Tudor house. This was originally to have been complemented by the Henry Moore sculpture that had inspired the lake's design. The Paradise Garden and Moss Garden are east of the house: the former is a complex arrangement of mixed borders, beds, arbours, fountains and arches, approached via stepping stones across a formal rectangular lily pond; the latter comprises concentric moss circles beneath a large plane tree.

The most celebrated parts of the garden are the Magritte-inspired Surrealist walk, which uses a trick of perspective, the urns not placed in order of size and the path narrowing, and then the climax, approached through a serpentine

tunnel in a yew hedge: a huge marble version of a small Ben Nicholson relief, prefaced by a long rectangular pool and surrounding yew hedge.

Jellicoe's use of sculptural elements was innovative in that he absorbed the work into the fabric of the garden (as with the Henry Moore), used traditional decorative elements in a contemporary manner (the urns) and rein-vented an art object so that it became part of the garden rather than an adornment to it (the Nicholson relief). Sculpture has rarely been deployed with such care and sophistication. The trajectory of the development of this interest in the twentieth century is as follows: first, the use of sculpture as ornament or decoration; second, sculpture placed in the garden as an artwork; third, sculpture made or conceived for its setting; fourth, site-specific sculpture; fifth, sculpture as non-sculpture, in that it is subsumed into the design and is indistinguishable from it generically. (This last phase has not actually occurred in practice as yet.)

Modernist sculptors such as Henry Moore and Barbara Hepworth were the first generation of artists to subsume their work successfully into a landscape or garden setting, although in most cases the piece was not created specifi-cally for a particular space. One of the most sophisticated twentieth-century gardens featuring a Moore piece is Dartington Hall, Devon, where Percy Cane worked after 1945, connecting up disparate spaces and adding the land-formed tilt-yard. Barbara Hepworth's own small garden at St Ives was realised with similar sensitivity, and there have been other effective attempts at creating an episodic garden defined by sculpture – Frederick Gibberd's design for his own garden at Harlow in Essex, begun in 1956, has received high praise. Individuals such as Lord Carrington at Bledlow in Buckinghamshire have built up significant collections of sculpture, well sited, and in the 1980s and 1990s a number of venues for large-scale sculpture were created, including Yorkshire Sculpture Park, near Wakefield, and Sculpture at Goodwood. These are essentially open-air art galleries.

Sculpture can be disastrous in a garden when it is added more as decoration than anything else. Hamblyn's Coombe near Dartmouth in Devon is an object lesson in how to do it properly. Here, sculptor Bridget McCrum has made places in her garden to accommodate her semi-abstract works, using hedges, slopes, trees, views across the River Dart and mowing regimes to offset the pieces to best effect.

Two ways of connecting art with the landscape in a potentially more profound way are through land art and site-specific art. In the mid-1960s, American artists such as Robert Smithson, Walter de Maria, Michael Heizer and

Robert Morris began to explore ways in which they could escape the confines of the gallery and work on a large scale, and they started to use landscape as a medium.

Land artists had an ambivalent attitude towards the natural world, alternately aggressive and nurturing, and they carefully sought out areas of wilderness or reclamation sites that they could manipulate for specific artistic ends. Robert Smithson's most celebrated work was the 'Spiral Jetty' (1970), a rock and mud spiral, 1,500 feet long and 15 feet wide, made by moving 6,650 tons of mud and salt crystal in the Great Salt Lake in Utah. Smithson's idea was to create a 'non-site' – his term for a place that transcends place. To paraphrase one of his own remarks: instead of putting a work of art on some land, he put some land into a work of art. The land-forming pioneered by land artists became one of the most fashionable working methods for landscape architects in the 1990s.

A site-specific attitude to sculpture also developed from the 1960s onwards at places such as Grizedale Forest in the Lake District, where scores of sculptures punctuate a variety of terrain, making a more profound relationship between sculpture and setting. Here, artists are encouraged to create works on site using available natural materials; Andy Goldsworthy and Richard Long are best known for working in this milieu. At Grizedale it is possible to imagine sculpture everywhere: there is up to fifteen-minutes' walk between each piece, and soon every blade of grass or tree stump starts to look like a sculpture. It makes the whole experience one of great sustained intensity. Other site-specific artists have worked successfully in garden settings, such as Ivan Hicks (at his own Garden in Mind, Hampshire, and at Groombridge Place, Sussex).

The history of sculpture in the twentieth-century garden is chequered to say the least. Although such artefacts seem to lend a spurious artistic legitimacy to gardens, which have always had a low status in the hierarchy of the arts, object-based art will often seem out of place in a garden setting unless it is conceived as an integral part of the garden rather than as an adornment to it.

BELOW:
● *Harewood House, Yorkshire (1995). The 9ft-tall figure of Orpheus (1984) by Astrid Zydower, which replaces the central fountain of Sir Charles Barry's parterre, is an unusually bold sculptural gesture in an historic setting.*

RIGHT:
● *Yorkshire Sculpture Park, near Wakefield (1999). 'Draped, Seated Woman' (1958) by Henry Moore, who pioneered outdoor siting of sculpture in the 1930s. The idea was taken up by private garden owners in the 1950s, and by the 1980s several open-air sculpture galleries had been established.*

8 · Romance and Restraint

1940–1969

The outbreak of the Second World War was to change everything in horticulture, as it did in most areas of life, but the impact on Home Front gardens was not immediately felt. At larger houses, entire staffs would eventually be conscripted and the house itself might even be requisitioned; while in more modest situations, back-garden plots would ultimately be given over to vegetable production in response to the government's patriotic 'Dig for Victory' campaign.

In the early phase of the war, however, there was considerable dissent in horticultural circles over what appeared to some to be a barbarous, politically expedient rout of the garden in the name of agricultural economy. *Gardener's Chronicle*, the weekly read for professionals and serious amateurs alike, was forthright, announcing just twenty days after the outbreak of war: 'This brings us to the question of whether it is advisable to dig up lawns in order to increase the area available for cropping. The answer is, No!' For many, the garden was part of what the nation was defending, so to destroy it voluntarily would be an admission of defeat before the fact. Their argument was that gardens and flowers would help boost national morale.

It was true that the war on the Home Front was not going to be won by digging for victory in Britain's gardens – mechanisation (tractors, chiefly), more intensive farming and the millions of acres of pasture, moor and marsh brought into cultivation did far more to lower Britain's food-import rate from two-thirds to one-third. But the nation launched into vegetable obsessiveness with gusto, lapping up the suicidal recipe exhortations of characters such as Potato Pete and Dr Carrot and gamely experimenting with exotic vegetables such as celeriac, endive, salsify and sweetcorn. There were Royal Horticultural Society vegetable demonstrations, model allotments at the Society's Wisley garden, and new horticultural clubs were set up. The number of allotments in Britain almost doubled during the war to 1.5 million. The conflict thus played an important part in horticultural education among homeowners, helping reinforce the notion, still strong in postwar years, of the garden as a version of a cottager's plot – essentially productive, but with flowers informally planted for ornament.

Every inch of spare land was considered for cultivation, partly for propaganda, 'we're all in this together' reasons. Grand London squares such as St James's and Tavistock were converted into allotments, and some of the salubrious balconies overlooking them became chicken runs. Bombsites were ingeniously converted into vegetable

■ *Crathes Castle, Kincardineshire (1937). The shrub borders at Sir James and Lady Burnett's acclaimed garden. Graham Stuart Thomas said, 'I have never seen another garden with even half the magic of this' – and that included his visit to Munstead Wood in Jekyll's lifetime.*

gardens; the moat of the Tower of London was given over to peas and beans; and allotments surrounded the Albert Memorial in Hyde Park. The swimming baths of the wrecked Carlton Ladies' Club became a piggery. In the countryside, most of the larger estates were already self-sufficient by virtue of their kitchen gardens; lack of manpower meant that the few gardeners who had not been called up concentrated on food production and left the ornamental gardens to fend for themselves.

In terms of decorative horticulture it was a time of great wretchedness, despite the protestations of leading gardeners early in the war. Gardens such as Glyndebourne in Sussex, where John Christie had by 1939 succeeded in making an exuberant cottage garden on a large scale with masses of delphiniums and campanulas, were put on hold for the duration (which all too often, in the case of a garden, means becoming overgrown). Vita Sackville-West swiftly turned part of Sissinghurst into an arable farm, and Winston Churchill's own garden at Chartwell was simply

closed up. But since there was no obvious expediency in ploughing up lawns and flower borders when there was so much pastureland readily available for such purposes, the County War Agricultural Committees (known as 'the War Ag') generally let smaller private gardens alone.

Given the constraints of supply and rationing, it was in the interests of individuals to grow their own fresh vegetables (although many did not). Landscape parks, on the other hand, were subjected to a concerted and fruitful ploughing campaign orchestrated by the War Ag. At Badminton, Gloucestershire, half the 1,200 acres of parkland had been ploughed by 1942, and the situation at Holkham in Norfolk was similar.

Demand for flowers continued unabated, however; if anything it was exaggerated in the circumstances. Early on in the war, the Ministry of Agriculture had instructed market gardeners to turn over flower production under glass to vegetables, and by 1943, transportation of flowers by rail had been made illegal. Flower smuggling broke out:

there were tales of flower-filled suitcases brought up to Covent Garden from the West Country, of cauliflowers with their hearts scooped out and filled with anemones, and even of a flower-filled coffin sent from Cornwall to London.

The war had interrupted a surge in the horticultural sophistication of gardeners in the mid- to late 1930s, and when it had finished it understandably took a while for gardeners to get back into their stride. The aesthetic-minded effusions of Jason Hill and his ilk, published just before the war, must have seemed a distant and irrelevant memory, telegraphs from quite another time. That kind of horticultural sophistication was not just considered inappropriate but was in any case unattainable for most gardeners, given the parlous state of the nursery industry and the unavailability of novelties and rarities. Instead,

there were a number of horticultural reactions to the depredations of post-war austerity in the late 1940s and early 1950s. In smaller gardens, there was great enthusiasm for vibrantly coloured annuals grown from seed – there was precious little colour anywhere else in life. The bright yellow 'Peace' rose, introduced via France in 1947 by the moustachioed nurseryman Harry Wheatcroft, was the popular hit of the post-war decade.

In numerous larger gardens, meanwhile, it took years for the borders and lawns to recover, and several did not recover at all. At many houses, hedges were unclipped, paving was strewn with weeds, topiary was shaggy, and the herbaceous borders had become unruly strips of weeds and grasses, with perhaps an untended shrub or two flowering wildly in all directions. This can all be seen in *Country Life* photographs of the period, although of course the parlous state of the garden is never commented upon in the articles. There is dilapidation and there is dilapidation: the Edwardian penchant for an air of mysterious ruin is quite different to the simple neglect of the post-war decade.

The Second World War and its aftermath had a far more decisive effect on gardens than the First, and in many ways it genuinely did mark the end of an era for the larger gardens and the start of a new one for the smaller ones. Taxation, the imposition of death duties and recession were to take their toll on the English country-house tradition, and although a few houses could be passed to the National Trust, several hundred were demolished in the 1950s and 1960s, as has been well documented in Giles Worsley's *England's Lost Houses* (2002). A single part-time gardener would now have to cope as best as he could where there might previously have been two or three full-time men, although new machinery was of some help.

In the sphere of professional design, there were nothing like the numbers of commissions in England after the war

compared with before, and the scale and expense involved was greatly diminished; there was simply not as much money in circulation for projects such as gardens. The war and its aftermath struck a body blow to ambitious gardening in England and it would not recover for the best part of half a century. Retrenchment and reassessment is the positive way of describing it; depression and destruction is perhaps more accurate.

Culturally, too, there were some crucial shifts, particularly from the mid-1950s onwards. The modest or suburban homeowner began to lay a claim to the style of the garden, and its use, in a way not seen before the war, when the emphasis had been on copying the gardens of grander houses. It was not quite a process of democratisation in action, but it did represent the beginnings of a greater sense of independence and confidence among garden-owners. In a way, one type of aspiration was simply eclipsed by another, as is often the case with domestic fashions – in this

case, and to simplify, the desire for a Cotswold manor house was replaced by the craving for what was being marketed as a modern lifestyle.

In the post-war years, design manuals such as George W. Hall's *Garden Plans and Designs* (1947) perpetuated the obsession with 'layout' seen in pre-war books, with bewildering numbers of near-identical plans of rectangular or square suburban gardens rigorously subdivided into lawn, vegetable patch, border, specimen trees and snaking paths. The approach was almost wholly horticultural: the point of the garden was growing plants, little else. Practical horticulture dominated the media's treatment of gardens, then as now – with Percy Thrower emerging as the leading media gardener, with a down-to-earth style that set the tone for television broadcasting, just as Cecil 'Mr' Middleton had for radio in the 1930s. Very gradually, design advice in books and magazines was altered to embrace the perceived leisure needs of the family, in the shape of more spacious crazy-paved terraces, rose gardens and lawns big enough for children to play on. Flower arranging became suddenly fashionable in the late 1940s and 1950s, particularly among the socially aspirational – it was a genteel pursuit which in

its own way encouraged women to view the garden and its produce as an extension of the home's decoration rather than a productive space presided over by the male.

The garden-centre concept arrived in Britain in the early 1950s. These outlets became the horticultural equivalent of the new American-style supermarkets, opening up a wealth of opportunity for gardeners with neither the time nor the confidence to deal with traditional plant nurseries. It was now possible for people to pursue their hobby on a more casual, spontaneous basis, cultivating a new attitude to their gardens in the process. The 'lifestyle garden' had arrived – although the proportion of 1950s homeowners who converted their gardens in this light is unquantifiable and should not be overestimated: the change in emphasis in smaller gardens was a very gradual process and probably only reached its apotheosis by the mid-1990s.

As the lifestyle garden slowly and fitfully emerged, a commentator such as Vita Sackville-West, whose *Observer* column began in 1947, struggled to make her writing relevant to those gardening on a smaller scale. Sackville-West and her husband had left their house at Long Barn and moved to Sissinghurst explicitly to escape the spread of

147

bungalows into adjacent fields – which were, paradoxically, themselves occupied by commuters seeking rural quietude. Yet Sackville-West clung to old certainties in her advice to urbanites: 'For my own part, if I were suddenly required to leave my own garden and to move into a bungalow on a housing estate, or into a council house, I should have no hesitation at all in ruffling the front garden into a wildly unsymmetrical mess and making it as near as possible into a cottage garden, which is probably the prettiest form of gardening ever achieved in this country in its small and unambitious way. I should plant only the best things in it, and only the best forms of the best things, by which I mean that everything should be choice and chosen.' This is the same kind of patronising vagueness practised by Gertrude Jekyll, and just as unhelpful to the average gardener at whom it is ostensibly directed.

How different was the approach of Lady Allen of Hurtwood and Susan Jellicoe (wife of Geoffrey Jellicoe, and an important contributor to his work, mainly through planting). Their 1953 book on gardens in a series called

'The Things We See' is a visual polemic for good modern design. The authors note that although modern houses can be 'mass produced', gardens cannot be, and ought instead be a reflection of the individual taste of the owner. In modern gardens two main trends are noticeable, they suggest: 'The first is a preference for fluidity and free,

▲ *Cottesbrooke Hall, Northamptonshire (1955). Within a decade of the end of the war, several gardens had returned to their pre-war splendour. The long border shown here effectively divides the landscape park (to the left) from Robert Weir Schultz's cellular Arts and Crafts layout lower down (to the right).*

▲ *Julians, Hertfordshire (1947). One of the few gardens to bounce back straight after the war. The gate piers to the walled garden are festooned in Rosa 'Etoile de Hollande' and choisya. Inside the walled garden was a delightful mass of herbaceous planting realised from 1940 by the owner, Mrs Pleydell Bouverie, in the exuberant manner of Norah Lindsay.*

● *The Salutation, Kent (1962). The view down the main borders from the raised east terrace at this 1911 Lutyens house. The garden was praised by Lanning Roper for its fusion of good planting and spatial awareness.*

natural lines as opposed to geometrical arrangements; the second is the breaking up of large spaces into smaller compartments whenever possible.' The proselytising impulse of the authors here is laudable, but their observation was accurate only with reference to the predilections of professional Modernist designers – it was not the reality of the suburban garden.

In larger gardens, one reaction to the disarray caused by war was the introduction of a severe, rectilinear style, usually in the shape of formal pools with seventeenth-century Dutch overtones. Lutyens had introduced one such pool at his last commission, Blagdon in Northumberland, in 1928. In the late 1940s, similar formal pools were used as tentative expressions of post-war confidence at Stonor Park, Oxfordshire, and Henley Hall, Shropshire. For the

public at large, a new kind of order was imposed on civic life through the creation of New Towns, such as Harlow, Stevenage and Hemel Hempstead. At Harlow the designer Frederick Gibberd moved fast: in 1949 the first residents moved in to enjoy the important open- and public-space component the landscape architect had introduced to the town's plan.

Designers such as Brenda Colvin, Frederick Gibberd, Geoffrey Jellicoe, Sylvia Crowe (who created the water gardens at Harlow), Frank Clark and Peter Youngman all found themselves working on post-war New Towns up and down the country, enthused with the sense of being involved in a social crusade and the necessity for meaningful gardens and open space in towns. The New Towns were the landscape correlative of the new Welfare State,

and, although they have inevitably dated, as social experiments they were far more successful than their high-rise architectural counterparts, which effectively bypassed the landscape or garden element in favour of green platforms to show off the sparkling new buildings – which, alas, did not sparkle for long.

For the landscape architects, it was not just a matter of social idealism: there was very little private work to be had in the straitened post-war conditions, so almost a whole generation of professionally trained garden and landscape designers found themselves drawn into the large-scale public and commercial sphere. Many of their ideas were realised in the various show gardens of the Festival of Britain on London's South Bank in 1951 – Peter Shepheard's use of large-leaved architectural plants was particularly noteworthy – but with a few exceptions, such as concrete planters, these did not go on to gain widespread currency. In fact, the story of post-war gardens has been somewhat monopolised by the New Town movement and its designers: the landscape profession has been better at articulating its history than the gardening world. Not everyone lived in a New Town, however, and there was much else going on that went unrecorded, except in *Country Life* and a few other publications.

In the pages of *Country Life* in this post-war decade-and-a-half, the emphasis was on retrenchment and practical horticulture, with few articles on new innovations at gardens. In an essay in *Country Life* on 15 March 1946, entitled 'The Future of Country House Gardens', Constance Villiers-Stuart suggests that informal herbaceous schemes might be the horticultural salvation at large gardens – it is salutary to note that much of her advice is aimed at gardens with Victorian parterres, which were still being kept up in large numbers in the 1930s (she recommends planting roses and lavender instead of annuals).

In some larger gardens, things were picking up by the early 1950s, however, and there was a particularly positive atmosphere surrounding developments in planting. A handful of great gardens showed by example what could be achieved and they shine out: Bodnant (featured in *Country Life* in 1949), the extravaganza garden par excellence; Bramdean in Hampshire, with its profuse borders, and Reggie Cooper's Knightstone, Devon (both 1950); Kiftsgate, next door to Hidcote in Gloucestershire, for its roses and sophisticated colour theming (1953); the superb borders at Cottesbrooke, Northamptonshire (1955); Groombridge Place, Kent, (1956), a garden repeatedly visited by *Country Life*; and, at the end of the decade, Newby Hall in Yorkshire (1959), always a benchmark of

● *Tintinhull, Somerset (1956).*
Phyllis Reiss used existing features, such as old yews and walls, to create the formal structure and dignified atmosphere for a new garden of discrete spaces, in which herbaceous plants were used in sophisticated planting schemes.

quality. One lesser-known garden that appears in startlingly good shape as early as 1947 is Julians, Hertfordshire, where Mrs Pleydell-Bouverie, who had acquired Reggie Cooper's house and garden in 1940, encouraged delightfully deep and unruly herbaceous borders which seem to meld into each other and form one herbaceous mass. Peter Healing's well-regarded garden at Kemerton, in Worcestershire, was also thriving at this time.

The interior designer John Fowler – who had worked in a nursery for a time in his youth – bought the hunting lodge at Odiham in Hampshire just after the war, and over the next three decades he made a garden with strong structural bones, clearly influenced by Hidcote (there was even a double row of pleached limes) but featuring a connoisseurial array of plants of his own choosing. He also advised others on gardens in an informal manner, although, as with Norah Lindsay, who worked in a similar way in a similar milieu, the true extent of his influence is difficult to gauge.

Despite the continuing popularity of these kinds of herbaceous gardens, in much of the literature of the time a rather masculine tone can be detected, with a growing stress on the use of shrubs for structure and colour as opposed to what was perceived as the more feminine appeal of the colour-themed border. Rhododendrons and other flowering shrubs had been popular garden plants for at least four decades, and some of the most celebrated collections were now reaching glorious maturity – at places such as Westonbirt, Sheffield Park and Bodnant. On a smaller scale, these plants were finally beginning to be assimilated into the garden, rather than being viewed as collectable artefacts.

In the austere post-war conditions, with labour in short supply, a collection of shrubs was an attractive alternative to a lavish herbaceous border. Serious plantsmanship was becoming widespread among the populace (*Country Life* began using Latin names in its picture captions in 1961). Knightshayes Court in Devon, made by the Heathcote-Amorys, is perhaps the best example of a post-war woodland garden, and its status was secured when the National Trust took it on in 1972. In the public sphere, the Savill Garden in Berkshire, made by Eric Savill, developed as one of the premier showcases of rhododendrons, azaleas and other exotic shrubs and trees.

In *A Diversity of Plants* (1953), the plant collector Patrick Synge describes the modern garden as '[dependent] for its effects on flowering trees and shrubs, combined with those displaying beauty of leaf, bark, form or berry and underplanted with naturalised bulbs and small herbs' (by 'herbs' he means herbaceous perennials). The mixed border has

been downgraded in favour of what he calls 'labour-saving' shrubs – the 'low-maintenance' fallacy emerged in the 1950s as an adjunct of lifestyle gardening and has never gone away. In his *Sunday Times* gardening column in 1954, Theo Stephens applauded pampas grass as a good exotic, and through the 1960s and 1970s it became fashionable as a stand-alone specimen plant, rather in the Victorian manner. It was now possible to contemplate making a garden without a herbaceous border.

Margery Fish has been mentioned in the context of her garden at East Lambrook Manor in Somerset, begun in 1938. Fish worked at the *Daily Mail* (her stickler of a husband, whom she slyly derides in her writing, had been the news editor, then editor). In her retirement she created a highly regarded cottage garden and gained fame as an author giving straightforward advice in economical prose.

ABOVE:
▲ *Tintinhull, Somerset (1956).* The combination of architectural garden design and innovative horticulture made Phyllis Reiss's garden hugely influential and a counterpoint to the cottagey effusions of her friend Margery Fish's garden at nearby East Lambrook Manor.

RIGHT:
▲ *St Paul's Walden Bury, Hertfordshire (1956).* The Garden of the Running Footman, named in honour of the Greek statue of the discus thrower, as re-interpreted by Geoffrey Jellicoe. The rotunda, flanking sphinxes and flight of steps, were all part of this imaginative reconstruction, with no great claims to authenticity.

Roughfield, Sussex (1950). The romanticism of Sissinghurst gave post-war owners of medium to large-sized gardens the confidence to work in a similar fashion – after all, few were able to employ full-time garden staff any longer. A tumbledown scene was now not just forgivable but desirable, and Vita Sackville-West had shown the way.

We Made a Garden (1956) was Fish's big success, and in it she sets out her stall regarding colour: 'We all have our preferences. Mine are for the pastel shades, for with them it is possible to have a riot without disagreement. Pinks, lavenders, soft blues and lilacs, with plenty of cream and white, never clash.' This is the kind of advice that is easy to follow. Fish disliked oranges, yellows and sealing-wax red, and did a great deal to popularise cranesbill geraniums as well as classic cottage plants such as delphiniums, lupins, nepeta, erigerons, achilleas and penstemons of all kinds. (A dislike of yellow is still a noticeable trait among traditional gardeners.) But Fish was also innovative: *Carefree Gardening* (1966), for example, contains thoroughly avant-garde chapters on ferns and grasses. And the idea of ground-cover planting was pioneered in England at East Lambrook – Fish wrote a book entitled *Ground Cover Plants* in 1964 – while in another book she popularised a positive attitude to gardening in shady situations. The garden at East Lambrook was not dependent so much on set-piece borders as on a sense of the garden as a tapestry that unfolds all around one, where the edges are blurred and all the spaces are filled up. Where Jekyll's idea of cottage-gardening was carefully organised, structurally and artistically, Fish's approach to planting was far more relaxed, with plants encouraged to self-seed anywhere.

These two dominant strands of thinking about herbaceous planting co-existed and fed into each other through the rest of the twentieth century, although it can be not just difficult but fruitless to try to distinguish the two: herbaceous gardens, constantly changing, are not like buildings, which are solid and fundamentally static; their stylistic influences cannot be pinned down in the same way. What we can be certain of is that Fish's literary career was integral to her success, and indicative of a wider trend: as gardening became more popularised and personalised, the social structure of horticulture changed and it became necessary for any ambitious or outspoken gardener to develop a writing career parallel to the horticultural one. This had been the norm for leading Victorian head gardeners, who would fire off letters and articles to the *Gardener's Chronicle*, and it is still the case today.

Lanning Roper was another journalist who commanded a loyal audience. He was gardens correspondent for the *Sunday Times* from 1951 to 1975, but his articles in *Country Life* in the 1950s and 1960s were his best, eclipsing most others in terms of their sensitivity to both plants and design. In his writing, Roper sought to clarify the relationship between garden and house, and to treat herbaceous plants in the context of the whole garden scene, not just the

borders. The several gardens he designed – including Coniston Cold, Yorkshire, Hillbarn House, Wiltshire, and the one in Onslow Square, London, that he made with his wife, Primrose Harley – are distinguished by their elegance and restraint, coupled with well-planned horticultural episodes and borders that are notable for their structural strength and presence.

For all his love of cottage plants, there is no doubt that Roper saw formal or architectural elements as the key to the garden. It was an approach similar to that practised by Ralph Dutton at Hinton Ampner and Oliver Hill in his later gardens, such as his own at Daneway, Gloucestershire (both were featured in *Country Life* in the mid-1950s). Hidcote was perhaps the key influence, however: like Lawrence Johnston before him, Roper was an Anglophile American who showed English gardeners the way. One of Roper's favourite gardens was Tintinhull, where Phyllis Reiss (also American) had since 1933 been crafting a garden that became the apogee of post-war elegance: a series of garden rooms in the Arts and Crafts manner, but relatively sparsely 'furnished' and dependent on numerous vistas for effect, as well as splashy herbaceous borders.

The designer Sylvia Crowe (like her colleague Brenda Colvin) worked in the garden arena when she could, and her *Garden Design* (1958) is perhaps the best touchstone for the post-war period. Her most famous remark encapsulates an emerging dichotomy among gardeners: 'There are two attitudes to plants in gardens. One is that the purpose of a garden is to grow plants, the other is that plants are one of the materials to be used in the creation of a garden.' This

LEFT:
◆ *Alderley Grange, Gloucestershire (1969).* The herb garden created by Alvilde and James Lees-Milne, with the sweet-scented damask rose 'Isphahan' towering above lavender and other herbs. Elsewhere, roses (shrub and floribunda) and a predominantly grey and soft-blue colour scheme featured.

RIGHT ABOVE:
◆ *Bulbridge House, Wiltshire (1965).* This garden typifies the prettiness and poise of the best 1960s gardening. The relatively formal sunken garden complements the house designed by Wyatt in 1794. Lanning Roper described its relaxed charm: 'All the colours are soft and well blended. Plants are chosen for effect, not rarity. Foliage is as important as colour.'

RIGHT BELOW:
◆ *Branklyn, Tayside (1966).* At the more informal end of gardening, Lanning Roper could also lavish praise on a plantsman's garden, filled with rarities (notably meconopsis, in this case). He admired the way the vistas and paths were arranged to lead the visitor on, and foliage plants used to create a sense of rhythm.

opposition was, for Crowe, resolved at Tintinhull, despite the old-fashionedness of its cellular layout: 'Its particular success lies in the contrast and proportion of its spaces, in the use of existing trees to pin down and unite the design, and in the beautifully contrived views … Pots and architectural features are used to give emphasis, but they are used with restraint … No plant, however lovely in itself, is grown unless it contributes to the picture, and those whose form and colour are needed again and again, such as *Senecio greyi* and bergenia, are constantly repeated. In spite of restraint it is anything but austere.' That last comment sums up this particular mode of English gardening in the 1950s.

Percy Cane was a journalist turned prolific garden designer, with a career spanning from the 1930s to the 1970s – at gardens such as Hascombe Court and King's House, both in Surrey, and Westfields, Bedfordshire. Cane was unusual in that he specialised in medium-sized gardens, almost always incorporating a substantial paved terrace. This helps give even his smaller gardens an airy feeling of spaciousness and width. His other speciality was in connecting up contrasting areas of one garden – he suggested that each garden should have two or three different tones, and was happy to oblige if his clients wanted a variety of features in quite a small space. Where possible, Cane also included a woodland glade, large lawns and formal stonework of the highest quality.

The historicist pulse in gardening was still beating away – Ralph Dutton's pre-war Hinton Ampner was still developing and widely admired – and in 1956 the leading Modernist Geoffrey Jellicoe began work at St Paul's Walden Bury in Hertfordshire, an early-eighteenth-century landscape garden. It was not anathema to Jellicoe, or other Modernists such as Crowe or Colvin, to work in a historical context: in fact, eighteenth-century landscape parks were a

major influence. Jellicoe described his approach at St Paul's, in which he imaginatively re-created glades, statue groups and other formal features, as 'neo-historicist'. (Perhaps the nearest Modernist equivalent to this attitude was Ezra Pound's doctrine of 'creative translation' of Chinese, troubadour and Anglo-Saxon poetry.)

There was sporadic interest in historical pastiche – in 1952 Vita Sackville-West gave her readers practical instructions on how to make a knot garden for Coronation year – but the era of garden history and restoration was to begin in the next decade, with the foundation of the Garden History Society in 1965 and, in the same year, the first large-scale restoration of the post-war era: Westbury Court in Gloucestershire. Garden-visiting would also be encouraged with the publication in 1964 of the first serious modern guidebook: *The Shell Gardens Book*, edited by Peter Hunt,

LEFT AND BELOW:
● *Odiham, Hampshire (1961).* Interior designer John Fowler's garden was the epitome of 1960s formal elegance. Gardens such as this pioneered the fashionable garden look of the 1970s and 1980s, in which a light touch was used to meld historicist elements with exuberant herbaceous plantings.

RIGHT:
● *Alderley Grange, Gloucestershire (1969).* The pleached lime walk in Alvilde and James Lees-Milne's garden viewed from the orchard garden. The trees were planted in squares of blue scillas and chionodoxa in spring, and blue lobelias in summer.

● *Eridge Park, Sussex (1965).* The swimming pool was created in 1958 after a section of the house, which had been rebuilt twenty years previously, was demolished to make it a more manageable size. Swimming pools sited adjacent to the house (or in this case orangery) became acceptable in the second half of the twentieth century.

with a clutch of eminent contributors. National Trust membership was steadily on the rise by this time.

In horticulture, interest in antique plants intensified from the mid-1950s as nurseryman Graham Stuart Thomas – the National Trust's gardens adviser from 1956 and a founder member of the Garden History Society – sought out and identified as many old shrub roses as he could, with the help of individuals such as the flower-arrangement guru Constance Spry and a few interested nurserymen, notably E. A. Bunyard, who had published *Old Garden Roses* as early as 1936. Like Jekyll before him, Thomas was a serious modern plantsman with a latent antiquarian sensibility. Vita Sackville-West was another valuable ally in what Thomas called 'the Quest'.

The shrub-rose cult was to continue to grow through the 1960s and 1970s, in company with Thomas's books on the subject, until they were a well-established part of the garden scene by the 1980s, with several nurserymen (such as David Austin and Peter Beales) catering to an eager international market. Shrub roses were not only fashionable and of historic interest, they were also perceived as labour-saving by anyone faced with large herbaceous borders: a healthy shrub rose can take up a lot of room. The taste for rare and antique plants of all kinds ultimately found form in the system whereby gardens with fine displays of individual species are given National Collection status by the National Council for the Conservation of Plants and Gardens, founded in 1978.

The 1960s was a period of romanticism and self-conscious prettiness in gardens, offset by formal features such as urns, statuary, clipped hedges, pools and scallop- or wavy-edged beds. From about 1958 a more private, domestic feel can be detected in many gardens – such as Houndsell Place, Sussex, Saltford Manor, Somerset, and the Red House, Bexleyheath, Kent – where there was an emphasis on the centrality of the lawn to the garden's life and a relaxed feel about the planting, so that the garden does not appear to have been designed at all. It is as if owners of medium to large gardens had become attuned to the idea of the garden as a private, domestic space, without

160

RIGHT:
● *Fiddler's Copse, Sussex (1964).*
Modernist inflections in a new terrace
by Bodfan Gruffyd, seen here from
the sliding doors of an extension to
the existing farmhouse. Gruffyd
flattened the lawn and removed trees
to open up views of the Weald,
whence the eye is directed by the
sweep of paving. John Brookes
designed the planting here.

BELOW:
● *Jenkyn Place, Hampshire (1965).*
The grass crossroads halfway down
the double herbaceous borders, filled
with clumps of tall flowering
perennials, such as verbascums*,*
achilleas*,* delphiniums*,* eryngiums *and*
lilies*. The stone coping emphasises*
the flowing edges of the border.

a permanent staff and with less emphasis on entertaining and impressing guests than in the pre-war era.

By about 1960, one can see full-blown romanticism in gardens such as Knightshayes, Chevithorne, Husheath Manor and the Salutation (a Lutyens house). In these gardens there is less of a sense that the herbaceous plants have been carefully placed and structurally arranged in the Jekyllian way, with subtle rhythms and colour gradations that surge and recede. Instead, sinuous lines, prettily designed groupings of flowers, careful architectural interventions and framing devices conspire to create an atmosphere of low-key domestic charm. Flowers are the focus, not profuse and apparently disorganised in the Fish manner, but treated as pretty specimens rather than part of a themed border. The soft contours and shapes of these gardens may also owe something to the organic

or biomorphic lines popularised in other areas of the decorative arts.

The world of flower power, psychedelia, hippies and sexual permissiveness is not reflected in gardens at this time – a reflection of the truism that on the whole people do not become interested in gardens until their thirty-fifth birthday. But the small and growing organic and self-sufficiency movement was becoming increasingly popular during the 1960s: journalist and organic pioneer Lawrence Hills had founded the Henry Doubleday Research Association in 1958; the Soil Association had been going since 1948, and Rachel Carson's *Silent Spring* of 1962 became a key text for the environmental movement.

Despite these nascent trends, the garden of the 1960s was not generally wild-looking, and in many cases the prettiness of the planting was offset by a modern edge to the hard surfaces, as at Coles, Hampshire, or Fiddler's Copse, Sussex, or else an old-fashioned formality, as at Alderley Grange, Gloucestershire (James and Alvilde Lees-Milne's house). At Haseley Court in Oxfordshire, Nancy Lancaster created a garden that seemed to encapsulate many of the ideas of the time: it has been described by Richard Bisgrove as 'a blend of formal axes and informal planting, reason and romance, cottage-garden charm and cosmopolitan joie de vivre'.

The most stylish designer of this period was Russell Page, who nevertheless seems doomed to relative obscurity in Britain because so much of his work was abroad and because so much has been lost. His greatest legacy is his memoir, *Education of a Gardener* (1962), perhaps the most eloquent meditation on gardens of the twentieth century. Page's design style was pared down and architectural, with formal arrangements of lawns and hedges punctuated by bursts of exciting planting where appropriate, as can be seen at The Cottage, Badminton, Gloucestershire. But it was his delicate control of open space that was his hallmark, as if he was moulding air rather than hard materials – here was a confidence simply to let less be more; after all, Page had worked in Paris for a number of years and started out as a Modernist, in partnership with Jellicoe.

While Page was dismissive of most herbaceous borders, which he called 'extensive and brightly coloured hay', he echoed Jekyll and Lutyens in his emphasis on the importance of a single idea underpinning a garden: 'The problem for a garden maker is always the same, and I always try to discover in what consists the significance of the site, and then base my general theme on that. For a theme of some kind, a basic idea, is essential. It will set the rhythm of your composition down to its smallest details.'

Page was a designer of grace and simplicity, with a style that was Modernist in spirit but looked safely Classical to traditional eyes. Indeed, Page hit out at the kind of garden which he could see all around, and which had become the basic template in England: 'The informal "gardeners' garden" … Its shapelessness and air of general confusion leave a sense of disquiet which no number of well-planted episodes can quite dispel. Even the largest and finest are often ill-articulated. The RHS's garden at Wisley comes to my mind as a series of charming incidents beautifully gardened but incoherent and unrelated to the site.' It was an acute observation but it was ignored, as the nursery trade and the gardening media conspired to perpetuate the idea of the garden as a repository for collections of plants.

Suddenly John Brookes arrived on the scene. Trained in the Nottingham parks system, Brookes joined Sylvia Crowe's office in the 1960s and contributed columns about modern gardening to *Architectural Digest* magazine from 1964. These writings were eventually collected and published as *Room Outside* (1969), and they revolutionised ideas about domestic garden design in England – even if they did not change the physical appearance of English gardens overnight. (The anti-lawn movement can, however, be traced back to Brookes.)

Strongly influenced by the Dutch designer Mien Ruys, who used decking, gravel and sculptural terracotta pots in her gardens, by Scandinavian style, and also by American Modernists working on a small scale (in a way that English designers had not) such as Thomas Church and Garrett Eckbo, Brookes set out to redefine the domestic garden in terms of its users rather than the plants growing in it. It was a response to a perceived need among homeowners for gardens that were relevant to their own lives, not the lives of people of another time and another context. In the preface to his book, Brookes was quite clear about his

agenda: 'I have tried to explain and illustrate the process of designing a garden which will not be merely a collection of plants but a useable extension of the home into the outdoor world.'

With his gridded garden plans, patios, gravel and architectural plants for smaller gardens, and his metal furniture, sculptural pots and outdoor lighting, Brookes was not advocating a low-maintenance garden – that concept was largely the invention of the retail industry – but railing against the typical suburban garden of lawn, path, rosebushes, birdbath and neat borders. His gardens are composed of interlocking geometric volumes conceived in three dimensions; it has been noted that his garden plans resemble abstract paintings by Piet Mondrian. Container planting, in the form of collections of pots on terraces, balconies or paved yards, became a major interest of many gardeners from this period, and has remained so ever since – the 1960s heralded an enthusiasm for terracotta pots which has not abated. In a small pamphlet of 1970 entitled *Garden Design and Layout*, Brookes encouraged garden-owners to think about design before decoration and forget the precedents of grander settings. There was indeed a gulf between the patrician sensibilities of the plantsmen and -women of previous generations and Brookes's own egalitarian instincts. He was also reacting against Jekyll by explicitly stating that a garden is not primarily a picture, but a place to be lived in.

The Danish-born designer Preben Jakobsen also found a client base for Modernist garden design on a domestic scale with an even more geometric style than Brookes, leavened by inventive herbaceous plantings. These ideas were realised on a landscape scale in the 1960s in the Span housing developments of the architect Eric Lyons working with the landscaper Ivor Cunningham and the developer Geoffrey Townsend (Jakobsen also contributed), in which small modern houses were arranged in an attractive and relaxed communal landscape of lawns, car parking spaces, and tree and shrub groupings. For these designers, atmosphere was just as important as function.

In some ways, Brookes was trying to do for gardens in the 1960s what Terence Conran was doing for interiors (the first Habitat shop had opened in 1964); the difference was, the garden revolution was based on ideas, not retail opportunities. Perhaps because of this, Brookes was nothing like as successful as Conran. Meanwhile, the model of the garden as Arts and Crafts pastiche still reigned supreme. Yet modern ideas about lifestyle needs were becoming ever more important: in all kinds of different ways, people were beginning to mould their gardens in their own image.

● Private garden, Knightsbridge, London (1979). The shape of things to come: a classic backyard rectangle, here divided into three sections (one of lawn and two of paving), with 'green' walls of wisteria, roses, ivy and other climbers. The concept of outdoor living was now becoming widely accepted.

9 · From Smart to Art
1970–1989

In the 1970s, with gardeners inspired by the ever-greater availability and knowledge of plants, the latent formalism of the previous decades was offset by a renewed focus on planting. The gardeners (and therefore garden writers) who commanded most respect and influence in the last quarter of the century tended to be those whose primary interest was in the diversity and potential of plant material, not in the design of the whole garden. Christopher Lloyd and Beth Chatto are perhaps pre-eminent in this respect, and Lloyd's classic *The Well-Tempered Garden* (1970) is a fitting prelude to the decade. The emphasis in these writers' gardens is firmly on a minute artistic appreciation of plant combinations planned for colour and structural effect through the seasons, not on the structural plan of the garden or its use.

Woodland gardens and collections of unusual shrubs were more popular than ever at this time, while the slightly fuzzy planting exhortations of cottage gardeners of previous generations were being replaced in many cases by a deeper and more serious botanical awareness. Often, it was a marriage between obsessive horticultural interest and a romantic sensibility. Plantsmanship was in the ascendancy.

The suitability of Britain's climate for growing a wide range of different plants is often commented upon, and the nursery trade – encouraged by several generations of plantsmen-cum-journalists – has done much to feed the desire for more and more new varieties, hybrids, and even species. While there have undoubtedly been numbers of worthwhile introductions (*Corydalis flexuosa* in the late 1980s, to name just one), there is a growing feeling that there are simply too many plants on the market. The non-specialist can easily become bewildered at the range available, and the garden centre, display nursery, and now internet stockists can encourage supermarket-style shopping, in which plants are dropped into the shopping basket singly and on a whim, with no clear idea of how they are to be used. This problem was identified by a minority of garden writers in each successive decade of the twentieth century – too much choice, too little discrimination – but it became ever more entrenched during the last third of the century. By 1980, the average

165

garden article in *Country Life* was little more than a long inventory of plant names and descriptions (rhododendrons were the main obsession), usually sited within a woodland or dell garden.

The structure of Christopher Lloyd's garden at Great Dixter was perhaps emblematic of this emphasis: the layout of the irregular compartments of clipped yew – created by Nathaniel Lloyd in collaboration with Lutyens in 1910 – remained exactly the same, while Lloyd pursued a policy of intense horticultural experimentation within them, as he still does today. In the best gardens of the period, this horticultural emphasis was leavened by a certain poise and control, in which the lines of the garden are still just discernible beneath a delightful mass of burgeoning planting. Sylvia Crowe's approving view of William Robinson's garden is perhaps relevant here: 'Gravetye … gives an example of how a plantsman's love of diversity can be contained within a unity of composition.' This has been a rare thing in twentieth-century gardens (E. A. Bowles and

Christopher Lloyd are among the few who have been able to achieve it).

The degree of romanticism depended on individual taste. John Codrington was a designer who pushed the wild look to its limits in his own garden of intimate spaces at Stone Cottage, Rutland. Stone paths and formal features were almost smothered with plants – rarities intermixed with quite ordinary plants in an artful jumble, and chosen for foliage and form as much as flower. This last emphasis became particularly widespread from the 1970s; it could be found to a high degree in a garden such as Coates Manor, Sussex. *Fatsia japonica* had been a fashionable plant in the 1960s, and now it found widespread popularity. This interest in foliage and plant rarities was brought indoors, with a marked increase in conservatories and house plants; cacti, for example, were a quintessentially 1970s interest.

James Russell was another designer working at the informal end of the spectrum, helping to inform and influence the taste for hardy perennials through his position

● *Barnsley House, Gloucestershire (1974). The aspirational appeal of Rosemary Verey's design made it, perhaps, the most influential new garden of the early 1970s. It was a fusion of Classical poise and high-level plantsmanship, with columnar Irish yews, smooth lawns and luxuriant borders.*

at Sunningdale Nurseries, one of the leading such establishments (Graham Stuart Thomas was in partnership there for several years). Russell could also work well in formal vein, as at Seaton Delaval, Northumberland, where he created a large box-hedged parterre in historicist spirit. In domestic gardens, this was an era when every terrace and wall had to be adorned with self-sown plants in crevices, when borders seemed to tumble out of their confines on to paths and lawns. The prettiness and delicacy of 1960s planting was overwhelmed by this sensuous abandonment: it felt as if the garden was overflowing itself, as can be seen at Wardes in Kent. Here the bones of the garden are blurred by an indistinct mass of plants. Enclosed gardens of well-defined episodes, originally conceived in an Arts and Crafts spirit, were considered old-fashioned and their architectural lines compromised by exuberant plantings – although this could also work to extremely good effect, as at Snowshill Manor, Gloucestershire.

As a general rule, 'professional' designers – the majority of whom were hardly professionalised – displayed the most artfulness. Rosemary Verey and her husband came to Barnsley House, Gloucestershire, in 1969, and the garden

rapidly became celebrated for its poise and detail, with set-piece features such as the Laburnum Walk and the Doric Temple providing a sense of distinction and pace amid romantic plantings. It was a garden self-consciously created in the spirit of Vita Sackville-West, and there was always a knowing, slightly detached air about it. Percy Cane was still working in the early 1970s and remained a considerable influence on younger designers, and at the start of

● *The Cottage, Badminton House, Gloucestershire (1976). Russell Page advised the Duchess of Beaufort here devising the system of hedged enclosures and paths.*

● *Windle Hall, Lancashire (1983). 'Smart' gardening was a pastiche mix of fashionable historical references. In this border – backed by roses 'American Pillar' and 'Seagull' – the feathery spires of Bassia scoparia lend a sense of cultured panache to lobelia, ageratum and chamomile.*

● *The Old Vicarage, Firle, Sussex (1975). The Anglophile American writer Lanning Roper led by example with elegant gardens that combined subtle plantsmanship with a refined sense of scale and proportion.*

the decade Anthony du Gard Pasley had set up in practice on his own after working in the offices of both Brenda Colvin and Sylvia Crowe. While structure is the keynote of Pasley's gardens – such as The Postern in Kent – he is a versatile designer whose work does not always betray his Modernist background.

Russell Page and Lanning Roper, both of whom had become well established in the 1960s, did a great deal of work in the 1970s – although most of Page's commissions were in France and Italy – and perhaps more than any other designers they achieved a sense of balance and decorum in terms of the proportions of open space, the size of terraces, the placing of planters and pots and the weighting of borders. This can be seen at Roper's English gardens, such as Hillbarn House, Wiltshire; Lower Hall, Shropshire; and the Old Vicarage, Firle, Sussex. The cottage garden was still an ideal for many homeowners, and Roper could provide this where necessary – Beechwood in Sussex, described as 'a simple country cottage garden', was illustrated in *Country Life* in 1976; indeed, the cottage ideal was repeatedly evoked in the magazine through the 1970s.

Perhaps the most notable popular craze in gardens of the 1970s was for dwarf conifers – the horticultural equivalents of flared trousers. Adrian Bloom of Bressingham Nurseries in Norfolk, whose father, Alan Bloom, had made his mark as a nurseryman and writer of respected guides to herbaceous plants, was the most successful promoter of these evergreens, which were available in many shades of green and yellow, including some scintillating acid tones that have become closely associated with gardens of this decade. Bloom's *A Year Round Garden* (1979) was a pæan to the virtues of evergreens, and his own bungalow garden was an extreme example of the trend: the vivid yellows and greens of the conifers, yews, pines and spruces, the pinks of heathers, the glaucous tones of the junipers and silver firs – all set in a lawned garden of circular beds and wavy-edged borders.

Heathers were often used as underplanting with conifers, and a 1950s invention of Alan Bloom's proved a novel way of showing off the plants: the island bed, which enabled 360-degree appreciation. This was a perfectly sensible development for a commercial nursery situation, in which the largest number of plants need to be showed off to the best possible advantage; it also found favour at professional institutions such as Harlow Carr in Yorkshire and Waterperry Manor in Oxfordshire. But its application in private gardens was often less successful, leading to lozenge-like blobs of planting beds dotted across lawns. Like most apparent innovations in gardening, this was not really a new idea – the Victorians had used similar methods

to show off their specimens, albeit with a little more panache. Another noticeable trend of the 1970s was the trough garden, in which stone or ceramic containers were used to display particularly alpine and succulent plants in gravelly soil (Joe Elliott's collection of troughs at Blundells, Gloucestershire, was most dramatic). Also popular was the raised bed – again ideal for the display of smaller specimens, if one's interests are wholly botanical.

In tandem with this interest in plantsmanship went a rather masculine consideration of the garden as a scientific or practical challenge. Organic gardening remained a niche interest, and chemicals of all kinds were still *de rigueur* in 1970s gardens. Books on 'garden planning' were preoccupied with problems of soil, drainage, composting, pond creation, greenhouses, rock gardening, lawn maintenance, sheds and other structures. The garden became the outdoor adjunct to the craze for do-it-yourself home maintenance and the number of machines (particularly electrical) used in gardens soared.

But the ideas about lifestyle that had come into focus in

the previous decade also found form in features such as swimming pools, climbing frames and slides for children, lightweight aluminium garden chairs and loungers, patios and barbecues. The trend for outdoor eating was certainly encouraged by wider experience of Continental habits, resulting from the rise of the package holiday, the books of cosmopolitan cookery writers such as Elizabeth David, and increased foreign travel in general. The title of H. G. Witham Fogg's *Creating a Luxury Garden* (1974) is indicative of the aspirational streak in garden style at this time. Perhaps the widespread adoption of the term 'patio' in the 1960s and 1970s is indicative of a kind of autonomy in gardens, a move away from the ideals of the larger-scale Arts and Crafts tradition: suburban gardens have patios, country gardens have terraces.

The *leitmotif* of gardening in the 1980s was the explosion in interest in garden history and plant heritage, boosted by 'The Garden' exhibition at the Victoria and Albert Museum in 1979, organised by Roy Strong, who led a revival of formalism specifically geared to the small garden.

ABOVE:
● *Strawberry House, London (1985).* Smart gardening in town. This garden, originally laid out in the 1920s by a theatre-set designer, became the perfect setting for a manicured 1980s garden of carefully rehearsed architectural and horticultural effects.

OPPOSITE ABOVE:
● *Barnsley House, Gloucestershire (1974).* The Classical temple and pool. Historical interpolations, such as this, became de rigueur at smart gardens of the 1980s as the cult of ultra-historicism and a dislike of modernity took hold.

OPPOSITE BELOW:
● *The Priory, Kemerton, Worcestershire (1986).* Peter Healing's renowned garden featured a 360ft-long x 18ft-deep double herbaceous border. Just beyond it, was this area, with stepping stones laid between informal plantings of phlox, allium, various eryngiums, astrantias and much more.

This enthusiasm for the past was partly fuelled by disillusionment with the vision of the future created by architects in the 1960s and 1970s – the 'Brutalist' tower blocks which now came in for sustained criticism. The 'period garden' became a genre in its own right, and in 1983 the H-word became enshrined in the new name for the Historic Buildings and Monuments Commission: English Heritage. In their books Graham Stuart Thomas and Penelope Hobhouse also contributed decisively to the popularity of historicism in gardens, with instructions on how to make all kinds of knots, parterres and arbours.

It was not just a matter of seventeenth-century and earlier precedent – landscape gardens such as Painshill, Surrey, were rescued from dereliction, and the 1980s saw the restoration of numbers of Edwardian gardens, often by private owners, which led to renewed appreciation of the Arts and Crafts movement. The restoration of the Jekyll – Lutyens garden at Hestercombe from 1973 had led the way, and in 1974 *Country Life* described the 'Edwardian terraces brought to life' at Nuneham Park, Oxfordshire. Penelope Hobhouse's own tenancy of Tintinhull from 1980 (by then it was owned by the National Trust) was extremely influential in this respect, since the framework of the garden was given life by her original planting ideas. In her books, Hobhouse has described how to integrate contemporary horticultural trends with historical settings or references.

There was also at this time a growing understanding of the international context of gardens and gardening, fostered principally through garden history. The Japanese garden, for instance, enjoyed a resurgence, particularly in the guise of dry gardens of gravel and sculptural stone. The Marchioness of Salisbury at Hatfield House, Hertfordshire, made a pioneer knot garden (1981), double avenues of mop-headed ilex and various other features, which were to inspire others to insert historical quotations into their gardens. Lady Salisbury had also designed knots at her previous garden, Cranborne Manor in Dorset, and at Highgrove for the Prince of Wales.

Potagers or ornamental vegetable plots were now just as fashionable as knot gardens (they had been popular even in the mid-1970s, when Rosemary Verey made an early potager at Barnsley House), which were themselves usually laid out in the formal French style, and herb gardening in all its guises was also chic. This was the heyday for the ornamental cabbage, most prized when delicately frosted, if not on the dinner table, and of lovage and other English herbs, lovingly labelled. Statuary even made a modest comeback, with a number of firms catering to a demand for high-quality replicas of seventeenth-and eighteenth-century

statues in reconstituted stone. The topiary shears also emerged from the shed again. Scholarship in garden history was now well established, and a new profession of landscape consultancy catered to the needs of the National Trust and private owners, as scores of gardens – mainly Edwardian and eighteenth-century landscape gardens – were restored and 'interpreted' for the public in lavish new visitor centres. Old walled gardens and their glasshouses, which had usually been neglected, built over or turned into car parks, came into focus, particularly after the 1987 television series *The Victorian Kitchen Garden*, and they began to be restored to working condition or else put to better use.

Historical awareness was to play its part in the formulation of one influential strand of garden-making in the early 1980s which might be termed 'smart gardening'. This was epitomised by Rosemary Verey at Barnsley House in its 1980s guise: an immaculate and conventionally minded version of Arts and Crafts, in which low box hedges, small formal pools, 'lollipop' topiary standards, brick paths, masses of lavender and white 'Iceberg' roses play a part, and soft pastel shades in flowers – all deemed to be in good taste – predominated. Even the wilder sections of these gardens seemed well organised. Historical inferences, such as small knots, espaliered fruit, Versailles planters and statuary (even obelisks), were integral to the look, which was predicated on restraint and genteel understatement.

ABOVE:
The Cottage, Badminton House, Gloucestershire (1976). The view towards the potager on the west side of the house, with a profusion of encroaching plants, including rosemary, lavender, senecio, phlomis, shrub roses and artemisia. This image represents an extreme of 1970s romantic planting.

RIGHT:
Newby Hall, North Yorkshire (1984). The unusual curving pergola, with long fronds of Laburnum vossii. *The 1984 article in* Country Life *was entitled 'The Garden that has Everything', and it was hardly an exaggeration. This was a garden that was a benchmark of quality for most of the twentieth century.*

Purples, deep plum and garnet were very 'smart' colours, as was anything understated and predominantly green, such as hellebores, epimediums and snowdrops. Lanning Roper had produced work of this type in the 1960s – the potager and formal-pool garden at Hillbarn House are good examples – and the Russell Page sense of poise and control was another influence, as was Dutton's classically spare Hinton Ampner.

'Smart' was a tone that can be detected in many gentry gardens at the time, including Windle Hall, Sherbourne Park, Wollerton Old Hall, Lord Carrington's Manor House, Bledlow, James and Alvilde Lees-Milne's garden at Essex House, Gloucestershire, Sir Frederick Ashton's Chandos Lodge, Suffolk, and Hardy Amies' gardens in London and at The Old School, Langford, Oxfordshire. Perhaps the architectural equivalent was the Post-

Modernist conceits of Quinlan Terry and Raymond Erith, created from the early 1970s onwards; Terry created garden buildings in a smart-garden context for Lord McAlpine at West Green House, Hampshire.

Despite its scholarly pretensions, the historical basis for smart gardening was in practice a mélange: the knots of English Tudor, the potagers of French seventeenth century, the Lutyens-designed curvilinear bench (which rapidly became a garden cliché), the eighteenth-century Classical temple or seat, and sculpture, sundials and other ornamental elements from various periods. As Arthur Hellyer, writing in 1986, observed of the Dutch Garden of box hedges at Parham House, it was called 'Dutch' for no clear reason except that 'it is relatively small and very neat'. The fallacious idea that modern garden restorations were somehow more authentic than earlier attempts was something that distinguished this late-twentieth-century version of historicism, especially after the development of garden archaeology and the establishment of a garden-restoration industry by the 1990s.

At their worst moments, 'smart gardens' appeared prissy and pretentious, but there were some good examples: the National Trust's Mottisfont Abbey, Hampshire, remade by Graham Stuart Thomas, contained many 'smart' elements in balance (in most gardens, 'smart' was in fact just one of many influences at work). In the 1970s, Mottisfont had also become the prime repository of Thomas's shrub-rose collections, and this cause became an important element of 'smart' gardening at places such as Goodnestone, Parham and Hazelby, where the old roses and statuary constituted a typical 1980s combination.

Perhaps our best guides to the smart-garden phenomenon are two books by Rosemary Verey and Alvilde Lees-Milne, *The Englishwoman's Garden* (1980) and *The Englishman's Garden* (1982), in which 'smart' is realised to varying degrees in different gardens, as could be seen in the work of contemporary designers such as Roddy Llewellyn, David Hicks, Peter Coats and (in the 1990s) Rupert Golby. Roy Strong has speculated as to whether this taste for manicured historicism in gardens was in part politically motivated (just as the New Town movement had been), as the traditional Conservative party came to terms with Margaret Thatcher and her populist appeal: 'If the landscape style accumulated overtones of the Left, can we argue that country house formality donned the weeds of the Right?' he asked. Viewed in this context, smart gardening can be seen as a retreat into history and nostalgia. After all, horticulture is the traditional pursuit of those who have failed in politics.

The horticultural extravaganzas of the previous decade continued to develop apace, made by gardeners driven on by a fascination with plants as opposed to fashionable design or the desire to make a specific intellectual statement. As well as great gardens like Nymans and Newby Hall, both illustrated to stunning effect in *Country Life* in 1984, examples such as Cobblers, East Sussex, and Benington Lordship, Hertfordshire, showed how considerations of architectural and structural setting were now almost completely subordinated to planting design. Private gardeners were beginning to achieve a standard of horticulture that eclipsed even the Edwardians in their heyday. The shrubs that had become popular in the post-war years – and that some commentators had feared would replace traditional herbaceous plants in the name of low maintenance – had been assimilated into the mixed border and were now playing a decisive part in effervescent planting schemes of great complexity and originality. Among the most respected private gardeners of the time were David Scott and Valerie Finnis at Boughton House, Northamptonshire; Lord de Ramsey of Abbots Ripton, Cambridgeshire (with the assistance of the designer Humphrey Waterfield); John Treasure at Burford House, Shropshire; Lady Anne Cowdray at Broadleas, Wiltshire; the painter John Hubbard of Chilcomb, Dorset; Lawrence Banks at Hergest Croft, Herefordshire; Peter Healing at the Priory, Kemerton, Worcestershire; the Hornbys at Pusey House, Oxfordshire; and Lionel Fortescue at The Garden House, Buckland Monachorum, Devon. In the majority of these gardens, a huge range of plants has been grown in a semi-formal setting: well-stocked borders and woodland gardens with lawns, enclosed spaces, formal pools and garden pavilions.

The horticultural predilections of the 1980s included a growing obsession with snowdrops (fashionable even into the twenty-first century, though less exclusive), and an interest in ferns and grasses, euphorbias of all kinds, cranesbill geraniums, hellebores, colchicums, grey and silver plants (eryngiums and *Melianthus major* for example), clematis, the larger-flowered dahlias (led by that irrepressible prelate, 'Bishop of Llandaff'), *Alchemilla mollis* on paths and in crevices, *Sedum* 'Autumn Joy', alliums of all sizes, the smaller narcissus, witch hazels, lilies and daylilies. The concept of the 'architectural' plant was now widely accepted, with several specialist nurseries providing specimens. Colourful annuals or biennials were considered infra dig – with exceptions such as the cottagey *Nigella damascena* (love-in-a-mist) – as were the heathers and conifers beloved by suburban gardeners of the 1970s, and

hybrid tea or floribunda roses (not ramblers, climbers or old shrub roses, in other words).

Notwithstanding the fact that many gardeners claim to be uninfluenced by fashion in horticulture, or even seek to deny its existence, most of these planting preferences were carried over into the 1990s. A growing recognition of the reality of a gardening orthodoxy led to an iconoclastic stance from a handful of writers, including Christopher Lloyd consistently in his columns (although he is so widely read that his views represent an orthodoxy in their own right), Connecticut-based Eleanor Perenyi, who published the witty *Green Thoughts* in 1981, and Mirabel Osler, whose *Gentle Plea for Chaos* (1988) struck a chord with many. 'We are too clever by half,' Osler declares. 'We read too many books, we take too many notes. We lie too long in the bath planning gardens. Have we lost our impulsive faculties?

Have we lost that intuitive feel for the flow and rightness of things; our awareness of the dynamics of a garden where things scatter where they please?' This was a reaction against smart gardening, knowing historicism and obsessive plantsmanship; it was an argument for carefree gardening in the Fish tradition.

Organic gardening was beginning to gain more of a following in the 1980s (Ryton Organic Gardens, the movement's showcase, opened in 1984), although it did not become a serious force until the 1990s, having been helped along by mainstream authors and broadcasters such as the BBC's Geoff Hamilton. The Prince of Wales also played a part through his interest in the burgeoning organic movement, as patron of the Ryton gardens and through his own example at Highgrove in Gloucestershire, where he was advised by the Marchioness of Salisbury on organic as

well as historicist gardening. He took some flak for his stance at the time but has been vindicated since by the growth of the organic food industry.

An ecological spirit was abroad in gardening: wild-flower meadows had become popular at larger gardens (including Great Dixter) in the 1970s, although Miriam Rothschild's was the first, at Ashton Wold, Northampton-shire. The 1970s had also seen a trend for self-sufficiency, or something like it, and renewed interest in vegetable gardening – although the fashion for 'the good life' was short-lived. The eco-impulse was to grow and grow until, by the early 1990s, even mainstream nurseries included a wild-flower-meadow collection in their seed range. Gardens designed to encourage birds, insects and other wildlife, as well as native plants, were promoted through the 1980s by ecologists like Chris Baines, but it was chiefly the plants that were to find popular appeal in succeeding decades. The sensitive plantsmanship of Beth Chatto, for example, was informed by an abiding sympathy with nature, and her emphasis on appreciating the natural char-acter and habit of plants in the wild was to influence a new generation of gardeners, including Dan Pearson.

In many gardens of the 1980s, however, there is a sense that the gardener is just blazing away in the mixed border – gardening to impress with no thought beyond that. One can often detect a certain knowingness, however, in gardens that have been restored by private individuals – Little Onn, Tapeley Court, Waystrode Manor and of course Tintinhull are examples – and on rare occasions a garden that 'grows in the mind', which is how Allen Paterson described the garden at Chilland in *Country Life* in 1982. At this time there also grew up a small but extremely influential body of garden experimentation by other indi-viduals involved professionally in the arts – notably the poet Ian Hamilton Finlay, the film-maker Derek Jarman, the art historian and curator Sir Roy Strong and his wife, the set designer Julia Trevelyan Oman, and (in the 1990s) the architectural theorist Charles Jencks and his wife, Maggie Keswick. Their examples had a slow-burn effect on English gardens, until by the late 1990s there was wide-spread evidence of confident, uncompromising self-expres-sion in gardens. These were not simply 'sculpture gardens' – lent a spurious artistic legitimacy by the placement of art objects – but gardens in which decorative yet meaningful artefacts played a part in the fabric of the design, conceived as integral to it rather than as adornments.

Ian Hamilton Finlay is a combative poet who made his name in the 1960s as part of the concrete-poetry movement. In 1966 in the shallow hills of Lanarkshire he began making the garden known as Stonypath, renamed Little Sparta after it began to be Hellenised from 1978. Finlay became known throughout Europe for his evocatively inscribed

The Laskett, Herefordshire (1997).

(above left): *The stag with golden antlers is one of several dramatic surprises in this singular garden, where gilding is a unifying decorative theme.*

(above right): *The Pierpont Morgan Rose Garden: every area is named in commemoration of an aspect of the owner's lives.*

(right): *The Silver Jubilee Garden, in which Julia Trevelyan Oman's professional experience as a set-designer is much in evidence.*

plinths carefully sited in landscape settings; Stockwood Park in Bedfordshire is another major work, and he contributed pieces to the permanent landscape around the Serpentine Gallery in London.

The garden at Little Sparta became a Classically inspired journey into the iconography of combat and revolution, with features including a stone submarine in the hosta-shaded Roman garden and silhouettes of Apollo chasing Daphne. Plantings enhance the varying moods of light and shade as the path moves through woodland clearings and then along paths of mown grass via a grenade gate and on towards an arresting and sinister gilded head lying in the undergrowth, inscribed 'Apollon Terroriste'. But the garden is not overpopulated with statuary. The climax is a series of inscribed stones set into Lochan Eck at the garden's fringes, bearing a quotation from the French revolutionary Saint-Just: 'The present order is the disorder of the future.' The whole garden is a pæan to the uncontrollable factors of life, from the global to the personal, expressed in a uniquely updated Classical and philosophical mode.

Strong and Oman began making their garden, The Laskett in Herefordshire, in 1973, and, as with Little Sparta, it only came into its own in the late 1970s and 1980s. The Laskett is a highly personal garden that has been built up gradually, section by section: an intensively designed series of at least 40 garden rooms, corridors and ante-chambers, ingeniously crammed into 4.5 acres and contained by high yew, *leylandii* and beech hedges which effectively cut out the rest of the world. Every area and every feature of the garden has been named after an event or person – it is above all an autobiographical garden, quite explicit in its terminology. Because of this, some people criticise The Laskett for self-aggrandisement, but that is not the feeling of the garden on the ground. Roy Strong described it thus: 'It is the portrait of a marriage, the family we never had or wanted, a unique mnemonic landscape peopled with the ghosts of nearly everyone we have loved, both living and dead.'

A series of monuments punctuate it, commemorating aspects of the couple's life, in a yellow-and-blue scheme which unites the decorative scheme of both garden and house, reminiscent of Clough Williams-Ellis's use of estate colours at Plas Brondanw. Gold leaf is also used on the ornaments. The garden is a decorative experience, with areas of relative informality and several long vistas. Its *modus operandi* is the element of surprise, and the sense of variety is enhanced by the many different levels and generally sloping terrain: it is quite a disorientating garden,

like getting lost in a mansion devised by Lewis Carroll. Strong claimed that the initial impulse to build this highly individual garden was to continue the tradition of the English country-house garden, and so it does – but the English garden of another, perhaps more confident age. In this sense, The Laskett could be placed in the context of the new awareness of garden history that Strong helped create in the 1980s, and a withdrawal from the perceived vulgarity of modern life that went with it.

Derek Jarman's beach garden at Prospect Cottage, Dungeness, Kent, is the only twentieth-century garden that has been accepted as a legitimate work of art by the wider arts and media establishment, and this is symptomatic of Jarman's artistic status as well as of the garden's innate power. Prospect Cottage feels as if it is in a different world

● *Little Sparta, South Lanarkshire (1996).*

The hand grenade gate (below), *the Corinthian capital, and the golden head inscribed 'Apollon Terroriste'* (right) *are among the sculptural and architectural fragments ranged round Ian Hamilton Finlay's garden in the Pentland Hills. The garden is a symbolic tour-de-force, which took on a militaristic tone after clashes with the local authority over the garden's artistic (and therefore taxable) status.*

to the 'smart gardens' made at this time. Horticulturally, the site is extraordinarily bad for gardening, with hardly any soil – just a pebble beach exposed to salty winds, with low rainfall, in the shadow of the Dungeness B nuclear power station. But horticulture alone does not make a good garden. It was begun in 1987 with a collection of pebbles strung as a necklace. Jarman gathered more and more stones and flotsam – old metal hooks, a chain coil, fishing-net floats, spiral pieces of iron – to make a garden that shouted defiance at the world with spiky totems. Jarman wrote: 'At first, people thought I was building a garden for magical purposes – a white witch out to get the nuclear power station … I invest my stones with the power of Avebury. I have read all the mystical books about ley lines and circles – I built the circles with this behind my mind.' Jarman reinforced the magical connotations by dressing as a shaman and shouting at passers-by when necessary. But his creation was essentially well suited to the site, with its huge, overarching pate of sky. There was also beauty and contrasting softness in his planting: Jarman found he could grow many flowers, including foxgloves, valerian, verbascums and broom, and lots of herbs, as well as sea kale, *Crambe maritima.*

The Dungeness garden became something of a cult, especially after it was 'discovered' by Christopher Lloyd, and it has had a considerable influence on the creative gardening scene – still-life ensembles of pebbles and sempervivums or sculpture made of flotsam glass with stones on a driftwood post could be seen reproduced in numerous gardens of the 1990s. Jarman's garden was liable periodically to be destroyed by wind and water, but that was part of the point: a shout of defiance from a man who was dying of Aids even as he made the garden. In one of his poems he wrote:

> Here at the sea's edge
> I have planted my dragon-toothed garden
> to defend the porch,
> steadfast warriors
> against those who protest their impropriety
> even to the end of the world.
> A fathomless lethargy has swallowed me,
> great waves of doubt broken me,
> all my thoughts washed away.
> The storms have blown salt tears,
> burning my garden,
> Gethsemane and Eden.

It is curious how poetry and gardening have always been so well matched.

⬛ *Prospect Cottage, Kent (1993).*

(opposite, above and left): *Film-maker Derek Jarman created this unlikely garden from 1987 using local coastal plants and found objects on the beach at Dungeness, in the shadow of a nuclear power station. The sculptural and shamanistic inferences of the garden have proved inspirational to many, and several homages to the Jarman garden have been made.*

10 · Making it Over
1990–1999

The early 1990s saw the continuation of the historicist theme of the mid- to late 1980s, with restorations proceeding apace at estates and larger gardens. The great storms of 1987 and 1990 which hit the south of England uprooted thousands of trees and were the catalysts for many such projects. On the domestic scale, there was sustained interest in the ornamental potential of historical features such as topiary, sundials and potagers, as well as a fashion for seeking out decorative architectural pieces from reclamation yards (something Vita Sackville-West had suggested back in 1954 and seen sporadically in gardens such as Frederick Gibberd's in the 1960s and Lanning Roper's Coniston Cold in the 1970s). In some ways, this reflected a deeply conservative strand of English gardening, in line with the emerging orthodoxy that the best thing that could happen to a garden was for it to be rediscovered, rescued and restored, or else made anew in homage to the past. This ethos was inspired by the continued popularity and perceived authenticity of restored gardens on the ground. It culminated, in the academic sphere, in the restoration of the Privy Garden at Hampton Court, and in the popular sphere in the marketing triumph that was The Lost Gardens of Heligan.

In the last decade of the century, everything that could be restored was restored, from the Victorian carpet-bedding schemes at Waddesdon and Harewood House, to eighteenth-century landscapes such as Stowe, Painshill and Hestercombe, to Arts and Crafts extravaganzas like Wightwick Manor and Gravetye. The majority of these restorations were achieved with great skill, delicacy and imagination, and they were also popular with visitors. In the public sphere, the Urban Parks Programme of the new Heritage Lottery Fund put many millions of pounds towards the restoration of High Victorian public parks, some of which were not particularly notable examples of the genre. Restoration was politically uncontroversial and apparently backed up by public opinion in surveys, whereas new design was liable to be railroaded at any moment (Kathryn Gustafson's aborted design for Crystal Palace Park in the late 1990s was a case in point).

This way of looking at gardens self-consciously through the prism of the past was given legitimacy by an ultra-historicist strain in garden history, which dictated that 'newness' as a concept was fundamentally flawed. As the garden historian Brent Elliott put it: 'Every modernism is parasitic upon historical revivalism ... Every original style is simply the dummy run for a future revival; and every style is better the second time around'. The counterargument to this is that while one can always dissect gardens and detect evidence of past styles, this does not necessarily negate the existence of originality and innovation: a garden is far too complex a cultural artefact and aesthetic experience to be reduced to a simple catalogue of historical references. The style of every garden represents a balance between ideas gleaned from history on the one hand, and on the other ideas that reflect contemporary culture, the spirit of the place, the garden's perceived use and the maker's own personality.

The assertion that historical awareness might underpin or direct all design was an extreme position, yet its acceptance was widespread in the last two decades of the century. It led to an assumption that conscious historical revivalism or full-blown restoration was the most appropriate way of dealing with gardens. This was a radical agenda that became normalised as orthodoxy in the gardens world. Such a position could not be sustained, and, by the late 1990s, assumptions about the authenticity of restoration and the cyclical nature of design were beginning to be challenged. Towards the end of the decade, the National Trust had changed its attitude to one of caution, and by the time it took on responsibility for William Morris's Red House in 2003, the policy was simply to leave the (undocumented) garden well alone.

Commercially, too, a modern scheme was now beginning to be considered a more exciting 'sell' than a historical pastiche. For the property developers who acquired Trentham in Staffordshire, the most attractive solution for the rejuvenation of Charles Barry's parterres was a dream team of modern plantsmen, whose remit was innovation rather than restoration. By the first years of the twenty-first century, it was almost as if restoration had been discredited and the fallacy of authenticity accepted. The beginnings of a new reluctance to intervene was demonstrated by the development of computerised 'virtual' restorations, to be shown in visitor centres rather than to be carried out on the ground.

In the domestic sphere, the most appropriate way of expressing historicism was felt to be through conscious or (more frequently) unconscious reference to Arts and Crafts gardens. There were now large numbers of high-quality restored Arts and Crafts gardens to visit – including the National Trust's Great Chalfield and The Courts, to name but two. The planting styles of exemplars such as these were extremely influential, and they were celebrated in the unprecedented number of features about gardens in magazines and in books. Improved quality of printing and paper in the mid-1980s – not to mention the move over to colour

LEFT:
▲ *Red House, Bexleyheath, Kent (2003).* The garden at Red House had been William Morris's horticultural laboratory for producing decorative specimens, but few records of its original appearance survived. When the National Trust acquired the house in 2003, it decided to hold off restoration plans for the garden.

BELOW:
▲ *Goddards, Surrey (1981).* A major exhibition on Edwin Lutyens in 1981 helped re-ignite interest in the Arts and Crafts movement as a whole, which grew through the 1980s and 1990s. Goddards is now owned by the Landmark Trust and it is possible to rent the house.

RIGHT:
▲ *Wightwick Manor, Staffordshire (1996).* The formal garden on the entrance front. Alfred Parsons designed the original planting scheme in 1887. Wightwick is now a National Trust property – the Trust was the prime mover in the restoration of Arts and Crafts planting schemes in the 1990s.

reproduction in magazines – had an appreciable influence on attitudes towards gardens and perhaps contributed to the widespread improvement in their design during this period. In terms of quality of horticulture and the sophistication of the average gardener, the 1990s marked a high point of the century for English gardens – and therefore an all-time high. Not since the 1930s had there been so many

fine gardens in existence in England. And now they were largely created and maintained by private owners rather than paid staff.

The look of these gardens was in almost all cases based on an appreciation of Arts and Crafts or its more manageable sibling, cottage gardening. This formed the core of ideas about the 'quintessential English garden', an aspirational concept which had gained widespread currency in the 1980s. This was itself a factor of the nostalgia of the closing decades of the twentieth century, demonstrated in the gardens world by the popularity of books such as *The Country Diary of an Edwardian Lady* (1977), films such as *The Draughtsman's Contract* (1982) – made at that perennial *Country Life* favourite, Groombridge Place – and 'heritage' television series such as *Brideshead Revisited* (1981).

For many gardeners in the late 1980s and 1990s, the watchword for garden style was 'old-fashioned', just as it had been at the beginning of the century. The potency of the cottage-garden ideal had remained undiluted throughout the twentieth century, but the desired architectural milieu had changed: for Edwardian gardeners it had been the stonework and topiary of seventeenth-century gardens, whereas for gardeners of the 1990s it was the Arts and Crafts gardens of the Edwardian era which were the inspiration. At innumerable gardens a rich and profuse planting style melded the structural and colour-themed prescriptions of Jekyll and classical Arts and Crafts, with the tumbledown cottage aesthetic in the Margery Fish and Sissinghurst tradition. Many of the best of these exuberant gardens were featured in the pages of *Country Life* in the

LEFT:
▲ *Newby Hall, North Yorkshire (1998).* The urn fountain in the Autumn Garden, with flowers grouped for structure as well as colour: chrysanthemums, dahlias, salvias, crocosmias, verbenas, hydrangeas and fuchsias.

RIGHT ABOVE:
▲ *Great Chalfield Manor, Wiltshire (1998).* View towards the entrance to the paved court, with dianthus and campanula in the foreground. National Trust tenants sensitively restored this Alfred Parsons garden through the 1980s and 1990s.

RIGHT BELOW:
▲ *Shore Hall, Essex (1999).* The paved terrace at the front of the house, colonised by a profusion of self-seeded chives, nepeta and thyme. This look of wild, sensuous abandon – in fact, carefully managed in most gardens – was at its zenith in the late 1990s.

1990s: Coverwood House, Surrey (1996), where the woodland garden colonises and subsumes the terraces; Howick Hall, Northumberland (1997) with its confident, ultra-relaxed planting; the massed plantings of Hemingford Grey, Cambridgeshire (1998); explosive borders at Elsing Hall, Norfolk, (1998); and cottage gardening on a giant scale at Sleightholmdale, Yorkshire (1995). In an article on Halecat House in Cumbria in 1990, the walls of the garden are described as 'successfully smothered' by plants – which would have been a contradiction in terms for Jekyll. But by this time her name was invoked as the inspiration for almost any garden dominated by complex herbaceous experimentation. The suggestion was that Arts and Crafts had come full circle.

But the planting was not typical of Edwardian Arts and Crafts. In the borders of the early to mid-1990s, masses of plants thrust against each other, bursting forth in impressive richness and variety, engorged with colour. Compared with Jekyll's borders, in which plants are allowed to breathe and relax and the garden does not seem to be trying too hard – and compared even with the plantings of the decades immediately preceding – many 1990s borders look like overstuffed, pumped-up, muscle-bound confections, packed to bursting point with flourishing and diverse plant material arranged in a complex and unremittingly rich tapestry of colours and shapes. There was no interval in which the visitor might mentally regroup before the next Technicolor onslaught; next to these Rococo effusions, Jekyll's plantings appeared positively spare.

Perhaps this manifestation of the herbaceous border might be seen as the last, most decadent phase of Arts and Crafts gardening: a period when theories of colour had become well established and gardens such as Hadspen in

Somerset could concentrate on minute, almost scientific gradations of colours in combination; a period when gardeners seemed to vie with each other to produce as many scintillating or unusual plant contrasts as possible. The result was gardens that appeared to be on steroids, so full of 'wow factor' that the attentive visitor came away either exhilarated and in awe of the spectacle of it all, or else exhausted, confused and faintly nauseous. There was, literally and metaphorically, no sense of proportion in many of these gardens, however enjoyable they were on a sensual level. Perhaps the English had simply got too good at gardening? There were numerous less hedonistic examples to be followed – Beth Chatto's 'jewel-box' approach, measured and delicate; the Classical restraint and careful balance in Penelope Hobhouse's designs; or the

BELOW:
● *Sleightholmdale, North Yorkshire (1995).* The walled garden on the valley side behind the house. Joyful, explosive and multi-coloured 1990s planting schemes did not shy away from strong colour contrasts. In this garden the spires of delphiniums, kniphofias, verbenas and hollyhocks vie for ascendancy.

RIGHT:
● *Howick Hall, Northumberland (1997).* Multi-coloured tulips in long meadow grass; in autumn, colchicums take up the story. Pretty meadows became objects of desire in the 1990s.

subtleties of Rupert Golby's plantsman approach at his Cotswolds design practice – but the taste for big borders was well entrenched by the mid-1990s and, as we shall see later on in this chapter, it took ideas from the Continent to temper this and move garden style in another direction.

While the general emphasis was on profuse planting in an Arts and Crafts mode, a taste for formality and Classicism prevailed in many gardens. In some ways this can be seen as a hangover from 1980s smart gardening, but the historical pieties of that period had been replaced by a witty and overtly Post-Modernist approach. George Carter's formal gardens epitomised the new style, while private owners such as Hugh Johnson at Saling Hall, Cambridgeshire, Roy Strong at The Laskett, Gervase Jackson-Stops at The Menagerie, Northamptonshire, and David Wheeler and Simon Dorrell at Bryan's Ground, Herefordshire, had also been working in this spirit, introducing visual tricks, ironic statuary, *trompe l'œil* decoration, knowing historical references, and surprising juxtapositions. It takes a certain confidence to garden in this way.

Arabella Lennox-Boyd was and is the garden designer with the most exclusive client list in England, and a similar relaxation of the strictures of smart gardening can be seen in her innovative and highly original work, which exists midway between the Italian formalism that is her birthright and the Arts and Crafts tradition of her adopted country. Kim Wilkie has developed an innovative creative approach for historical work at gardens such as Heveningham Hall in Suffolk, where he introduced a turf amphitheatre to a Capability Brown park. Anthony Noel makes bright, witty, bijou gardens in a style inspired by the pretty formalism of the 1960s and the spatial awareness of Russell Page.

Modernism – in the guise of a brand of retro-chic based on mid-century Scandinavian and American models – had by now developed a niche in the retail sector through Habitat, The Conran Shop and numerous other high-end outlets. Magazines such as the cult classic *Wallpaper*

(founded in 1996) ensured that this was the look of choice for fashionable, aspirational, cosmopolitan urbanites. In the mid-1990s, the style achieved a new level of democratisation through the success of the Ikea stores from Sweden, which offered the clean, functional appeal of Modernism at budget prices. As is usually the case (for practical as well as cultural reasons) gardens were slower to pick up on the trend. In the early 1990s, one of the few designers with Modernist credentials was Dan Pearson, who offered a unique mix of high-level plantsmanship and contemporary structure – such as decking, smooth rendered walls and modern furniture.

But there was a growing appetite for gardens that echoed Modernist retro-chic, as evinced by the success of Pearson and Terence Conran's *The Essential Garden Book* (1998), and a niche interest in modern garden furniture. London-based designer Stephen Woodhams created a series of chic urban

gardens featuring his trademark galvanised steel planters – usually partnered with the spiky, architectural or silvery (and preferably all three) plants that were *de rigueur* at this time – which soon filtered into the mainstream and became something of a cliché of 1990s design. The turning point was perhaps the 1997 Chelsea Flower Show, at which Christopher Bradley-Hole's Modernist garden of smooth walls, Classical inscriptions and stately irises and grasses won the award for best garden in show. Significantly, perhaps, it beat into second place the *Country Life* centenary show garden in the next plot: a contemporary version of traditional Arts and Crafts, it seemed dated and irrelevant next to its neighbour. For the first time ever in English gardens, Modernism had become smart.

The phenomenon of the garden-makeover television programme did much to popularise the idea of the functionalist garden. Dan Pearson had, in fact, fronted the first such series in the early 1990s: Channel 4's *Garden Doctors*, in which the race-against-time aspect of the format was less of a feature than it subsequently became, and many of the programme's designs stood up well. But it was the BBC's *Ground Force*, launched in 1997 and starring Alan Titchmarsh and Charlie Dimmock (who became a gardening sex symbol), which found mass appeal and spawned many imitators.

The garden-makeover concept unites gardeners in a chorus of disapproval, since it seems to deny all that is precious about gardening – chiefly the fact that it is a process not a product, as Sylvia Crowe put it. In addition, the standard of design and decoration in these gardens often left much to be desired and was reflected in the standard of garden furniture and other objects available in DIY superstores and at Royal Horticultural Society shows such as Hampton Court, where decorative objects began to be more in evidence than plants. But the programmes were enormously popular with viewers as entertainment and perhaps tapped into a genuine desire for a solution to the problem of how to use gardens and how to envisage them.

The makeover embraced the concept of the garden as a space for eating, playing, working and entertaining, and chimed with the popular idea of the garden as an 'outdoor room'. The rise in house prices had meant that property was now by far the most important investment for most individuals, who were also likely to move house more often, so a garden was now seen as a shrewd investment of time and money. In reality, few homeowners attempted to make over their own gardens; instead, they picked up Neo-Modernist ideas such as decking and mixed them with more conventional ornaments and planting schemes.

All this was anathema to the existing generation of traditional gardeners, reared on Arts and Crafts principles and aspirations, and it horrified even Modernists, who saw the tenets of good design being cheerfully debased on prime-time television. But for television's 'lifestyle gardening', perhaps we should read 'Modernist gardening': at the heart of the makeover format is the assumption that a garden should reflect the personality and interests of the owners. Generally in the media, the assumption had been that a garden should reflect the personality and interests of Vita Sackville-West. Thirty years after the publication of John Brookes's *Room Outside*, the idea of the functionalist garden had finally found wide appeal, but it took another industry to achieve it: the garden revolution had indeed been televised.

▲ *The Garden House, Buckland Monachorum, Devon (2001).*

(below): *The Cretan Cottage Garden, part of 10 acres of paddocks – in addition to Lionel Fortescue's original two-acre garden – which Keith Wiley developed in an eclectic, adventurous and wholly contemporary horticultural spirit to wide acclaim in the 1990s.*

(right): *The South African Garden, where the planting is intended to mimic natural habitats, an idea popular at the more sophisticated end of 1990s horticulture and long promoted by influential figures such as Beth Chatto and Dan Pearson.*

Towards the end of the decade, a Modernist outlook became associated with a generally more individualistic take on garden-making. Gordon Taylor and Guy Cooper's seminal book *Paradise Transformed* (1996) had been a surprise success, showcasing for the first time a wealth of innovative international work which was to resonate into the twenty-first century. *Country Life* had been the first magazine to feature the gardens of Ian Hamilton Finlay and Derek Jarman, and now also Charles Jencks, who had created with his wife Maggie Keswick from 1990 a 'garden of cosmic speculation' near Dumfries, an explicit landscape metaphor for scientific theory possessed of a surreal beauty. The most striking and decoratively appealing feature is the 400-feet-long, S-shaped earthwork wave which twists sinuously round a smooth pond, warping away from it in terraces to embrace another much smaller arc of a pond on the other side.

The example shown by Jencks and other contemporary gardeners, coupled with the retail success of Modernism, led to the identification of a new market in the gardens world and the launch at the end of the decade of *New Eden* magazine from the *Country Life* stable. This square-format, glossy production was aimed at a core audience of thirty- to forty-somethings interested in all types of modern gardens as well as practical horticulture. Just as it had with the first wave of Modernism in the 1920s, *Country Life* was again strenuously promoting contemporary designers. *New Eden* was a critical success and proved to be commercially buoyant, but those are not the only important factors in the corporate world and the magazine lasted less than two years.

Yet contemporary gardening was not going to wither away. One of the new strands in international contemporary garden design identified and promoted by *New Eden* was Conceptualism: a school of thought that emerged from Modernism, Post-Modernism, Pop Art, and the example of artists such as Isamu Noguchi and Robert Smithson. Conceptual garden design is based not on the existing sense of place or topography, but on a single, strong, unifying idea inspired by the place's history, ecology or intended

use. The role of the artist is therefore paramount and the old idea of nature as a legitimate guiding force for design is rejected. The key figure in this movement is Boston-based landscape architect Martha Schwartz, while on the West Coast, Topher Delaney also utilises the Conceptual armoury of artificial materials (particularly plastics), bright colour, surreal scaling and a sense of humour.

In Britain, Paul Cooper was a lone figure through the 1990s, creating Conceptualist gardens in which new materials and technologies feature strongly. Tony Heywood also works in Conceptualist vein, creating garden installations or happenings that straddle the gap between the garden and contemporary art. The materials used, if not the Conceptual basis for the design, were assimilated into other gardens during the 1990s, and it was not surprising to find in new gardens Astroturf, aluminium decking, rendered concrete walls, modern lighting of all kinds, stretched nylon sails, outdoor hi-fi systems, stainless-steel cascades, and even white screens used for films and atmospheric slide shows.

The temporary or semi-temporary nature of much Conceptualist work is part of its aesthetic, and this made it particularly well suited to a new phenomenon of the 1990s: the contemporary garden show, consisting of up to twenty-five gardens which remain in situ from around June to October. The first of these shows was at Chaumont in the Loire Valley, and it was followed by similar Expos at Gothenburg in Sweden, Lausanne in Switzerland, and Metis in Canada. In Britain, the annual Westonbirt Festival of Gardens ran from 2002 to 2004, the year in which the Cornerstone Festival in California began. Conceptualist design outfits thrive in this atmosphere, and although the thought-provoking gardens they create are not designed to be practical in a private garden setting, it must be admitted that neither are those at more conventional shows.

On a more down-to-earth level, plantsmanship continued to be an enduring obsession through the 1990s. The cult gardeners of previous decades, such as Christopher Lloyd and Beth Chatto, were more revered than ever, and a new generation of commentators – Carol Klein, the Popes of Hadspen and Marilyn Abbott, among others – emerged to satisfy the demand for discussions about colour and the decorative appeal of specific plants. For many keen gardeners, this topic remains at the heart of gardening.

Concerns about climate change led to an emphasis on gardening in a more 'Mediterranean' manner, using herbs and plants that thrive in dry conditions. This conveniently complemented the prevailing fashion for silvery-leaved, succulent, glaucous and spiky plants, and encouraged a

vogue for a new range of plants from Australasia, notably tree ferns. Books by Myles Challis and Heidi Gildemeister were influential in this respect, while Beth Chatto's dry garden, converted from a gravel car park, emerged as a leading exemplar of the look, as did Denmans, where John Brookes continued the gravel gardening envisaged by its previous owner, Joyce Robinson. Of symbolic importance was Christopher Lloyd's decision, in 1994, to replace the rose garden at Great Dixter with an exotic garden defined in glorious Technicolor by orange cannas, red dahlias, strappy-leaved banana plants and the purple filigree of *Verbena bonariensis*. The ambitious Neo-Arts and Crafts

garden at the Old Vicarage, East Ruston, Norfolk – featured widely in the press – also boasted a wide range of exotic plants from warmer climes juxtaposed with more traditional subjects.

But warmer summers certainly did not put an end to traditional planting interests. The craze for snowdrops (only among the cognoscenti at first) continued unabated, and, as ever, certain plants took a star turn in gardens for a few seasons. To take one example as representative: *Cerinthe major* 'Purpurascens' emerged as a connoisseurial favourite in the mid-1990s, available from specialist nurseries; by the end of the decade it could be found in garden superstores (the same might be said of numerous grasses). Anna Pavord's bestselling book *The Tulip* (1999) led to a surge in interest – not that the flower had ever been

unpopular – and at the end of the decade Sarah Raven and Graham Rice led a cheeky revival of interest in bright annual flowers. By the mid-1990s, the pastel shades of cottage gardening had become unfashionable and searing colour was promoted instead. Organic gardening also began to be perceived as the norm rather than the exception (Kew and the RHS had set an example), while the strong links between food and gardens were explored in the media.

But of all of these strands of influence, the dominant one was still the idea of the wild garden. In more forward-looking or fashionably minded gardens, a wild-flower meadow had by the early 1990s become a necessary adjunct to stunning borders in the garden proper. Many were showcased in *Country Life* at this time – for example Feeringbury, Little Bowden and Sticky Wicket – and *Gardens Illustrated* magazine, which had been launched in 1993, made the relaxed virtues of meadow gardening its defining feature.

The 1990s woodland garden, comprising masses of naturalised bulbs and shade-loving plants, was nurtured in the same spirit. The idea was essentially a reprise of William Robinson: that the garden should look entirely natural, despite the presence of rarities and exotics. A more radical development of this idea was proposed by Jill, Duchess of Hamilton in *English Plants for Your Garden* (2000), a veritable manifesto of eco-friendly gardening (with butterflies particularly in mind) which suggested that non-native species should be phased out of gardens in favour of not just native but local species. Among the new artistic class of gardener, a search for meaning had emerged as the key concern. On a popular level, it was lifestyle and use that defined the garden, but among keen gardeners, ecology had transformed the garden's appearance. The underlying message was that unsullied nature represented the key to redemption – moral, emotional and ecological.

Into this atmosphere emerged the New Perennials movement in planting design, pioneered in Holland and the German public-parks system. By the close of the century, this had become the most important single movement in English gardening, informing the work of gardeners and designers at all levels. The New Perennials look consists of massed perennial plants and grasses, laid out in naturalistic drifts that sway in the wind and look their best in late summer. In essence, the idea was not new – its lineage could be traced back a century and more – but it had never before been conveyed to the gardening public in so explicit a fashion.

The leading member of the movement was the Dutchman Piet Oudolf, whose first work in England was the massive farmyard at Bury Court, Hampshire, where the owner, John Coke, was an early enthusiast. Oudolf's books, and those of Noël Kingsbury, the chief English exponent of New Perennials, led to the existing interest in wild flowers, meadows, woodland gardens, self-sown bulbs, and ecological or organic gardening being reconceived in the light of this new coherent movement of planting design.

Serious horticultural interest in the look was reflected in Oudolf's commission to create a new double border at the Royal Horticultural Society's Wisley garden, while on a

◆ *Shoreditch Electricity Showroom, London (2000). Featured in* New Eden: *artist Cathy de Monchaux created a roof garden – round the bulb-festooned 1920s copper dome – of orderly pots repeat-planted with miniature patio roses, sunflowers, festuca grass and sweet peas, backed by tomato plants.*

LEFT BELOW:
◆ *Jestico House, London (1999). Featured in* New Eden: *a modern house designed by the architect-owner and set in an old orchard. A decked platform, flanked on one side by a bank of lavender, surrounds the glass-walled building – the epitome of retro-Modernist styling.*

popular level, the acceptance of grasses in all their variety into the garden scene was notable. Perhaps the most radical aspect of the approach was that colour theming was usually disregarded entirely at the planning stage (at least that was the claim). This was anathema to traditional border designers. There was also scepticism regarding New Perennials' efficacy on a small scale and some concern about what seemed to be a relatively limited palette of plants. But New Perennials injected some much-needed innovation and vim into the British herbaceous border. It was a genuinely refreshing alternative that also – crucially – seemed to chime with the times.

As well as attracting designers whose work is defined by planting – such as Isabelle Van Groeningen and Brita von Schoenaich – the New Perennials pattern appealed to Modernists such as Bradley-Hole and Brookes, and it has

influenced the planting style of many others, such as Tom Stuart-Smith and Dan Pearson, in more subtle ways. In effect, English gardening at the end of the twentieth century and in the first years of the twenty-first was witnessing a slow and decorous collision between the tail end of English Arts and Crafts and the influx of these new ideas from Europe.

It seems likely that the development of gardens in England in the twenty-first century will continue to be characterised by slow processes of development and the absorption of new influences: gardening is not something that changes overnight, but in cycles of decades and half-decades. And the individualistic streak will probably continue to deepen as the garden becomes more widely perceived as a sphere for personal expression. Accordingly, the art world may come to a realisation that gardens represent the most profound expression of the interaction between mankind and nature – that they might be viewed not as just outdoor installations but as dynamic works of art that engage with the power of place.

Plantsmanship will always be a strong facet – perhaps the strongest – of the English gardening scene, but perhaps New Perennials will instill more widely a holistic conception of planting in the garden, in which overall effect is considered before the minutiae of border planning and plant combinations. The move towards organic methods and an ecological understanding of gardening is likely to accelerate and become irreversible; gardens, where ecological problems are dealt with in miniature, may provide a metaphor for the conundrum of our apparently deteriorating planet.

The biggest shift of the twentieth century in terms of gardens, however, was the massive increase in ownership of gardens of small and medium size, which went hand in hand with house-building booms. The major challenge of the century had been to identify and to popularise a coherent design vocabulary relevant to small gardens and their users. In this aim, twentieth-century garden design can be seen to have signally failed. The likelihood of it rising to the challenge in the twenty-first century depends on whether the garden continues to be viewed as an escapist fantasy or as a beautiful and functional adjunct to contemporary life. Which of these two models represents success is a matter of personal opinion.

LEFT:
◆ *Westonbirt Festival of Gardens, Gloucestershire (2002). Artist-embroiderer Candace Bahouth made this garden of plastic flowers for the Westonbirt Festival. This was one of several international shows that followed in the wake of the one at Chaumont in the Loire Valley, encouraging the burgeoning conceptual strand in garden design.*

SELECT BIBLIOGRAPHY

Abrioux, Yves, *Ian Hamilton Finlay: A Visual Primer*, Reaktion, Edinburgh, 1985.

Alfrey, Nicholas [ed] Daniels, Stephen [ed], and Postle, Martin [ed], *Art of the Garden*, Tate, London, 2004.

Allen of Hurtwood, Lady, and Jellicoe, Susan, *The Things We See: Gardens*, Penguin, London, 1953.

Amherst, Alicia, *A History of Gardening in England*, Bernard Quaritch, London, 1895.

Aslet, Clive, *The Last Country Houses*, Yale University Press, London, 1982.

Aslin, Elizabeth, *The Aesthetic Movement: Prelude to Art Nouveau*, Elek, London, 1969.

Batson, Henrietta M., *The Summer Garden of Pleasure*, Methuen, London, 1908.

Beard, Geoffrey, *Thomas H. Mawson, 1861–1933*, University of Lancaster, Visual Arts Centre, 1976.

Bisgrove, Richard, *The National Trust Book of the English Garden*, Viking, London, 1990.

—, *The Gardens of Gertrude Jekyll*, Frances Lincoln, London, 1992.

Blomfield, Reginald Theodore, *The Formal Garden in England*, Macmillan, London, 1892.

—, *Memoirs of an Architect*, Macmillan, London, 1932.

Bloom, Alan, *A Year Round Garden*, Floraprint, 1979.

—, *A Plantsman's Perspective*, Collins, London, 1987.

Boothby, Robert, *I Fight to Live*, Victor Gollancz, London, 1947.

Bowles, Edward A., *My Garden in Summer*, T. C. & E. C. Jack, London, 1914.

—, *My Garden in Spring*, T. C. & E. C. Jack, London, 1914.

—, *My Garden in Autumn and Winter*, T. C. & E. C. Jack, London, 1915.

Boyle, Eleanor Vere (EVB), *Days and Hours in a Garden*, Elliot Stock, London, 1884.

—, *A Garden of Pleasure*, Elliot Stock, London, 1895.

—, *Seven Gardens and A Palace*, John Lane, London and New York, 1900.

—, *Peacock's Pleasaunce*, John Lane, London and New York, 1908.

Bradley-Hole, Christopher, *The Minimalist Garden*, Mitchell Beazley, London, 1999.

Bradley-Hole, Kathryn, *Lost Gardens of England: From the Archives of Country Life*, Aurum Press, London, 2004.

Brookes, John, *Room Outside*, Thames & Hudson, London, 1969.

—, *Garden Design and Layout*, Queen Anne Press, London, 1970.

Brown, Jane, *Gardens of a Golden Afternoon*, Penguin, London, 1982.

—, *Lanning Roper and his Gardens*, Weidenfeld & Nicolson, London, 1987.

—, *Eminent Gardeners*, Viking, London, 1990.

—, *Sissinghurst, Portrait of a Garden*, Weidenfeld & Nicolson, London, 1990.

—, *Lutyens and the Edwardians*, Viking, London, 1996.

—, *The English Garden through the 20th Century*, Garden Art Press, Woodbridge, 1999.

— and Bryant, Richard, *A Garden and Three Houses* [Peter Aldington], Garden Art Press, Woodbridge, 1999.

—, *The Modern Garden*, Thames & Hudson, London, 2000.

Burnett, Frances Hodgson, *The Secret Garden*, 1911.

Cane, Percy, *Modern Gardens, British and Foreign*, The Studio, London, 1926.

—, *Garden Design of Today*, Methuen, London, 1934.

—, *The Earth is My Canvas*, Methuen, London, 1956.

—, *Creative Art of Garden Design*, Country Life, London, 1967.

Casteras, Susan P. [ed], *Richard Redgrave: 1804–1888*, Yale University Press, New Haven & London, 1988.

Chatto, Beth, *Plant Portraits*, Dent, London, 1985.

—, *Gravel Garden*, Frances Lincoln, London, 2000.

Chivers, Susan, and Wolozynscka, Suzanne, *The Cottage Garden: Margery Fish at East Lambrook Manor*, John Murray, London, 1990.

Clark, Herbert Francis, *The English Landscape Garden*, Pleiades Books, London, 1948.

— and Jones, Margaret Elizabeth Noël, *Indoor Plants and Gardens*, Architectural Press, London, 1952.

Coats, Peter, *The House & Garden Book of English Gardens*, Webb & Bower, Exeter, 1988.

Collens, Geoffrey and Wendy Powell [ed], *Sylvia Crowe,* Landscape Design Trust, Reigate, 1999.

Colvin, Brenda, *Land and Landscape*, John Murray, London, 1947.

Cook, Ernest Thomas, *Gardens of England*, A. & C. Black: London, 1908.

Cornforth, John, *The Inspiration of the Past: Country House Taste in the Twentieth Century*, Viking, London, 1985.

—, *The Search for a Style: Country Life and Architecture, 1897–1935*, Andre Deutsch, London 1988.

Cox, Euan Hillhouse Methven, *The Modern English Garden*, Country Life: London, 1927.

Cran, Marion, *The Garden of Ignorance*, Herbert Jenkins, London, 1913.

—, *Garden Talks by Marion Cran*, Methuen, London, 1925.

—, *I Know a Garden*, Herbert Jenkins, London, 1933.

Crowe, Sylvia, *Tomorrow's Landscape*, Architectural Press, London, 1956.

—, *Garden Design*, Country Life, London, 1958 [revised 1994].

—, 'William Robinson', in *Hortus*, No. 1, 1987.

Cumming, Elizabeth, *The Arts and Crafts Movement*, Thames & Hudson, London, 1991.

Davey, Peter, *Arts and Crafts Architecture* (revised edition) Phaidon, London, 1995.

Dean, David, *The Thirties: Recalling the English Architectural Scene*, Trefoil in association with Royal Institute of British Architects Drawings Collection, London, 1983.

Dick, Stewart, *The Cottage Homes of England*, Edward Arnold, London, 1909.

Dresser, Christopher, *Unity in Variety, as Deduced from the Vegetable Kingdom*, London, 1859.

—, *Popular Manual of Botany*, Edinburgh, 1860.

—, *The Art of Decorative Design*, London, 1862.

Du Cane, Ella and Florence, *The Flowers and Gardens of Japan*, Adam & Charles Black, London, 1908.

Dunbar, Evelyn, and Mahoney, Cyril, *Gardeners' Choice*, G. Routledge & Sons, London, 1937.

Durant, Stuart, *Christopher Dresser*, Academy Editions, London, 1993.

Dutton, Ralph, *The English Garden*, B. T. Batsford, London, 1937.

—, *Hinton Ampner: A Hampshire Manor*, B. T. Batsford, London, 1968.

Edwards, Joan, *Gertrude Jekyll: Embroiderer, Gardener and Craftsman*, Bayford, Dorking, 1981.

Elgood, George S, *Italian Gardens*, Longmans, London, 1907.

Ellacombe, Henry Nicholson, *In my Vicarage Garden and Elsewhere*, John Lane, London & New York, 1902.

Elliott, Brent, *The Country House Garden: From the Archives of Country Life, 1897–1939*, Mitchell Beazley, London, 1995.

—, 'Historical Revivalism in the 20th Century', essay in *Garden History*: 'Reviewing the Twentieth-Century Landscape', 28:1 (2000).

Ewing, Juliana Horatia, *Mary's Meadow*, Christian Knowledge Society, London, 1886.

Fearnley-Whittingstall, Jane, *The Garden: An English Love Affair*, Weidenfeld & Nicolson, London, 2002.

Festing, Sally, *Gertrude Jekyll*, Viking, London, 1991.

Fish, Margery, *We Made A Garden*, Faber, London, 1956.

—, *Cottage Garden Flowers*, Collingridge, London, 1961.

—, *Ground Cover Plants*, B. T. Batsford, London, 1964.

—, *A Flower for Every Day*, Studio Vista, London, 1965.

—, *Carefree Gardening*, 1966.

Ford, G., *'The Cottage Controversy', in Nature and the Victorian Imagination*, edited by U. C. Knoepflmacher and G. B. Tennyson, University of California Press, Berkeley, and London, 1977.

Gloag, M. R., *A Book of English Gardens*, Methuen, London, 1906.

Godfrey, Walter Hindes, *Gardens in the Making*, B. T. Batsford, London, 1914.

Golby, Rupert, *The Well-Planned Garden*, Conran Octopus, London, 1994.

Gorer, Richard, *The Flower Garden in England*, B. T. Batsford, London and Sydney, 1975.

Gradidge, Roderick, *Dream Houses, The Edwardian Ideal*, Constable, London, 1980.

—, *The Surrey Style*, Surrey Historic Buildings Trust, Kingston-upon-Thames, 1991.

Greensted, Mary, *The Arts and Crafts Movement in the Cotswolds*, Sutton, Stroud, 1993.

Gunn, Fenja, *Lost Gardens of Gertrude Jekyll*, Letts, London, 1991.

—, essays on Percy Cane in *Hortus*, No. 51 and No. 52, 1999.

Hadfield, Miles, *A History of British Gardening* (revised edition), Spring Books, London, 1969.

— [ed], *The Gardener's Companion*, J. M. Dent & Sons, London, 1936.

Haigh, Diane, *Baillie Scott: the Artistic House*, Academy Editions, London, 1995.

Halén, Widar, *Christopher Dresser*, Phaidon, London, 1990.

Hall, George W., *Garden Plans and Designs*, W. H. and L. Collingridge, London, 1947.

Hall, Michael, *The English Country House: From the archives of Country Life 1897–1939*, Mitchell Beazley, London, 1994; reprinted 2001 by Aurum Press, London.

Hamilton, Jill, Duchess of, *The Gardens of William Morris*, Frances Lincoln, London, 1998.

—, *English Plants for your Garden*, Frances Lincoln, London, 2000.

Hamilton, Walter, *The Aesthetic Movement in England*, Reeves & Turner, London, 1882.

Hancock, Ralph, *When I Make a Garden*, G. T. Foulis & Co, London, 1936.

Haslam, Richard, articles on H. Avray Tipping's houses and gardens, in *Country Life*, December 6, 13, 1979.

Hay, Thomas, *Plants for the Connoisseur*, Putnam, London, 1938.

Hellyer, Arthur, *The Amateur Gardener*, W. H. & L. Collingridge, London 1948 (revised and reprinted into 1990s).

— [ed], *Amateur Gardening Picture Book of Gardens*, W. H. and L. Collingridge, London 1956.

— [ed], *Amateur Gardening Garden Plans and Designs*, W. H. and L. Collingridge, London, 1961.

Helmreich, Anne, essay 'The Marketing of Helen Allingham: The English Cottage and National Industry' in Adams, Steven, and Robins, Anne G., *Gendering Landscapes*, Manchester University Press, 2000.

Henslow, Geoffrey, *Garden Architecture* Dean & Son, London, 1926.

Hill, Jason, *The Curious Gardener*, Faber & Faber: London, 1932.

—, *The Contemplative Gardener*, Faber & Faber: London, 1940.

Hitchmough, Wendy, *Arts and Crafts Gardens*, Pavilion, London, 1997.

Hobhouse, Penelope, *Private Gardens of England*, Weidenfeld & Nicolson, London, 1986.

—, *National Trust Book of Gardening*, Pavilion, London, 1986.

—, essay on Phyllis Reiss and Tintinhull in *Hortus*, No 1, 1987.

—, *Garden Style*, Frances Lincoln, London, 1988.

—, *Painted Gardens: English Watercolours, 1850–1914*, Pavilion, London, 1988.

—, *Penelope Hobhouse's Garden Designs*, Frances Lincoln, London, 1997.

—, *The Story of Gardening*, Dorling Kindersley, London, 2002.

Hort, Arthur, *Garden Variety*, E. Arnold & Co., London, 1935.

Hunt, Peter [ed], *The Shell Gardens Book*, Phoenix House in association with George Rainbird, London, 1964.

Hyams, Edward, *English Cottage Gardens*, Nelson, London, 1970.

Jacques, David, 'Modern Needs, Art and Instincts: Modernist Landscape Theory', essay in *Garden History*: 'Reviewing the Twentieth-Century Landscape', 28:1 (2000).

Jarman, Derek, *Derek Jarman's Garden*, Thames & Hudson, London, 1995.

Jekyll, Francis, *Gertrude Jekyll: A Memoir*, Jonathan Cape, London, 1934.

Jekyll, Gertrude, 'Colour in the Flower Garden', *The Garden*, August 26, 1882.

—, 'Colour', *The Garden*, November 25, 1882.

—, 'The English Garden 200 Years Ago', *The Garden* No. 670, 1884.

—, *Wood and Garden*, Longmans, London, 1899.

—, 'Formal to Free', *Country Life* Vol. 58, Nos 1504 and 1505, 1900.

—, *Home and Garden*, Longmans, London, 1900.

—, *Old West Surrey*, Longmans, London, 1904.

—, *Some English Gardens, After Drawings by G. S. Elgood*, Longmans, London, 1904.

—, *Colour in the Flower Garden*, Country Life/George Newnes, London, 1908.

—, *Old English Household Life*, B. T. Batsford, London, 1925.

—, 'The Small Garden', *Country Life* Vol.90, No.2863, 1926.

—, *A Gardener's Testament* [selected journalism], Country Life, London, 1937.

Jellicoe, Geoffrey, and Shepherd, J. C., the Younger, *Italian Gardens of the Renaissance*, Ernest Benn: London, 1925.

— and Jellicoe, Susan, *Modern Private Gardens*, Abelard-Schuman, London, 1968.

—, essay on Ditchley in *Garden History*, Vol.10 No.1, 1982.

— with executive editors, Patrick Goode and Michael Lancaster, *Oxford Companion to Gardens*, Oxford University Press, 1986.

—, *The Studies of a Landscape Designer over 80 Years*, Garden Art Press, Woodbridge, 1993.

Jencks, Charles, *The Garden of Cosmic Speculation*, Frances Lincoln, London, 2003.

Johnson, Robert Vincent, *Aestheticism,* Methuen, London, 1969.

Lacey, Stephen, *The Startling Jungle*, Viking, London, 1986.

Lambourne, Lionel, *The Aesthetic Movement / Lionel Lambourne*, Phaidon, London, 1996.

Lancaster, Osbert, *Homes Sweet Homes*, John Murray, London, 1939.

Lloyd, Christopher, *The Well-Tempered Garden*, Collins, London, 1970.

—, *Other People's Gardens*, Viking, London, 1995.

Lloyd, Nathaniel, *Garden Craftsmanship in Yew and Box*, Ernest Benn, London, 1925.

Lockwood, Mary Smith, and Glaister, Elizabeth, *Art Embroidery*, Marcus Ward & Co, London, Belfast, 1878.

Marsh, Jan, *Back to the Land: The Pastoral Impulse in England, from 1880 to 1914,* Quartet, London, 1982.

Martineau, Alice, *The Herbaceous Garden*, Williams & Norgate, London, 1913.

Mawson, Thomas, *The Art and Craft of Garden Making*, B. T. Batsford and G. Newnes, London, 1900.

Mowl, Timothy, *Historic Gardens of Gloucestershire*, Tempus, Stroud, 2002.

—, *Historic Gardens of Dorset*, Tempus, Stroud, 2003.

—, *Historic Gardens of Wiltshire*, Tempus, Stroud, 2004.

Musson, Jeremy. *The English Manor House: From the archives of Country Life,* Aurum Press, London, 1999.

Nichols, Rose Standish, *English Pleasure Gardens*, Macmillan Co, New York, 1902.

—, *Italian Pleasure Gardens,* Williams & Norgate, London, 1929.

Nicolson, Nigel, *Portrait of a Marriage: Vita Sackville-West and Harold Nicolson*, Weidenfeld & Nicolson, London, 1973.

— [ed], *Vita and Harold: The Letters of Vita Sackville-West and Harold Nicolson*, Weidenfeld & Nicolson, London, 1992.

Osler, Mirabel, *A Gentle Plea for Chaos*, Bloomsbury, London, 1989.

Ottewill, David, *The Edwardian Garden*, Yale University Press, New Haven, London, 1989.

Oudolf, Piet, with Kingsbury, Noël, *Designing with Plants*, Conran Octopus, London, 1999.

Page, Russell, *The Education of a Gardener*, Collins, London, 1962.

Pavord, Anna, *Hidcote Manor Garden* [guidebook], National Trust, London, 1993.

Pearson, Dan, and Conran, Terence, *The Essential Garden Book*, Conran Octopus, London, 1998.

Perenyi, Eleanor, *Green Thoughts*, Random House, New York, 1981.

Peto, Harold, *The Boke of Iford*, Libanus, Marlborough, 1994 (reprint).

Plumptre, George, *The Latest Country Gardens*, Bodley Head, London, 1988.

—, *The Garden Makers*, Pavilion, London, 1993.

—, *Great Gardens Great Designers*, Ward Lock, London, 1994.

—, *Classic Planting*, Ward Lock, London, 1998.

Powers, Alan, *Oliver Hill: Architect and Lover of Life*, Mouton Publications, London, 1989.

—, *The Twentieth Century House in Britain: From the Archives of Country Life*, Aurum Press, London, 2004.

Quest-Ritson, Charles, *The English Garden: a Social History*, Viking, London, 2001.

Redgrave, Richard, *An Elementary Manual of Colour*, London, 1853.

—, *Manual of Design*, London, 1876.

Reynolds, Gwynneth [ed], and Grace, Diana [ed], *Benton End Remembered*, Unicorn, London, 2002.

Richardson, Margaret, *Architects of the Arts and Crafts Movement*, Trefoil in association with the Royal Institute of British Architects Drawings Collection, London, 1983.

Richardson, Tim [ed], *The Garden Book*, Phaidon, London, 2000.

Ridley, Jane, *The Architect and his Wife*: A *Life of Edwin Lutyens*, Chatto & Windus, London, 2001.

Robinson, William, *The Parks, Promenades and Gardens of Paris*, John Murray, London, 1869.

—, *The Wild Garden*, John Murray, London, 1870.

—, *The English Flower Garden*, John Murray, London, 1883.

—, *Gravetye Manor*, John Murray, London, 1911.

Roper, Lanning, *Successful Town Gardening*, Country Life, London, 1957.

—, *Hardy Herbaceous Plants*, Penguin Books, London, 1960.

Sackville-West, Victoria, *In Your Garden*, Michael Joseph, London, 1951.

—, *In Your Garden Again*, Michael Joseph, London, 1953.

—, *More For Your Garden*, Michael Joseph, London, 1955.

—, *Even More for Your Garden*, Michael Joseph, London, 1958.

Schaffer, Talia [ed], *Women and British Aestheticism*, University Press of Virginia, Charlottesville, 1999.

—, *The Forgotten Female Aesthetes*, University Press of Virginia, Charlottesville, 2002.

Scott, Mackay Hugh Baillie, *Houses and Gardens*, George Newnes, London, 1906.

— and Beresford, Arthur Edgar, *Houses and Gardens*, Architecture Illustrated, London, 1933.

Scott-James, Anne, *The Cottage Garden*, Allen Lane, London, 1981.

Sedding, John Dando, *Garden Craft Old and New*, Kegan Paul & Co, London, 1895.

Shepheard, Peter, *Modern Gardens*, Architectural Press, London, 1953.

Sitwell, George, *An Essay On the Making of Gardens*, John Murray, London, 1909.

Sitwell, Osbert, *Noble Essences*, Macmillan, London, 1950.

Spencer, Robin, *The Aesthetic Movement*, Studio Vista, London, 1972.

Spens, Michael, *Gardens of the Mind: The genius of Geoffrey Jellicoe*, Antique Collectors' Club, Woodbridge, 1992.

—, *The Complete Landscape Designs of Geoffrey Jellicoe*, Thames and Hudson, London, 1994.

Stansky, Peter, *Sassoon: The Worlds of Philip and Sybil*, Yale University Press, New Haven, London, 2003.

Strong, Roy, *Small Period Gardens*, Conran Octopus, London, 1992.

—, *Garden Party: Collected Writings, 1979–99*, Frances Lincoln, London, 2000.

—, *The Laskett*, Bantam, London, 2003.

Sudell, Richard, *Landscape Gardening*, Ward Lock, London, 1933.

Synge, Patrick, *A Diversity of Plants*, Geoffrey Bles, London, 1953.

Tankard, Judith B., *Gertrude Jekyll: A Vision of Garden and Wood*, John Murray, London, 1989.

—, essay on 'Gardening with Country Life' in *Hortus*, No 30, Summer 1994.

—, *Gertrude Jekyll at Munstead Wood*, Sutton, Stroud, 1996.

—, *Gardens of the Arts and Crafts Movement*, Abrams, New York, 2004.

Taylor, G. C., *Garden Making by Example*, Country Life, London, 1932.

—, *The Modern Garden*, Country Life, London, 1936.

Taylor, Gordon and Cooper, Guy, *Paradise Transformed*, Monacelli Press, New York, 1996.

Thomas, Graham Stuart, *The Old Shrub Roses*, Phoenix House, London, 1955.

—, *Recreating the Period Garden*, Collins, London, 1984.

—, *Recollections of Great Gardeners*, Frances Lincoln, London, 2003.

Tilden, Philip, *True Remembrances*, Country Life, London, 1954.

Tillyard, Stella, *The Impact of Modernism, 1900–1920*, Routledge, London, 1988.

Tinley, George, *Colour Planning of the Garden*, T. C. and E. C. Jack, London, 1924.

Tipping, H. Avray, *English Gardens*, Country Life, London, 1925.

—, *The Garden of Today*, Martin Hopkinson, London, 1933.

Tooley, Michael J., *Gertrude Jekyll*, Michaelmas, Witton-le-Wear, 1984.

Triggs, Harry Inigo, *Formal Gardens in England and Scotland*, B. T. Batsford, London, 1902.

—, *Garden Craft in Europe*, B. T. Batsford, London, 1913.

Tunnard, Christopher, *Gardens in the Modern Landscape*, Architectural Press, London, 1938.

Venison, Tony, article on Rodmarton Manor in *Country Life*, Vol 160, 1976.

—, article on Snowshill Manor in *Country Life*, p1178, 1980.

Verey, Rosemary [ed], and Lees-Milne, Alvilde [ed], *The Englishwoman's Garden*, Allen Lane, London, 1980.

— [ed], and Lees-Milne, Alvilde [ed], *The Englishman's Garden*, Allen Lane, London, 1982.

—, *Good Planting*, Frances Lincoln, London, 1990.

Waterfield, Margaret, *Flower Grouping in English, Scotch and Irish Gardens*, Dent, London, 1907.

Waymark, Janet, *Modern Garden Design: Innovation Since 1900*, Thames and Hudson, London, 2003.

Weaver, Lawrence, and Jekyll, Gertrude, *Gardens for Small Country Houses*, Country Life / George Newnes, London, 1912.

Wolseley, Frances Garnet, *Gardens: Their Form and Design*, Edward Arnold, London, 1919.

Woudstra, Jan, 'The Corbusian Landscape: Arcadia or No-Man's Land', essay in *Garden History*: 'Reviewing the Twentieth-Century Landscape', 28:1 (2000).

Wright, Walter P., *The Perfect Garden*, Grant Richards, London, 1908.

—, *The New Gardening*, Grant Richards, London, 1912

Yorke, F. R. S., *The Modern House*, Architectural Press, London, 1934.

—, *The Modern House in England*, Architectural Press, London, 1937.

Youngman, Peter, essay on 'New towns, 1945–55', in *Landscape Design* No.275, November 1998.

INDEX

Page numbers in italic refer to illustrations

Abbots Ripton, Cambridgeshire 176
Abbotswood, Gloucestershire 78, 118
Abbott, Marilyn 200
Aberconway, Lord 7, 98, 106, 118
Acton, Arthur 94, 117
Adams, Robert *138*
Adcote House, Shropshire 13
Adie, Button and Partners 128, 131
Alderley Grange, Gloucestershire *156, 159*, 161
Aldington, Peter 133
Allen, Lady 148
Allingham, Helen 15
Allington Castle, Kent 78, 105
Amherst, Alicia 16
Amies, Hardy 174, 177
Ammerdown, Somerset *106*
Angell and Imrie 94
Anglesey Abbey, near Cambridge 97
Antony House, Cornwall *138*
Architectural Digest 162
Arley Hall, Cheshire *74*, 75
Art of Decorative Design, The 33
Artworkers' Guild 18
Ascott House, Bedfordshire 10
Ashcombe Tower, Devon 131
Ashford Chace, Hampshire *59*, *65*, 66
Ashridge Park, Hertfordshire 76
Ashton, Sir Frederick 174
Ashton Wold, Northamptonshire 178
Astor, Nancy 80
Astor, William Waldorf 97
Athelhampton Hall, Dorset 20, 52, *53*
Austin, David 160
Avebury Manor, Wiltshire 53

Bacon, Francis 17
Bahouth, Candace 203
Baillie Scott, Mackay Hugh 7, 47, 56, 66, 69, 70
Baines, Chris 178
Baker, Sir Herbert 101, 105
Balls Park, Hertford 94
Banks, Lawrence 176
Barcelona Pavilion 121, 133
Barn, The, Hampshire 64
Barnsley House, Gloucestershire *166*, 167, 171, *171*, 172
Barnsley, Edward 18, 36
Barnsley, Ernest 18, 52, 64
Barnsley, Sidney 52
Barrow Court, Somerset 52, *66*
Barry, Sir Charles 18, 140, 186
Batson, Mrs Stephen 79
Beacon Hill, Essex 80, *85*
Beales, Peter 160
Beauchamp, Lord and Lady 58
Beaufort, Duchess of 169
Beechwood, Sussex 169
Belvoir Castle, Leicestershire *14*
Benington Lordship, Hertfordshire 176
Bentley Wood, Sussex *122*, *123*, 126–127, 131
Benton End, Suffolk 90
Berenson, Bernard 94
Beth Chatto Garden, Essex *200*
Bibury Court, Gloucestershire 26
Biddulph, Claud 64
Biddulph family 65

Billington, Jill 133
Bisgrove, Richard 161
Blackburn, Tom 38
Blagdon Hall, Northumberland *146*, 149
Blenheim Palace, Oxfordshire 107
Blickling Hall, Norfolk 80
Blomfield, Reginald 16, 18, 26–27, 52, 93
Bloom, Adrian 169
Bloom, Alan 169
Blow, Detmar 59, 64, 107
Blundells, Gloucestershire 170
Bodnant, Denbighshire 7, *87*, 98, *106*, 118, 150, 152
Book of Garden Design, The 62
Boothby, Robert 98, 100
Borde Hill, Sussex 76
Bottengoms Farm, Essex 88
Boughton House, Northamptonshire 176
Bowles, E. A. 84, 166
box hedges 55, 64, 65, 69, 107, 125, 167, 172, 174, 177
Boyle, Eleanor Vere 15, 21–22, 43, 75, 85, 115
Brabazon, Hercules 35
Bradell, Darcy 122
Bradfield, Devon *18*
Bradley-Hole, Christopher 121, 134, 194, 203
Bramante, Donato 36
Bramdean, Hampshire 150
Branklyn, Tayside *157*
Bressingham Nurseries, Norfolk 169
Brickwall, Sussex *19*, 20, 75
Brideshead Revisited (TV) 188
Bridge House, Surrey 94, *95*, *99*
Britten, Benjamin 90
Britwell Salome, Oxfordshire *165*
Broadleas, Wiltshire 176
Brockenhurst Park, Hampshire *20*, 25
Brookes, John 121, 133, 161, 162, 194, 200, 203
Brown, 'Capability' 25, 40, 128, 193
Brownsea Castle, Dorset 108
Bryan's Ground, Herefordshire 192
Buckhurst Park, Sussex 94
Bulbridge House, Wiltshire *157*
Bunyard, E. A. 160
Burford House, Shropshire *174*, 176
Burne-Jones, Georgina 37, 38
Burnett, Frances Hodgson 76
Burnett, Sir James and Lady 144
Burton Manor, Cheshire 58
Bury Court, Hampshire 202
Buscot Park, Oxfordshire 94, *98*
Buttersteep House, Berkshire 132, *133*

Caerhays Castle, Cornwall 87
Cambo Hall, Fife *193*
Cameron, Julia Margaret 24–25
Campsea Ashe, Suffolk 25, *25*
Cane, Percy 73, 126, 139, 158, 167
Capon, Kenneth 131
Carefree Gardening 155
Carrington, Lord 139, 174
Carroll, Lewis 180
Carson, Rachel 161
Carter, George 192
Castle Drogo, Devon 105
Cave, Walter 52

Challis, Myles 200
Chandos Lodge, Suffolk 174
Chaplin, Charlie 98
Charles, Prince of Wales 171, 177
Charters, Berkshire *129*, 131
Chartwell, Kent 144
Chatto, Beth 90, 165, 178, 190, 194, 200
Chelsea Flower Show 73, 107, 194
Chelwood Vetchery, Sussex 93
Cheney Court, Wiltshire 107, *138*
Chequers, Buckinghamshire 83
Cherkley Court, Surrey 9
Chermayeff, Serge 121, 122, 126
Chevithorne, Devon 161
Chevreul, Michel-Eugène 33
Chilcomb, Dorset 176
Chilland, Essex 178
Chiswick House, London 22, *23*, 25
Christie, John 144
Church, Thomas 128, 162
Churchill, Winston 98, 104, 144
Claremont, Surrey 25
Clark, Frank 130, 149
Clark, Kenneth 98
Clifton Hall, Nottinghamshire *16*
Cliveden, Berkshire 80
Coach House, The, Dorset *198*
Coates Manor, Sussex 166
Coats, Peter 174
Cobbetts, Surrey 78
Cobblers, East Sussex 176
Cock Rock, Devon 132
Codford, Wiltshire 26
Codrington, John 166, 174
Coke, John 202
Cold Ashton Manor, Gloucestershire 55
Colefax, Sybil 55
Coles, Hampshire 161
Coleton Fishacre, Devon 55, *64*
Colour in the Flower Garden 44
Colvin, Brenda 149, 157, 158, 169
Compton End, Hampshire *76*, 78
Coniston Cold, Yorkshire 157, 185
Connell, Amyas 121, 125
Conran, Terence 162, 193
Contemplative Gardener, The 87
Conway, Martin 78
Cook, E. T. 78
Cooper, Guy 198
Cooper, Paul 200
Cooper, Reggie 54–55, 100, 113, 150, 152
Cornforth, John 52
Cornwell Manor, Oxfordshire 97, *109*, *143*
Cothay, Somerset 54, *54*, 55, 113
Cottage Gardening 15
Cottage, The, Badminton House, Gloucestershire 161, *168*, *172*
Cottesbrooke Hall, Northamptonshire *148*, 150
Country Diary of an Edwardian Lady, The 188
Country Life 7, 20, 21, 22, 24–26, 47, 55, 69, 73, 75, 76, 80, 82, 85, 90, 93, 95, 108, 112, 128, 130, 145, 150, 152, 155, 157, 166, 169, 171, 172, 176, 178, 188, 194, 198, 199, 202
Court Farm, Gloucestershire 63
Courts, The, Wiltshire 186

Coverwood House, Surrey 189
Cowdray, Lady Anne 176
Cowley, Herbert 30
Cran, Marion 48, 84
Cranborne Manor, Dorset *24*, 25, 171
Crathes Castle, Kincardineshire *144*
Crawley, George 82
Cray Clearing, Oxfordshire *120*, 133
Creating a Luxury Garden 170
Crowe, Sylvia 133, 149, 157–158, 162, 166, 169, 194
Crowhurst, Surrey 26
Crowhurst Place, Surrey *58*, *82*
Crystal Palace Park 185
Cunningham, Ivor 162
Curious Gardener, The 88, 130

D'Oyle Carte, Mr and Mrs Richard 55
Daily Mail 152
Daneway Manor, Gloucestershire 52, 157
Dartington Hall, Devon 139
David, Elizabeth 90, 170
Dawber, E. Guy 52
De Maria, Walter 139
de Monchaux, Cathy 203
de Noailles, Vicomte 125
de Ramsey, Lord 176
Deanery Garden, Berkshire *41*, 47
Delaney, Topher 192
Denmans, Sussex 200
Derry and Tom's roof garden 69
Derwent Hall, Derbyshire 25
Devey, George 9, 18, 20
Dillistone, George 70, 105
Dimmock, Charlie 194
Ditchley Park, Oxfordshire *104*, 108
Diversity of Plants, A 152
Dorrell, Simon 192
Dowles Manor, Worcestershire *147*
Draughtsman's Contract, The (film) 188
Dresser, Christopher 31, 33–34
Drew, Jane 130
Du Cane, Ella and Florence 80, 82, 85, 87
Dûchene, Achille, 107
Dumbarton Oaks, USA 94
Dutton, Ralph 94, 108, 157, 158, 174

East Anglian School of Painting and Drawing 90
East Lambrook Manor, Somerset 77, 152, 155
Easton Lodge, Essex *100*
Easton Neston, Northamptonshire 107
Eaton Hall, Cheshire 9, *13*, 34, 107
Eckbo, Garrett 162
Education of a Gardener 80, 161
Edwardian Garden, The 52
Egerton, Lady Louisa 17, 20
Elgood, George Samuel 17
Elizabeth and Her German Garden 116
Ellacombe, Canon 79
Elliott, Brent 108, 122, 185
Elliott, Joe 170
Elsing Hall, Norfolk 189
Eltham Palace, London *199*
England's Lost Houses 145
English Flower Garden, The 10, 12–13
English Garden, The 108
English Heritage 171

English Plants for Your Garden 202
English Pleasure Gardens 16, 18
Englishman's Garden, The 174
Englishwoman's Garden, The 174
Enville Hall, Staffordshire 13
Eridge Park, Sussex *160*
Erith, Raymond 174
Essay on The Making of Gardens, An 95
Essential Garden Book, The 193
Essex House, Gloucestershire 174, *176*
Etwall, Derbyshire 25
Evelyn, John 17, 43
Ewing, Juliana Horatia 15
Exbury, Hampshire 87

Fairhaven, Lord 97
Falkner, Harold 78
Faringdon House, Oxfordshire *192*
Farnsworth House, Illinois 134
Farrer, Reginald 85
Feeringbury Manor, Essex 202
Felley Priory, Nottinghamshire *2*
Fenwick, Guy 62
Fenwick, Mark 78, 118
Fermor-Hesketh, Sir Thomas 107
Festival of Britain 150
Fiddler's Copse, Sussex 161, *161*
Finlay, Ian Hamilton 7, 178, 180, 198
Finnis, Valerie 176
Fish, Margery 77, 152, 155, 177, 188
Flower, Mr and Mrs Wickham 46
Flowers and Gardens of Japan 82
Fogg, H. G. Witham 170
Folly Farm, Berkshire *42*, 43, *44*, *45*
Formal Garden in England, The 16
Formal Gardens in England and Scotland 16
Fortescue, Lionel 176, 194
Foster, Myles Birket 15
Fowler, John 152, 158
Freud, Lucian 90
Friar Park, Henley 87
Fulbrook House, Surrey *37*

Garden Architecture 69
Garden Craft in Europe 17
Garden Craft Old and New 16, 18
Garden Design 157
Garden Design and Layout 162
Garden Doctors (TV) 194
Garden History Society 158, 160
Garden House, The, Buckland Monachorum, Devon 176, *194*, *195*
Garden in Mind, Hampshire 140
Garden in the Suburbs, A 69
Garden Making by Example 69
Garden of Cosmic Speculation, The, Scottish Borders *201*
Garden of England 78
Garden of Ignorance, The 84
Garden of Pleasure, A 22
Garden Plans and Designs 147
Garden, The 10, 40, 46
Gardener's Chronicle 143, 155
Gardens for Small Country Houses 58, 63
Gardens Illustrated 202
Gardens in the Modern Landscape 126, 127
Garrowby Hall, Yorkshire *146*
Garsington Manor, Oxfordshire 97
Geddes, Sir Eric *127*, 130
Gentle Plea for Chaos 177

George, Sir Ernest 52, 93
Giardino Giusti, Verona 95
Gibberd, Frederick 139, 149, 185
Gildemeister, Heidi 200
Gill, Irving 125
Gimson, Ernest 18, 52
Gledstone Hall, Yorkshire *94, 105*
Glyndebourne, Sussex 144, *145*
Goddards, Surrey *37, 47, 186*
Godmersham Park, Kent 80
Golby, Rupert 174, 192
Goldsworthy, Andy 140
Gooday, Leslie 131
Goodnestone Park, Kent 174, *176*
Grammar of Ornament, The 33
Gravetye, Sussex 12, 166, 185, *199*
Great Chalfield Manor, Wiltshire 53, 186, *189*
Great Dixter, Sussex 83, 84, 166, 178, 200
Great Fosters, Surrey 55, 106
Great Tangley Manor, Surrey 46, *63*, 118
Green Thoughts 177
Greenaway, Kate 34
Gribloch, Stirlingshire *128*, 131
Grizedale Forest, Lake District 140
Grocock, George 64
Groombridge Place, Sussex 52, 140, 150, 188
Groote Schuur, South Africa 101
Gropius, Walter 121
Ground Cover Plants 155
Ground Force (TV) 194
Gruffyd, Bodfan 161
Guévrékian, Gabriel 125
Gunn, Fenja 47
Gunnersbury, London 10
Gustafson, Kathryn 185
Guthrie, Leonard Rome 93
Gwynne, Patrick 125, 130

Haddon Hall, Cheshire 20, *21*
Hadrian's Villa, Tivoli 97
Hadspen, Somerset 190
Haig, General 98
Hale, Kathleen 90
Halecat House, Cumbria 189
Halifax, Countess of 147
Hall, George W. 147
Hallingbury Place, Essex 70
Hambling, Maggi 90
Hamblyn's Coombe, Devon *136*, 139
Hamilton, Geoff 177
Hamilton, Jill, Duchess of 202
Hampshire Manor, A 108
Hampton, Anthony *see* Hill, Jason
Hampton Court, Herefordshire 76
Hampton Court Palace, 20, 185
Hamstone House, Surrey 131
Hancock, Ralph 69, 73, 107, 125
Hardwick Hall, Derbyshire 17, *17*, 20, 52, 78
Harewood House, Yorkshire *140*, 185
Harley, Primrose 157
Harleyford Manor, Buckinghamshire *74*, 76
Harlow Carr, Yorkshire 169
Harlow water gardens 149
Hartham Park, Wiltshire 94, *94*
Hascombe Court, Surrey *72*, 158
Haseley Court, Oxfordshire 161
Hatfield House, Hertfordshire 20, 171

Hazelby House, Hampshire 174
Healing, Peter 152, 170, 176
Hearst, William Randolph 105
Heathbrow, Hampstead, London *131*, 131
Heathcote-Amory family 152
Heatherbank, Surrey 79
Heizer, Michael 139
Heligan, The Lost Gardens of 77, 185
Hellyer, Arthur 174
Hemingford Grey, Cambridgeshire 189
Henley Hall, Shropshire 149
Henry Doubleday Research Association 161
Henslow, Geoffrey 69
Hepworth, Barbara 139
Herbaceous Garden, The 87
Hergest Croft, Herefordshire 176
Heronden, Kent *142*
Herstmonceux Castle, Sussex 55, *57*, 105
Hestercombe, Somerset *46*, 47, *47*, 48, *48*, 108, *167*, 171, 185
Heveningham Hall, Suffolk 193
Hever Castle, Kent 97, 105
Hewell Grange, Worcestershire 76
Heywood, Tony 200
Hicks, David 165, 174
Hicks, Ivan 140
Hidcote Manor, Gloucestershire 7, 18, 55, 65, 80, 83, 111–113, *116*, 117–118, *117, 118, 119*, 150, 152, 157
Higgins, Hal 131
High and Over, Buckinghamshire *121*, 125
High Glanau, Monmouthshire 82, *84*, *90*
High Hascombe, Surrey, *see* Sullingstead
High Sunderland, Selkirk *127*, 131, 133
Highcliffe Castle, Hampshire 105
Highgrove, Gloucestershire 171, 177
Hill, Jason 83, 87, 88, 130, 145
Hill, Oliver, 51, 66, 78, 93, 97, 121, 125, 133, 139, 157
Hill, The, London *96*
Hillbarn House, Wiltshire 157, 169, 174
Hilles, Gloucestershire *58*, 64
Hills, Lawrence 161
Hinton Ampner, Hampshire 94, 108, 157, 158, 174
History of Gardening in England, A 16
Hobday, E. 15
Hobhouse, Penelope 171, 190, 199
Holkham Hall, Norfolk 144
Holland House, London 25
Homewood, The, Surrey *124, 125*, 130, 131
Hopes and Fears for Art 36
Horder, Percy Morley 55, 56
Houndsell Place, Sussex 160
Houses and Gardens 69
Howick Hall, Northumberland 189, *191*
Hubbard, John 176
Hudson, Edward 22, 41,108
Hughenden Manor, Buckinghamshire 25
Hunt, Peter 158

Huntercombe Manor, Buckinghamshire *15*, 21–22, 43
Hussey, Christopher 46, 133
Hyères, France 125
Hyver Hill, Hertfordshire 130

I Know a Garden 48
Ideal Home Exhibition 73, 122, 128
Iford Manor, Wiltshire 54, *92*, 93
Indoor Plants and Gardens 130
Institute of Landscape Architects 73
Island, Steep, Hampshire 108
Italian Gardens 17
Italian Gardens of the Renaissance 108
Italian Pleasure Gardens 94
Italian Villas and their Gardens 95

Jackson-Stops, Gervase 192, 200
Jacobsen, Arne 133
Jakobsen, Preben 133, 162
James, the Hon. Robert 'Bobby' 78, 79, 118
Jarman, Derek 178, 180, 183, 198
Jekyll, Gertrude 7, 9, 16, 17, 20–22, 27, 29, *29*, 30–31, 33–34, 35–41, 43–48, 52, 58–59, 62, 63, 66, 73, 75, 77, 78, 79, 80, 82, 83, 85, 90, 94, 95, 98, 101, 115, 116, 118, 136, 144, 148, 155, 160, 162, *167*, 171, 188, 189–190, 193
Jellicoe, Geoffrey 104, 108, 122, 133, 134, 136, 139, 148, 149, 152, 158, 161
Jellicoe, Susan 148
Jencks, Charles 7, 178, 198, 200
Jenkyn Place, Hampshire *161*
Jestico House, London *202*
Johnson, Hugh 192
Johnston, Lawrence 55, 80, 94, 111–112, 116, 117–118, 157
Joldwynds, Surrey *132*
Jones, Inigo 65, 88
Jones, Owen 33
Julians, Hertfordshire 55, *148*, 152

Kaufmann and Benjamin 125
Kelmscott Manor, Oxfordshire 37, *51*
Kemsing St Clere, Kent 107
Kent, William 94
Keswick, Maggie 178, 198
Kiftsgate, Gloucestershire 118, 150
Kildwick Hall, Yorkshire 76
Kiley, Dan 128
King's House, Surrey 158
Kingsbury, Noël 202
Kingston Bagpuize House, Oxfordshire *196–197*
Kirby, Ian 200
Kitchin, George Herbert 76, 78
Klein, Carol 200
Knebworth, Hertfordshire 10
Knightsbridge garden, London *163*
Knightshayes Court, Devon 152, 161
Knightstone, Somerset 55

La Pietra, Florence 94, 117
Lacey, Stephen 77
Lambay Castle, County Dublin 105
Lancaster, Nancy 161
Land's End, Leicestershire 128
Landmark Trust 186
Landscape Gardening 70
Lane End House, Buckinghamshire 88
Laskett, The, Herefordshire *164*, *178*, *179*, 180, 192

Latham, Sir Paul 55
Le Corbusier 121, 122, 125, 127, 130
Le Nôtre, André 65, 107
Leeds Castle, Kent 105
Lees Court, Kent *88*
Lees-Milne, James and Alvilde 157, 158, 161, 174, 177
Leighton, Frederic, Lord 34
Leith Hall, Aberdeenshire *145*
Lemoine nursery, France 87
Lennox-Boyd, Arabella 193
Leonardslee, Sussex 87
Lett-Haines, Arthur 90
Levens Hall, Cumbria 20, 34
Leverhulme, Lord 97
Lindisfarne Castle, Northumberland 105
Lindsay, Nancy 88
Lindsay, Norah 55, 80, 82, 83, 88, 100, 108, 118, 148, 152, 193
Little Boarhunt, Hampshire *62*, 65
Little Bowden, Leicestershire 202
Little Onn Hall, Staffordshire 178
Little Paddocks, Berkshire *90*
Little Sparta, Lanarkshire 178, 180, *180, 181*
Little Thakeham, Sussex *38, 39*
Littlecote Manor, Wiltshire *73*
Llewellyn, Roddy 174
Lloyd, Christopher 84, 165–166, 177, 183, 200
Lloyd, Nathaniel 83, 166
Long Barn, Kent 113, 147
Long, Richard 140
Longford Hall, Derbyshire 10
Longleat House, Wiltshire 20
Loos, Adolf 121, 125
Lord Leycester Hospital, Warwick *192*
Lorne, Francis 132
Lost Gardens of Gertrude Jekyll 47
Lovejoy, Derek, and Partners 132, 134
Lower Hall, Shropshire 169
Lowesby Hall, Leicestershire 107
Lowther, Colonel Claude 55, 56
Lubetkin, Berthold 130
lupins 33, 73, 74, 87, 155, 199
Lutyens, Edwin 7,13, 27, 29, 30, 34, 36, 38, 40–41, 43–48, 51–52, 58–59, 62, 63, 64, 66, 70, 73, 78, 82, 93, 94, 101, 105, 108, 113, 117, 118, 147, 149, 161, 162, 166, 171, 186
Lyons, Eric 162
Lytes Cary Manor, Somerset 53
Lyme Hall, Cheshire *6*

Macartney, Mervyn 52
Madresfield Court, Worcestershire 56
Mallet, Sir Louis 52, 53–55, 118
Mallows, Charles Edward 47, 58, 64
Mangles, Henry 45
Manor House, The, Bledlow, Buckinghamshire *138*, 139, 174
Manor House, The, Sutton Courtenay, Berkshire 55, 80, *80, 83*, 88
Manual of Colour 33
Manual of Design 34
Martineau, Alice 87
Marlborough, Duke of 107
Marsh Court, Hampshire 47, *100*, 105
Mary's Meadow 15
Mathern Place, Monmouthshire 83, *84*
Mawson, Thomas 58, 63, 64, 70, 73, 88, 97, 105

McAlpine, Lord 174
McCrum, Bridget 136, 139
McGrath, Raymond 127, 128
Menagerie, The, Northamptonshire 192, *201*
Messel, Colonel and Mrs Leonard 55
Metroland 69
Middleton, Cecil 'Mr' 147
Mies van der Rohe, Ludwig 121, 125, 131, 133
Millmead, Surrey 78
Milne, Oswald 55, 65
Modern House in England, The 125
Modern House, The 125
Modern Painters 35
Mondrian, Piet 162
Montacute House, Somerset 17, 20, 52
Moor Close, Berkshire *50*, 66, *66-67*
Moore, Henry 122, 126, 139, 140
Morris, Cedric 90
Morris, Robert 140
Morris, William 29, 33, 36–38, 40, 43, 51–52, 58, 64, 65, 70, 85, 186
Mottisfont Abbey, Hampshire 174
Mountains, Essex 80, 82, *86*
Mounton House, Monmouthshire 83, *91*
Muir family 118
Munstead Wood, Surrey *28, 30, 31, 32, 34, 39–41, 43–47*, 115, 144
My Garden in Summer 84
My Old World Garden and How I Made It In A London Suburb 69
Myddelton House, Enfield 84

Nash, John 88
National Council for the Conservation of Plants and Gardens 160
National Trust 80, 111, 145, 152, 160, 171, 172, 174, 186, 188
Naudin, Claude 33
Nesfield, W. A. 107
Nether Lypiatt Manor, Gloucestershire *55*, 56
New Eden 199, 203
New England, Surrey *134, 135*
Newby Hall, North Yorkshire 150, *173*, 176, *188*
Newton, Ernest 52
Ney, Reyner 131
Nichols, Rose Standish 16, 18–20, 25, 94
Nicholson, Ben 136, 139
Nicholson, William 29
Nicolson, Harold 54, 55, 98, 111, 113, 113, 115
Nicolson, Nigel 115
No. 16 Kevock Road, Lasswade, Midlothian *126*, 131
No. 41 Trafalgar (now Chelsea) Square, London *139*
No. 48 Storeys Way, Cambridge 69
Noble Essences 56
Noel, Anthony 193
Noguchi, Isamu 199
North Landing, Suffolk 131
North Luffenham Hall, Rutland *60–61*
North Mimms, Hertfordshire 12
Nuneham Park, Oxfordshire 171
Nymans, Sussex *54*, 55, 176

Oakwood, Surrey 79
Observer 111, 116, 147
Odiham, Hampshire *158*

Olantigh, Kent *132*
Old Buckhurst, Sussex 108
Old Garden Roses 160
Old Rectory, The, Burghfield,
  Berkshire *167*
Old School, The, Langford,
  Oxfordshire 174, *177*
Old Sleningford, North Yorkshire *184*
Old Vicarage, The, East Ruston,
  Norfolk 201
Old Vicarage, The, Firle, Sussex 169,
  169
Old Vicarage, The, Rickling, Essex
  198
Old West Surrey 38
Oman, Julia Trevelyan 165, 178, 180
Onslow Square, London 157
Orchardleigh Park, Somerset *11*
Orchards, Surrey *35*, 47
Osler, Mirabel 177
Ottewill, David 52
Oudolf, Piet 202
Overbecks, Devon *200*
Owlpen, Gloucestershire 53

Packwood House, Warwickshire 20,
  75, *75*
Page, Peter Randall 138
Page, Russell 79, 80, 118, 161–162,
  169, 174, 193
Painshill, Surrey 171, 185
Panshanger Hall, Hertfordshire 10
Paradise Transformed 198
Paradisi in sole, paradisi terrestris 15
Parham House, Sussex 174
Paris Expo (1925) 122
Parkinson, John 15
Parsons, Alfred 63, 188
Parsons, Beatrice 15, 78
Pasley, Anthony du Gard 169
Paterson, Allen 178
Pavord, Anna 201
Peacock's Pleasaunce 85
Pearson, Dan 178, 193–194, 203
Penshurst Place, Kent *8*, 20, 52
Perenyi, Eleanor 177
Perfect Garden, The 69
Peto, Harold 54, 90, 93–95, 97, 98,
  101, 108
Pinsent, Cecil 94
Plas Brondanw, Gwynedd 97, 180
Platts, The, Hampshire 108
Pleasance, The, Lothian 107
Pleydell-Bouverie, Mrs 148, 152
Pollen, Francis 121, 133
Popular Manual of Botany 33
Port Lympne, Kent 54, *81*, *93*, 98,
  100–101, *102–103*, 104–105, 108
Portmeirion, Wales 97
Postern, The, Kent 169
Pound, Ezra 158
Powers, Alan 122
Powis Castle, Powys 13
Prior, E. S. 52
Priory, The, Kemerton,
  Worcestershire 152, *171*, 176
Prospect Cottage, Dungeness, Kent
  180, *182*, 183, *183*
Pusey House, Oxfordshire 176
Puslinch, Devon 76
Pye, William 138

Quest, The 36

Raven, Sarah 201

Red House, Bexleyheath, Kent 37, 46,
  70, 160, *186*
Redgrave, Richard 33–34
Reiss, Phyllis 150, 152, 157
Renishaw Hall, Derbyshire 95
Repton, Humphry 41
Rhodes, Cecil 101
rhododendrons 55, 74, 79, 87, 90, 127,
  152, 166
Ricardo, Halsey 52
Rice, Graham 201
Ridley, Jane 30
Rivington, Lancashire 58
Robinson, Joyce 200
Robinson, William 10, 12–15, 26–27,
  29, 35, 40, 47, 74, 79, 85, 116, 166,
  199, 202
Rodmarton Manor, Gloucestershire
  18, 36, 64, *64*, 65, 111, 115
Room Outside 133, 162, 194
Roper, Lanning 149, 155, 157, 169,
  174, 185
roses 33, 43, 48, 55, 65, 69, 78, 79, 83,
  84, 87, 88, 90, 111, 112, 115, 116,
  117, 132, 145, 148, 150, 157, 160,
  162, 169, 172, 174, 177, 200
Rosetti, Dante Gabriel 20, 75
Rothschild family 10
Rothschild, Miriam 178
Roughfield, Sussex *154*
Rowe, Ernest 15
Royal Horticultural Society (RHS)
  143, 162, 194, 201, 202
Ruckmans, Surrey 62
Ruskin, John 22, 29, 35
Russell, James 166–167
Ruys, Mien 162
Ryton Organic Gardens 177

Sackville-West, Victoria 'Vita' 90, 94,
  111–113, 115–118, 144, 147–148,
  155, 158, 160, 167, 185, 194
St Ann's Hill, Surrey 127
St Catherine's College Oxford 133
St Catherine's Court, Somerset *20*
St Donat's Castle , Glamorganshire
  105
St Nicholas, Yorkshire 78, *79*, 118
St Paul's Walden Bury, Hertfordshire
  153, 158
Saighton Grange, Cheshire *77*
Saling Hall, Cambridgeshire 192
Salisbury, Marchioness of 171, *177*
Saltford Manor, Somerset 160
Saltwood Castle, Kent 105
Salutation, The, Kent *149*, 161
Sandbeck, Yorkshire 77
Sapperton, Gloucestershire 52
Sargent, John Singer 98
Sassoon, Sir Philip 54, 80, 93, 98,
  100–101, 104–105, 108
Savill, Eric 152
Savill Garden, Berkshire 152
Scarborough, Celia, Lady 77
Schultz, Robert Weir 64, 148
Schwartz, Martha 192
Scott, David 176
Scrubey, William 64
Sculpture at Goodwood 139
Seager, Stanley 136
Seaton Delaval, Northumberland
  167
Secret Garden, The 77
Sedding, John Dando 16, 18, 26, 41,
  43, 52, 63

Sedgwick Park, Sussex 25
Selfridge, Gordon 105
Serenity, Surrey *130*, 131
Serpentine Gallery, London 180
Serre de la Madone, France 118
Seven Gardens and A Palace 43
Shaw, George Bernard 98
Shaw, John Byam 24
Shaw, Richard Norman 52
Sheffield Park, Sussex 152
Shell Gardens Book, The 158
Shepheard, Peter 150
Shepherd, J. C. 108
Sherbourne Park, Warwickshire 174
Shore Hall, Essex *189*
Shoreditch Electricity Showroom,
  London *202*
Shrubland Park, Suffolk 18
Shute House, Dorset 136
Silent Spring 161
Sissinghurst Castle, Kent 7, 54, 55, 65,
  77, *110*, 111–118, *111*, *112*, *113*, *114*,
  115, 144, 147, 155, 188
Sitwell, Osbert 56, 95, 98
Sitwell, Sir George 95
Skibo Castle, Inverness-shire 105
Sleightholmdale, North Yorkshire
  189, *190*
Smithson, Robert 139–140, 199
Snowshill Manor, Gloucestershire 56,
  56, 167
Soane, Sir John 101, 105
Soil Association 161
Some English Gardens 17, 34, 78
Span (architectural practice) 121, 132,
  162
Spence, Basil 131
Spry, Constance 160
Stammers, John 133
Stannard, Lilian 15
Stanwick Park, Yorkshire *9*
Stephens, Theo 152
Sticky Wicket, Dorset 202
Stockwood Park, Bedfordshire 180
Stoke Park, Buckinghamshire *10*
Stokes, Leonard 52
Stone Cottage, Leicestershire 166, *175*
Stonor Park, Oxfordshire 149
Stonypath, Lanarkshire 178
Stowe, Buckinghamshire 185
Strachan, Arthur Claude 15
Strawberry House, London 170
Strong, Sir Roy 165, 170, 174, 178,
  180, 192
Stuart-Smith, Tom 203
Sturry Court, Kent 76
Suarez, Diego 94
Sudeley Castle, Gloucestershire 25, *88*
Sudell, Richard 70
Sullingstead (High Hascombe), Surrey
  40
Summer Garden of Pleasure, The 79
Summerson, Sir John 127
Sunday Times 152, 155
Sunningdale Nurseries 167
Sutton Courtenay *see* Manor House,
  The
Sutton Place, Surrey 136, *136*, *137*,
  139
Swinstead, George Hillyard 69
Synge, Patrick 152

Tapeley Court, Devon 178
Tayler and Green 131
Taylor, G. C. 69–70

Taylor, Gordon 198
Tecton Group 130
Tennyson, Lord Alfred 20
Terry, Quinlan 174
Thomas, Francis Inigo 20, 52, 53, 93,
  95
Thomas, Graham Stuart 43, 77, 88,
  144, 160, 167, 171, 174, 177
Thonger, Charles 62
Thrower, Percy 147
Tigbourne Court, Surrey *36*
Tilden, Philip 78, 93, 104–105
Tintinhull, Somerset *151*, *152*,
  157–158, 171, 178, 199
Tipping, H. Avray 24, 70, 73, 78,
  82–83, 85, 90, 94
Tirley Garth, Cheshire 64
Titchmarsh, Alan 194
topiary 18, *19*, 20, 75, 78, 83, 88, 98,
  108, 116, 118, 138, 172, 185, 188
Townhill Park, Hampshire 93
Townsend, Geoffrey 162
Treasure, John 174, 176
Tree, Ronald and Nancy 104, 108
Trent Park, Hertfordshire 54, 80, 98,
  100–101, *108*
Trentham Hall, Staffordshire 18, 186
Triggs, Harry Inigo 17, 59, 62, 65
Tring Park, Hertfordshire 10
Tritton family 80
Trower, Seymour 98
True Remembrances 104
Tugendhat House, Czech Republic
  131
Tulip, The 201
tulips 33, 54, 82, 87, 190, 193
Tunnard, Christopher 121, 122,
  126–128, 130, 134
Turn End, Buckinghamshire 133
Turner, J. M. W. 35
Turner, Thackeray 63
Tusmore House, Oxford 94
Twentieth Century House in Britain, The
  122
Tyringham Hall, Buckinghamshire
  101, 105

Unsworth, W. F. 59, 66
Upper Wolves Copse, West Sussex
  131, *131*

Valewood Farm, Surrey 66, *68*, *69*, 78
van Groeningen, Isabelle 199, 203
Venison, Tony 90
Verey, Rosemary 166, 167, 171, 172,
  174
Versailles, France 104
Viceroy's House, Delhi 105
Victoria and Albert Museum 170
Victorian Kitchen Garden, The 172
Villa d'Este, Tivoli, Italy 104
Villa I Tatti, Florence, Italy 94
Villa Maryland, France 95
Villa Medici, Florence, Italy 104
Villa Rosemary, France 95
Villa Savoie, France 121, 125
Villa Sylvia, France 95
Villiers-Stuart, Constance 150
Vizcaya, USA 94
von Armin, Countess 116
von Schoenaich, Brita 203
Voysey, Charles 47, 52

Waddesdon Manor, Buckinghamshire
  10, 185, *185*

Wade, Charles Paget 55–56
Walberswick, Suffolk 26
Walker, W. H. Romaine 52, 55, 106
Wallpaper 193
Wardes, Kent *52*, 53–54, 118, 167
Wargrave, Berkshire 40, 47
Warley Place, Essex 79
Warwick, Countess of 101
Waterfield, Humphrey 176
Waterperry Manor, Oxfordshire 169
Waterston Manor, Dorset *55*, 56
Wayford Manor, Somerset 90, 93
Waystrode Manor, Kent 178
We Made a Garden 155
Weaver, Lawrence 26,
Webb, Philip 46, 47, 63, 69
Well-Tempered Garden, The 165
West Bitchfield, Northumberland 78,
  78
West Dean, Sussex 52, 94
West Green House, Hampshire 174
Westbrook, Surrey 63
Westbury Court, Gloucestershire 158
Westfields, Bedfordshire 158
Westminster, Duke of 34, 107
Westonbirt, Gloucestershire 87, 152
Westonbirt Festival of Gardens,
  Gloucestershire 200, *203*
Westwood Manor, Wiltshire 53
Wharton, Edith 95, 117
Wheatcroft, Harry 145
Wheeler, David 192
When I Make A Garden 125
Wightwick Manor, Staffordshire 63,
  185, *187*
Wild Garden, The 10, 12
Wilde, Oscar 40
Wildwood, Perth and Kinross 131
Wiley, Keith 194
Wilkie, Kim 193
Williams, J. C. 87
Williams, Mrs Leslie 69
Williams-Ellis, Clough 97, 108, 180
Willmott, Ellen 79
Wilson, E. H. 78
Wilson, G. F. 79
Wilton House, Wiltshire 10, *12*
Windle Hall, Lancashire *169*, 174
Wisley, Surrey 79, 143, 162, 202
Witley Park, Surrey 132
Wollerton Old Hall, Shropshire 174
Womersley, Peter 131
Wood and Garden 33, 34, 44
Woodfalls, Hampshire 122
Woodhams, Stephen 193
Woodhouse, Violet Gordon 55, 56
Worsley, Giles 145
Wright, Frank Lloyd 125, 131
Wright, Walter P. 69
Wyatt, James 157
Wyndcliffe Court, Monmouthshire
  83

Year Round Garden, A 169
yew hedges 21, 34, 36, 43, 53, 56, 59,
  64, 69, 78, 83, 95, 98, 115, 180
Yews, The, Cumbria *71*
Yorke, F. R. S. 125
Yorkshire Sculpture Park 139, *141*
Youngman, Peter 149

Zydower, Astrid 140